WE WON'T
GO BACK

WE WON'T GO BACK

Making the Case for

Affirmative Action

CHARLES R. LAWRENCE III

and MARI J. MATSUDA

HOUGHTON MIFFLIN COMPANY

Boston   New York   1997

For information about permission to reproduce selections from this book,
write to Permissions, Houghton Mifflin Company, 215 Park Avenue South,
New York, New York 10003.

For information about this and other Houghton Mifflin trade and reference
books and multimedia products, visit The Bookstore at Houghton Mifflin
on the World Wide Web at http://www.hmco.com/trade/.

Library of Congress Cataloging-in-Publication Data
Lawrence, Charles.
  We won't go back : making the case for affirmative action /
Charles R. Lawrence III and Mari J. Matsuda.
      p.   cm.
ISBN 0-395-79125-1
1. Affirmative action programs — United States. 2. Race discrimination —
United States.   I. Matsuda, Mari J. II. Title.
HF5549.5.A34L38   1977
361.6 — DC20   96-46158   CIP

Printed in the United States of America

QUM 10 9 8 7 6   5 4 3 2 1

Contents

[III]

THE WELCOME TABLE:
EXPANDING AFFIRMATIVE ACTION

Preface

I WAS SEVEN YEARS OLD, sitting in the back seat of our family's old Plymouth, when my mother turned around, leaned over the seat, and said to her three children, "If Mommy and Daddy tell you to get down, you get on the floor and stay there until we tell you to get up." She pointed to the deep seat well beneath our dangling feet, her voice stern.

"Why?" one of us asked.

"Because," she answered, "where we are going there may be people who want to hurt us."

My brother Bill and I remember this moment in June of 1963, such an unusual one in our protected childhood. Our family was driving to a Los Angeles motorcade honoring Medgar Evers, assassinated earlier that week in Jackson, Mississippi, because he had been organizing poor Blacks to stand up for their rights.

Why, we wondered, would our parents take us where there was danger? We learned the answer in pieces. We were picket-line babies, pushed in buggies before we could walk on marches for labor rights, for civil rights, for peace. We learned that our parents were different, brave, and sometimes despised for their work.

In the aftermath of McCarthyism we were young and protected from much, but not all. A letter arrived one day from the Minute Men, a violent hate group, threatening to kill our parents. I can't remember how I found out about this, but I know it was indirect. It was not until I was an adult that I learned of the seven jobs my father lost because the FBI harassed his employers; about the closed-door meeting at the local Japanese American Citizens League, where, after bitter argument, the board narrowly voted not to eject my father as "un-American." As a child I was told some things, and other things I watched and learned.

It is a good life, my siblings and I learned, to share in the civil rights struggle; to seek "brotherhood," that patriarchal but stirring word used by my parents' generation. At one of those early 1960s' civil rights marches in Los Angeles, I remember my father walking at the head of the parade, a handsome Nisei man strategically placed alongside a Mexican, a Negro, a Gentile, and a Jew, each carrying an American flag.

This was before the days of Black Power and the New Left. It was a time when claiming brotherhood across race lines could get you shot dead in the street, when the symbols of patriotism were deployed to make what was then a radical statement for a person of color: I Am an American. Some of the men who marched in those days wore military uniforms and displayed Purple Hearts. My dad often wore a Disabled American Veterans hat. The military insignia were worn in proud defiance, without the cynicism and sense of tragedy those symbols carried when my family marched again, a decade later, alongside Vietnam veterans who wore their medals in protest.

"Lady, how can you bring your children here? You should be ashamed!" a heckler yelled at my mother when we marched in the Moratorium — the first major nationwide protest against the Vietnam War. I remember feeling intense self-consciousness, but my mother smiled, ignored the hecklers, held her head high, and marched on.

I'd seen that smile before when I followed her, door to door, to campaign for Tom Bradley, when he first ran for a Los Angeles City Council seat in 1963. She believed then that the election of a Black man to public office would revolutionize the city and, not incidentally, be good for the Japanese Americans.

When we got to my friend Erin Sullivan's house, I told my mother we shouldn't bother; the Sullivans would never vote for Bradley. "How do you know?" she asked.

I didn't want to confess that I had sat in their living room and looked at my shoes, saying nothing, while Mr. Sullivan, our genial, bagpipe-playing neighbor, shouted epithets at Cassius Clay on the television. "Mom, I just know. Don't try it." Mom put on the same smile she later used to face down the hecklers and headed up the walk to the Sullivans', Bradley brochures in hand.

"Oh, you're for Bradley," Mrs. Sullivan said at the door. "We've already decided to vote for him. He's for education." It was one of those curious lessons in which what I already knew became evident. I knew, at age seven, that American racism was perverse, and that within that perversity existed unpredictable moments of connection. I knew Mr. Sullivan was both a good neighbor and a racist, a man who could rail against nonwhites yet insist that I take seconds when I sat at his table. I knew that his Irish pride was not unlike my father's Okinawan pride, and I loved it when the sound of his bagpipes carried through the air of our midtown L.A. neighborhood.

I didn't know then that I was living in a fragile sociological ecosystem, that the bagpipes floating over the taco stand corridos and mixing with a hundred hand-held radios emitting Aretha was not a sound mix destined to last in the city. I learned in that neighborhood how to chop liver in a wooden bowl, how to dance "ballin' the jack," how a teacher I adored could be unthinkingly cruel to a girl who could speak only Spanish. I stared in wonder at a gory crucifix over one friend's bed; snuck with another friend into her grandmother's bedroom to watch her unwrap treasures — a feather fan, a mesh coin purse — remnants of a golden life before the Holocaust. I learned rhyming games like "This Way, Valerie," which I later read about in anthropology texts — part of oral traditions come to L.A. streets from West Africa via Mississippi. I learned an anthropologist's rule: culture is never static. Culture exists in interaction with time, place, and, most important, other cultures.

One day my best Jewish friend moved to the Westside, my other best white friend to the Valley, and then we moved, back to my mother's home in Hawaii. My parents explained the move to us: they wanted safer schools, a better life for their children. Our lovely Los Angeles neighborhood, where many-hued children played together despite the prejudices they were quickly learning from the larger culture, was suffering the abandonment called "white flight," which also encompassed many middle-class people of color who foresaw urban decay.

In Hawaii I learned to negotiate a whole different set of cultural interactions. Japanese Americans held visible positions of power, even though they were still kept out of the fancy country clubs and the boardrooms of *haole* — white — corporations. Native Hawaiians were poised to begin their "renaissance," following the lead of Black nationalists, and they seemed to resent whites and Japanese Americans equally. Sorting out who was more privileged than whom was at once complicated and easy. My brothers and I worked our way through the halls of public schools where Hawaiian kids sniffed glue from wadded-up pieces of terry cloth and "high-jacked" lunch money from middle-class Asian kids who were tracked into college prep. Meanwhile, anti-personnel weapons lacerated Asian children in Vietnam and bombs fell on Cambodia. In locker rooms, in classrooms, at the meetings and protests our parents dragged us to, we felt the complexities of our relationships with people who were different from us; we learned the different ways in which the world inflicts cruelty on those designated less valuable.

What we learned was that race is complicated, is connected to class, and is situational and knowable. It is these lessons that inform what I know about affirmative action today: what makes sense in rectifying injustice is inevitably tied to time and place. That contingent reality is no excuse for inaction. It's just not that complicated, when you walk through halls where children are destroying their own brain cells at age thirteen, to understand that some people need more help than others to make it in this world.

It is a blessing of my life that my first encounters with school and community were intercultural. Today, almost none of the students at the law schools where I teach grew up in integrated communities. The cost of social segregation is an absence of comfort with difference, a static notion of race, and an inability to talk about racism. Over the years, I have learned to expect the anger, tears, and frustration that erupt in the classroom when we discuss affirmative action. Words like "blame," "innocence," "racist" — even the word "white," which calls attention to the race that isn't — all of these words are triggers for emotions, weighted with a social power and symbolism that stall conversation. I don't want to watch yet another generation of young people unable to speak about race. In writing about affirmative action, I seek the language of my first schoolyard: of frank curiosity about how others live in this world, of nuanced management of open confrontation, of varied talents allowed, sometimes grudgingly but still unfailingly, always to play.   — MJM

* * *

IN JANUARY 1987, I was on my way to teach my first constitutional law class as a Stanford law professor. I was one of two African Americans on the law faculty, the second hired in the school's history. I was the new kid on the block, and this was my first day at my new school. Dressed in gray slacks, a pin-striped, button-down shirt, blue tie loosened at the collar, and a blue blazer, I passed a colleague in the hall who kidded me about my formal attire. He wasn't wearing a tie, nor did he need to. He had lived on this block for a while. But as my father said, "If you're going to preach a radical sermon, dress conservatively." I have followed his admonition to the extent that my wardrobe and sense of style will allow.

A familiar tightness in my chest, a knot in my gut on that day evoked another first schoolday thirty-five years earlier. My family had moved from a deteriorating Black neighborhood in New York City to the suburb of Rockland County, and I was about to begin the third grade. My sisters and I would be the only Black kids at our new school. I sat in a seat near the back of Mr. Gurkey's bus and felt the stares in my direction as each new group got on, the quick glances followed by whispered conversation. I wondered whether these kids had ever seen a Black kid before, if they would ever be my friends.

On my first day at Stanford I wondered the same thing. I had decided not to begin my class with the traditional discussion of Chief Justice Marshall's justification of judicial review, but with a story from my childhood, a story of my earliest memories of constitutional discourse, of how the classmates at my new school became my friends despite the daily lessons in racism we learned from our history books and television sets, despite the sentiments of the adults who had posted a hand-painted sign at the entrance of the local lake resort: NO NIGGERS, JEWS, OR DOGS ALLOWED.

My story actually begins in Mrs. Rose's fourth-grade class at the South Main Street School in Spring Valley, New York, where I was one of two Black kids in the class. It was 1952. Three of us were wearing ALL THE WAY WITH ADLAI buttons amidst a sea of I LIKE IKE. And when Mrs. Rose allowed us to bring our radios to listen to the Subway Series between the Yankees and the Dodgers, five of us cheered our hearts out for the Bums from Brooklyn and against what was then America's team, the Yanks. Eisenhower and the Yankees won, and "under God" was inserted into the Pledge of Allegiance between "one nation" and "with liberty and justice for all."

That spring my family traveled south to visit relatives. We packed picnic lunches and dinners to avoid the humiliation of being sent to the back door of diners. My parents had grown up in Mississippi and were veterans at coping with Jim Crow.

In May of 1954, *Brown* v. *Board of Education of Topeka, Kansas,* was decided. Although I'd heard of the NAACP and had met Thurgood Marshall at a church dinner, this was the first time I can remember hearing about the Supreme Court. Nine white men in black robes had lifted from our heads the veil of legally sanctioned segregation. There was much rejoicing in my house, but even at the tender age of ten, I sensed that *Brown* was not so much a benignly bestowed gift as the fruit of a hard-fought struggle. Even at this young age, I understood that the struggle had just begun.

While I sensed intuitively that the Constitution protected only those who protected themselves, I also had a naïve idealism about the nature of political struggle. I was able to speak to my classmates face to face. We played ball and cut class together and fought over whether Mickey Mantle or Willie Mays was the better center fielder. When, as a high school student, I picketed the local Woolworth and asked my white buddies not to patronize it because Woolworth stores in the South would not serve Blacks at the lunch counter, they honored my request. I was a friend whose humanity was important to them. They promised only to shoplift and not to buy. When a pacifist organization in which my parents were active sponsored a Pete Seeger concert, the local chapter of the American Legion picketed the hall. It was a cold day, and my father and I served coffee to the picketers, most of them fathers of my classmates, and talked politics with them.

I decided to tell this story to my first constitutional law class for several reasons. It was a way to introduce myself, to say, "This is who I am and what I stand for." It was also a parable about the meaning and importance of constitutional debate. A constitution defines who we are as a community. It describes our national temperament and character; it is a mode of self-articulation; and it is an expression of our continuing capacity for creative action — our responsibility for collectively shaping ourselves. My story of our ability as children to engage one another, of our willingness to explore conflicting values, and, through that exploration, to discover the values we share, is an aspirational paradigm. It is a vision of what constitutional politics might be at its best. Finally, my account is a tentative articulation of shared experience and ideals. In some small but important way my story is also my listeners' story. It provokes thought and feeling, a moment of insight or understanding that says, "You have been there, too." It is an invitation to my students to say who they are, to bring their own gifts to our struggle to shape our community, and to be their best selves.   — CRL

WE WRITE not simply as individuals, but as individuals who are connected to multiple communities. Our first communities are our families of origin, from whom we inherit a lifetime's vocation of struggle for civil rights. Our parents taught us that this struggle is not just about individual advancement, nor only about the advancement of one's racial group. The struggle for human dignity is for all human beings. Those who would live off the toil of others, those who would sign restrictive covenants, those who would bomb a church, are also part of the human family. This is the complicated and difficult lesson we learned in the classroom of our first teachers, our parents, Kimi and Don Matsuda and Margaret and Charles Lawrence. They taught us that the struggle to make a place at the table for ourselves was also a struggle to free the souls of those who would exclude us. This is the lesson we hope to bring to our understanding of affirmative action. We were raised by folks who believed in and embraced the collective, the human family in its entirety. We start — in our lives and our work — from their stories.

Kimiko Ogata grew up barefoot, poor, and loved on a sugar plantation at Makawele, Kauai, Hawaii. One of ten children born to immigrant plantation workers, she learned from her mother the basics of plantation ethics: go when someone is sick, make peace when there is feuding, don't make yourself "high" — above others.

She also learned from young Nisei teachers on the plantation a false truism: in America, all are equal; anyone can succeed through hard work and education. Against the odds, she made those platitudes come true for herself, graduating from college to become a gifted teacher of young children and of their teachers. Along the way, she also became a radical. If you ask what did it, she will tell you it was the plantation —

watching her parents' generation used like workhorses, with no rights
or dignity, for the all-powerful sugar companies that controlled Hawaii's economy and politics.

She joined the legions of idealistic young college students who
fought for unions and the democratization of Hawaii. Coming of age in
the 1930s and 1940s, she was part of a mass movement for social change
that struggled for economic justice along with racial justice. Like the
many dreamers of her time, she believed in the truly egalitarian society:
no rich, no poor, no hunger, no war.

On a cross-country trip to a national Nisei for Wallace meeting,[1]
Kimi car-pooled with Don Matsuda, a handsome young veteran and
labor organizer. He told her the story of his life, and listened intently to
her story in turn. The son of an Okinawan antiimperialist-socialist father, Don grew up in a community of radicals — working-class Okinawans who studied Marx, Lenin, Tom Paine, and Thomas Jefferson in
their eager search for liberating ideas. In coming to America, the Okinawans sought not only economic survival, but also a world of potential freedom, individual rights, and workers united in struggle for a
better life.

The Okinawans' bitter hatred of Japan did not save them from internment along with Japanese Americans during World War II, nor did
Jefferson's Constitution protect them from deportation and persecution
in times of anti-Red hysteria. Despite such violations of their humanity,
the need to fight fascism and claim U.S. citizenship rights led progressive Okinawans to support the U.S. war effort. Don volunteered for
combat duty in World War II, leaving behind his mother in her internment camp barrack. He survived some of the worst battles of that war
— Anzio, Monte Cassino, the Lost Battalion rescue — but most of his
comrades did not. He was the only survivor to return home from his
original machine gun squad. After the war, he worked in the steel mills,
in the days when organized crime's hit men joined forces with the
company to keep out progressive unions. He once left an organizing
meeting to get the coffee, and returned to find the room destroyed by a
bomb. A Golden Glove champ — young, brave, and single — he laughs
when he speaks today of the risks of that time.

Don and Kimi married and moved to Los Angeles just as McCarthyism hit. Their idealistic work for labor rights and interracial "brother-

hood" suddenly made them targets. Threats, blacklists, and FBI harassment resulted in lost jobs and going without. The family survived on
the money Don earned doing small repair jobs. He was of the generation who knew how to fix things, back in the days when most things
were made to fix rather than be thrown out. Thus they raised their three
babies, on modest payments made by fellow radicals who needed an
antenna adjusted or a radio repaired. All the while, they never stopped
walking the picket lines.

When the War on Poverty came, Kimi signed up. She trained teachers for Headstart and worked with young mothers who were organizing a national movement for welfare rights. She walked confidently
through housing projects that even the police were afraid to enter, to
involve parents in decisions about their children's schooling. She believed in the goodness and talent residing in all human beings, and
acted on that belief. For her, children had to come first. There is no child
we cannot reach, and the costs of child neglect return tenfold to haunt
our streets.

To have lived with these two is to know the quiet contentment that
comes from believing that change is inevitable. When asked by her
impatient children, "What's the point?" as she set out on yet another
door-to-door campaign, Kimi would snap back, "We ended lynching."
We put on our walking shoes, carried petitions, organized study
groups; people were dying, and we stopped it. Her "we" is largely
unknown today. In her life she felt — and still feels — the complete and
powerful company of others like herself, organized and ready to struggle for the great day when all will live in peace, down by the riverside.

Charles Lawrence II was raised in rural Mississippi. His mother and
father were teachers at Utica Normal and Industrial Institute. The Black
families who lived in the hills and bottomlands of Hinds and Copiah
counties sent their children to Utica to learn the three R's and a trade.
Many of his parents' students worked in the fields by day and came to
school at night, paying their school fees in produce when that was all
their families could afford.

Utica was a small, deeply religious Black community, surrounded by
a hostile world of rigid racial hierarchy and violence. Charles watched
Mr. McAdney, a prosperous Black landowner and patron of the school,

enter by the back door when he did business with the white bank in town, and more than a few times he heard his parents speak in hushed tones of a Black man lynched in some nearby town.

At Morehouse College and Atlanta University, Charles's teachers — men like John Hope and W.E.B. Du Bois — taught a "social gospel": there should be no division between the work of scholars, political activists, and servants of the people. Charles learned these lessons and later taught them to students at Fisk University and Brooklyn College and to his children. He kept for his son a special letter dated June 6, 1943. "My dear sir," it read. "Congratulations on your advent into this astonishing world. I hope that you will be able to do something towards straightening it out. Very truly yours, W.E.B. Du Bois." The infant Charles Radford Lawrence III was thereby inducted into Du Bois's circle of activist scholars.

Charles had heard about Margaret Morgan, the beautiful and brilliant premed student, well before he laid eyes on her. Her parents were known to all in the Negro community of Vicksburg, Mississippi.[2] Margaret's father was an Episcopal priest; her mother a teacher at the small school run by the church. As a child, Margaret followed her father through Vicksburg's poor neighborhoods while he carried food to the hungry and laid "healing hands" on the sick. She was nine when she decided to become a doctor.

At fourteen Margaret moved to New York to live with her aunts in Harlem and finish high school, and at sixteen she went to Cornell, where she was the only Black undergraduate. When she was later denied admission to Cornell's medical school, despite a stellar academic record, the dean told her it was because they had admitted a Negro twenty-five years earlier, and "it didn't work out . . . He got tuberculosis."

Years later, when Margaret returned to Cornell to give a lecture, she took her children to meet the family for whom she had worked as a maid in exchange for room and board. They were a white couple who expressed joy and pride at Dr. Lawrence's success. After the visit, the young doctor turned around in the front seat so that she could look directly at her children in the back. "You may hear some white people say that you can't trust the Negroes you employ because 'they will steal.' This is a racial stereotype. We are no more prone to theft than any other group. Sometimes working people do have to take something for their families when their employers do not pay them enough. When I worked for the people you just met, I would sneak peanut butter from the refrigerator because they did not give me enough to eat."

Margaret became a pediatrician and then a child psychiatrist and psychoanalyst, founding and directing an interdisciplinary mental health team at Harlem Hospital. "Our job," she would say, "is to search out the ego strengths of young Harlem families, in the hospital, on the streets, in the childcare centers — wherever young children are to be found."

When Margaret discovered she was pregnant with her first child, her husband was on a civil rights march to Washington with A. Philip Randolph. Margaret and Charles were activists, and their new family would not change this. They stood in vigils, preached at churches, and spoke at conferences. Always, they took their children with them.

"I believe peace to be indivisible," Charles would say. "We have a responsibility as Negroes to work for equality and for morality in the world, not for the sake of minority groups, but for the sake of a very sick world." This was his and Margaret's vocation: to make a wounded world whole.

Charles and Margaret loved to sing together with their children: songs in the church choir, songs around the piano, a blessing sung before meals, a song sung by a parent to a child at bedtime. Most often it was spirituals and hymns, songs of praise and protest. When they sang "Walk together, children. Don't you get weary. There's a great camp meeting in the Promised Land," it was a joyful, loving song, and their children knew it was about their parents' work. "I'm gonna walk and never tire," they sang, and we children believed them, because we'd seen them do it all our lives.

We introduce Don and Kimi and Charles and Margaret here because we are their children, and we write from what they taught us. In a co-authored book, the tradition is to blend the voices into one narrator. Our politics, however, compel a different choice. We reject the notion that there is one universal authority and instead follow the tradition of feminist and other liberationist writers who choose to write in their own voices, from their own subjectivity, in protest against the detachment of the standard authorial voice.

Who we are and our genealogies are relevant to what we believe and to how the reader will respond to us. We write together because we are in solidarity in our support of affirmative action, but we will at times write separately in this book to let the reader know, in our most direct and immediate voice, what our experience brings to our analysis.

In a world divided radically by race and gender, a Black man and an Asian woman sometimes see things differently. We strive to retain this separate vision as a strength of analysis. The choice of multiple voices is not just style; it is substantive. Our defense of affirmative action is a defense of bringing human beings together from a multiplicity of experience, bringing them together as Who They Are, with their genealogies intact. Human beings can live and flourish side by side without sacrificing their individual humanity. There is a place for this, although we do not yet live there. This is the dream of peace that runs through the world's major religious traditions and through our great secular religion of constitutionalism. It is a dream reflected in the practice of affirmative action.

WE WON'T
GO BACK

Introduction

ONE OF OUR FRIENDS presses the mute button whenever a commercial comes on the television. It is his small rebellion against a hundred messages intended to subvert his values. Too often the mute button runs the other way, however, closing out dissent and sheltering the dominant view from challenge. Defending affirmative action often feels like talking to someone who owns the remote control to all human discourse. The words explaining affirmative action, carefully chosen to cross great divides, disappear; mouths move, but no one listens. At the outset, in writing this book, we face a clash of world views that makes give-and-take difficult.

One impetus for our writing this book was our frustration with the rhetoric infusing the public debate over affirmative action. Whether they support or reject affirmative action as a remedy for racial and gender subordination, most people define it as taking from one to give to another. Newspaper editors write of their reluctant support for a harsh remedy. Some, in fact, compare affirmative action to chemotherapy: a horrible but necessary cure.[3]

In contrast, we see affirmative action as a gain for all, an affirmation of democratic values. To our minds, ending racial and gender subordination in our country will liberate all of us and allow us to know the fullness of a community in which all talents are nurtured, all gifts brought to the table for the greater good. We write for our sisters who bear the scars of patriarchy's violence on their bodies; for the children who grow up poor because their mothers can't earn a living wage. As activists and writers, we fight patriarchy first for the sake of the women and children who are hurt, objectified, erased, and impoverished by it. We support affirmative action for women because women need the chance to go to school, to earn a decent living, to get away from the danger that dependency on men too often means. We fight patriarchy for the batterer as well. A world in which he doesn't have to dominate in order to claim a place for himself is a better world. Because we want this world, because we believe affirmative action is part of the journey to it, we write this book.

We have watched, with mounting dismay, as opponents and proponents of affirmative action speak past one another in the growing darkness. At a recent congressional hearing on a bill to end affirmative action in the federal government, for instance, the arguments, though made at the same table, were so disjunctive in premise and belief that they seemed to come from unrelated planets.

Representative Susan Molinari attacked affirmative action as "a program to confer special benefits on designated groups to achieve not equal opportunity but equal results."[4] Kingsley Browne, a law professor from Wayne State, argued that affirmative action "shifted the focus of decision-making from the relevant criterion of merit to the irrelevant criteria of race, sex, and ethnicity."[5]

Pro–affirmative action testimony focused on the reality of discrimination. Marcia Greenberger, from the National Women's Law Center, was armed with statistics: "95 to 96 percent of the senior managers of *Fortune* 1000 and *Fortune* 500 companies are male . . . women physicians earned 53.9 percent of the wages of male physicians . . . women received only 9.6 percent of doctorate degrees in engineering . . . 65 percent of working women earn less than $20,000 annually, and 38 percent earn less than $10,000."[6]

In the popular mythology surrounding affirmative action, we hear a different story from the one Ms. Greenberger attempted to portray with statistics. Early on, opponents of affirmative action knew their best tactic was to convince white men that affirmative action was taking their jobs, their educational opportunities, their life chances. The rhetoric of reverse discrimination and racial preference erases the statistical reality of inordinate advantage and preference that come from being white and male in this country, creating a surreal landscape for public debate.

Which world is the real one?

- The *Washington Post* reports that the wages of college-educated African Americans are dropping in comparison to similarly educated whites, with the earnings gap growing throughout the 1980s, belying the popularly held notion that education cancels out discrimination.[7]
- On another day, the *Post* runs a feature on a local high school basketball coach, known for his emphasis on "fundamentals." The feature describes the heartache and drama involved in the first few weeks of practice, when the coach must eliminate from the school's team roster most of those who hope to play. The coach is white, as are most of the students and all of the teachers at this private, suburban school. A white student who is cut from the team mutters to the reporter, "They don't keep any white kids unless they're over six-six."[8]
- *Ms.* magazine runs a story on women who rely on affirmative action programs to enter blue-collar professions. Women, the article points out, are .7 percent of plumbers and pipefitters, 1.7 percent of crane and tower operators, 1 percent of carpenters. Women want skilled trade jobs, because those are the only ones in which high school graduates can earn enough to support a family. Wages in the building trades are more than twice as high as those in "women's jobs" requiring comparable education, such as a dental hygienist or childcare worker. The article describes the harassment, ridicule, and discrimination these women — many of whom are single mothers trying to get off welfare — face when they enter the building trades.[9]
- Meanwhile, back in Congress, Clint Bolick — known for his attacks on Lani Guinier — testifies that "affirmative action has absolutely no relevance whatsoever to people who are outside the economic mainstream. In fact, it harms them because it sweeps these serious social problems under the carpet of racial preferences."

In her book *The Rooster's Egg*, Professor Patricia Williams describes attending a commercial law conference:

I stood with a group of Real Hungry Men, jockeying for position next to a table loaded with nice little creampuffs and fruit-filled cookies. "My wife wants to move to Chicago to be nearer her family," said one, scooping up a plateful of raspberry thins, "but I told her to forget it. Nobody's hiring white guys anymore."[10]

And yet, of the several hundred lawyers in attendance at the conference, Williams notes:

"there was a modest sprinkling of women in the crowd, perhaps fewer than a third. There were maybe ten Asians. I was one of two black women, and as far as I could tell, there were no black men, no Hispanics, no Native Americans, and not a single Pacific Islander. So who is it that's getting hired if not white guys?"[11]

- A philosophy professor from the University of Michigan warns that "preferential affirmative action on our campus (as on many campuses around the nation) has driven race relations among us to a point lower than it has ever been. The story is long and complicated and has many variants, but the short of it is this: give preference by race and you create hostility by race. And for that we Americans are paying, and we will pay a dreadful price."[12]
- In contrast, researchers at the same university reported that there are positive interethnic interactions on college campuses. Minority students regularly studied and dined with students from other races, interacting across racial lines more frequently than did white students. The study found that "55 percent of blacks, 69 percent of Asians, 78 percent of Chicanos, and 21 percent of whites reported dining with someone of a different race while in college."[13]

In this book we ask how to bring these two worlds together. We know the dominant world because we move within it: the world of disappointed white men who think their place on the team or their job in Chicago was stolen and given to someone without merit in an unfair game of racial preference. We also recognize a second world because we move within it as well — the world constrained by ancient and unacknowledged privileges determining that women become nurses' aides and men become plumbers, that Black men can't get a cab on the streets of the nation's capital, that outspoken Asian women are a threat to the natural order of things.

A clash in perspective of this kind is not resolved by taking away affirmative action, the immediate impetus for the clash. Returning to a segregated world — and this is exactly what the end of affirmative action would mean — will do nothing to erase racial tension or to resolve our lack of mutual understanding. We answer in these pages the charges that affirmative action breeds incompetence and resentment, that it hands out favors on the bases of race and gender, that it takes from white men and ignores the poor. In answering the charges, we strive also to hear them. The facts may be wrong — the young lawyer who believes women and minorities are getting all the jobs may not have his statistics right — but feelings are never wrong. If he feels anxiety about his job and his life chances, about disruption of race and gender hierarchies, those feelings are real, and we are bound to address them.

The policy of affirmative action comes out of a history that makes it an imperative. It is not an idea cooked up in the abstract. It is an idea born of a struggle — the same struggle that made our parents radicals. But the affirmative action debate, as it is largely presented, focuses on abstract ideas outside of social context — ideas like "colorblind" discussed without the history of racism; ideas like "preference" discussed outside the context of widening class division; ideas like "merit" discussed without reference to social structures like patriarchy.

Our work is about context and history and acknowledgment of culture. We are where we are, with the huge bloody problem delicately referred to as "race relations," because of a history. Women live the lives they do — whether worrying about their weight or struggling for dignity in the workplace — because of a social condition called gender.

This book tells of the early struggles around affirmative action. The news here is that there is no news. None of the arguments put forth today adds anything to the debate set out nearly twenty years ago at the time of the first attack on affirmative action. Ultimately, the result in any contest over affirmative action has less to do with quality of argument than with the social forces behind the debate. At the time of that first assault, in the late 1970s, an organized, grassroots movement for race and gender equality waged an effective fight back. The result was an uneasy compromise: watered-down affirmative action programs remained in place alongside a new rhetoric of "reverse discrimination."

While we believe that social struggle determines outcome, we also believe that ideology is part of that struggle. What people think and believe, the language they use, and the power of that language to evoke feeling and action are potent forces in the affirmative action battle.

In this book we seek to understand the terms of the affirmative action debate by asking the anthropologist's questions. What would a person have to know and believe about the world in order to make these arguments? Under what world view do they make sense? Who believes that, but for affirmative action, jobs, places at the university, government contracts, and other goodies are handed out according to merit? Why do we need to believe this? We hear many arguments against affirmative action: it stigmatizes beneficiaries, it causes resentment, it disadvantages "successful" minorities, it is discrimination against white men. We explore these arguments in our discussions of meritocracy, stigma, and interethnic conflict.

We consider women's position in affirmative action. Do women need affirmative action, and if so, where are they in the debate? Organized feminist groups have raised valiant defenses of affirmative action, yet women, as this nation's one potentially unbeatable voting block, are not, on the whole, taking an aggressive pro–affirmative action position. We ask why, and offer some answers, as well as a defense of affirmative action that comes from feminist theory.

The war over culture — the PC bashing, ethnotrashing debate that paints multiculturalism as voodoo academics — is also something we put at the center. What do sexual harassment, racial name calling, burning crosses, and anti-Semitism have to do with affirmative action? We think they are the heart of it. The criticism of Eurocentrism; the raising of the Women Question; the so-called cant of race-sex-class that has changed how we think and how we understand the world of ideas, are direct results of affirmative action.

New people bring new ideas, and new ideas are a threat. Someone will inevitably complain that "it's not the same anymore," that people can't say what they want to say, or that new and trivial work is sapping the dignity of the field. No crosses burn when hierarchies are fixed and people stay in their places. The tension created by shifts within hierarchy is what causes eruptions and backlash, name calling, and even violence. Affirmative action counters the belief that the other should "stay in her place." PC bashing, antimulticulturalism, and harassment are about saying "go back, go back," and so is the attack on affirmative action.

Affirmative action is affirmative. It is action in the face of what history hands us. In the last part of this book, we consider the need for apology and reparation; we look history in the eye. There is no shame and indeed great glory in acknowledging past wrong and committing ourselves to its rectification. This is certainly not the only reason for affirmative action, but it is one we call on in our belief that righting past injustice is part of the task of righting current injustice.

Finally, we do not divide our demand for public inclusion through affirmative action from other means of inclusion. Certainly ending poverty, particularly the poverty of children, is an immediate imperative if any of the words of democracy are to make sense. A democratic government residing in the people presumes that people have basic shelter, food, clothing, education; in short, that they survive.

This book thus offers a vision of affirmative action that includes those disadvantaged by class, as well as those excluded for other social reasons, including homophobia. Nondiscrimination is not enough when powerful state-supported forces systematically keep some people out of the social world: devalued, silenced, casually violated. In a time when many say affirmative action has gone too far, we say it has not gone far enough, and argue for aggressive expansion of existing programs.

Behind the rhetoric of the debate, there are real people. We introduce a few of the beneficiaries of affirmative action in order to give it a human face. The brief portraits in this book are an invitation to the reader to think in concrete terms: what people are in the room because of affirmative action, and what would we lose if they were no longer there? We know legions of people who are proud and talented beneficiaries of affirmative action, whose lives are just as remarkable as the few we present in these pages.

We want readers to feel the presence of these individuals, to feel, as we do, the excitement and promise of their work. The parsimonious language of "quota" and "preference" cannot begin to do justice to their lives; nor, for that matter, can our limited efforts convey all that is rich and wonderful about them. They are introduced here to show how affirmative action works, and to represent the thousands of others who are still shut out, still waiting for the chance that affirmative action can provide.

Affirmative action is part of a human dream, one that we venture to call universal. All human beings want good, useful, decent lives for themselves and their children. No one feels right when passing the homeless on the streets; no one takes true comfort in the guns and alarms and bars that we use to protect ourselves from crime; no one wants to say, on the last day, "I lived only for myself, with no care or concern for others." This is, ultimately, a spiritual book, written by an atheist and an Episcopalian. Affirmative action is an expression of the best parts of the human condition. It affirms the human family, our connectedness, our inevitable interdependency, and our potential to live generous lives. The anti–affirmative action rhetoric is bluster covering a dark and anxious vision of the human condition: get what you can for yourself, and guard every bit with care, lest someone undeserving take it from you. There is no mercy for you; so should you grant none to any other. Certainly much of human history is marked by that credo, but life under it is unsatisfying, fearful, and sad.

There is joy in deciding to take on the whole world as home, treating every path as sacred, treating every person as deserving of respect and care, taking less so that all the children are fed, needing less so that your soul can sleep in peace.

This we learned at our parents' table. It is the heart of affirmative action and the reason for this book.

[I]

DEEP RIVER

---

*The Historical Lineage
of Affirmative Action*

---

[1]

Born in Rebellion:
The Deep Meaning of
Affirmative Action

The black revolution is much more than a struggle
for the rights of Negroes. It is forcing America to
face all its interrelated flaws — racism, poverty, and
militarism. It is exposing the evils that are rooted
deeply in the whole structure of our society. It reveals systemic rather than superficial flaws and suggests that radical reconstruction of society itself is
the real issue to be faced. — *Martin Luther King, Jr.,*
1968[1]

O N   A   W I N T E R   D A Y   I N   1955, a diminutive forty-three-year-old
Black woman defied the Montgomery, Alabama, law requiring
segregation on the city buses and refused to move from her seat to make
room for a white man. "My feet were tired," she explained later. Asked
what was on her mind, Mrs. Rosa Parks answered, "This is what I
wanted to know . . . When and how would we ever determine our rights
as human beings?"

Montgomery Blacks boycotted the city buses; they walked to work
and organized car pools. They gathered in mass meetings that filled the
churches to overflowing. The city's response was to indict a hundred
leaders of the boycott and send many to jail. White employers threatened to fire Black employees if they continued to participate in the
boycott. Segregationists bombed four Black churches and the home of
Dr. Martin Luther King, Jr., the young minister who emerged as one of
the boycott's most eloquent leaders. Through it all the buses stayed
empty.

The Black people of Montgomery would not turn back; they under-stood what Rosa Parks meant when she said her feet were tired. They knew the humiliation of riding in the back of the bus, but more than that, they understood the import of her question. Their humanity was at stake, and they alone would determine the full measure of their rights. Dr. King was only reminding them of what they already knew when he told them their protest was not merely about segregated buses but about things that "go deep down into the archives of history."

A few years later, on February 1, 1960, four freshmen at A & T College, a Negro college in Greensboro, North Carolina, took seats at a Woolworth lunch counter restricted to whites. When they were denied service, they refused to leave, and Woolworth closed the lunch counter for the rest of the day. The next day they returned. Again they were refused service, and then, day after day, they and other Black students came to sit in dignified silence, waiting to be served or arrested.

Thus began the sit-in movement, which, within a matter of weeks, spread to fifteen cities in five Southern states. By the end of the year tens of thousands of young people had participated in demonstrations, and over 3600 people were put in jail. These young people, mostly Black, some white, sacrificed the safety and security of school and family to face violent mobs and police clubs, to defy the power of established society. They were the "new abolitionists," who saw agitation and dis-ruption as the essence of democracy.[2]

Following closely on the heels of the first sit-ins came the Freedom Rides. In South Carolina, Alabama, Tennessee, and Mississippi, Free-dom Riders, demonstrating against segregated facilities on interstate bus lines, were attacked by mobs with iron bars, their buses set afire. Local police jailed Freedom Riders after standing by while they were beaten. FBI agents ignored advance warnings of threatened violence, watched the beatings, and took notes.

Meanwhile, throughout the South, SNCC and the Southern Chris-tian Leadership Conference were organizing local Black people to regis-ter to vote and protest against racism. In Albany, Georgia, alone, twenty-two thousand Black people went to jail. In Birmingham, Ala-bama, thousands of schoolchildren, ranging in age from six to eight-een, faced police clubs, tear gas, dogs, and high-power fire hoses, and on an infamous bloody Sunday in Selma, Alabama, state troopers at-tacked marchers with billy clubs, bullwhips, tear gas, and trampling horses. In the space of only three months during 1963, the Department of Justice recorded 1,412 civil rights demonstrations. Rosa Parks's protest had ignited a massive rebellion and a consciousness-raising among the Black community that would inspire the struggle for years to come.

Congress responded at last in 1964 by passing civil rights legislation that made segregation illegal in most public accommodations and provided legal remedies for individuals denied employment opportunities because of their race. In 1965 it passed a comprehensive federal voting rights act that gave Southern Blacks their first meaningful access to the ballot. While these laws represented significant victories, pressure for change at the grassroots level remained unabated; the new civil rights laws alone could not alter the substantive condition of Black people's lives. Tens of thousands had not suffered jailings and beatings and the deaths of loved ones just to see the WHITE and COLORED signs come down. The movement had always been about much more than that. The movement was about what Dr. King called "the radical reconstruction of society itself." It was about changing not just the text of the laws but the facts of inequality.

The formal equality written into the new antidiscrimination laws was often unenforced and, even when implemented, was clearly not a fundamental solution to historically entrenched racism and poverty. In February 1963 the unemployment rate for whites was 6.1 percent, for nonwhites, 13.3 percent,[3] and a fifth of the white population had incomes below the poverty line, compared with half of the Black population.[4]

The new abolitionists understood that only when the conditions of poverty and the prerogatives of privilege were eliminated would all persons truly belong to America. They knew that this required the elimination of institutional barriers to inclusion, not just the outlawing of open bigotry. In this realization lay the seeds of the struggle for affirmative action.

The militant, nonviolent protest movement that swept the South in the early sixties turned north in the later part of the decade, erupting into insurrection in scores of cities. In 1964 and 1965 there were Black uprisings in Cleveland, New York, Chicago, Philadelphia, and Jersey City. In Los Angeles, the Black community of Watts erupted in the most violent urban outbreak since World War II.

Nonetheless, the veterans of the nonviolent movement continued their work in the South. And on June 6, 1966, James Meredith, who four years earlier had been accompanied by federal marshals when he enrolled as the first Black at the University of Mississippi, set out on a 220-mile "march against fear" through his native state. He began the walk virtually alone, with only four supporters accompanying him. The march seemed a quixotic personal crusade at a time when even the stalwarts of the civil rights movement had grown weary of marches. On the second day he was ambushed by a white unemployed hardware clerk from Memphis, who fired three shotgun blasts from a thicket beside the road. An Associated Press photographer captured the scene of Meredith writhing on the ground in a pool of blood. Meredith was rushed to a Memphis hospital, where, after emergency surgery, he recovered from his wounds, but he was unable to complete the march.

Leaders from all of the major civil rights organizations rushed to Mississippi to continue Meredith's march. It was crucial to resist old-style Southern intimidation. For more than two years, SNCC workers had been organizing in communities along the planned route of the march, and it fell naturally to them to make sure the march went forward. In a matter of hours, Meredith's lonely walk became what one *New York Times* reporter called "the biggest parade since Selma."

It was on June 16 that Stokely Carmichael, the chairman of SNCC, first introduced the nation to the slogan "Black Power." Carmichael's impassioned speech that evening to marchers in Greenwood, Mississippi, was enthusiastically received. He told his largely Black audience that they couldn't count on whites for support or help, that they had to do it on their own. Blacks were being sent off to fight in Vietnam, but at home they were second-class citizens. They couldn't vote and had no rights in the communities where they lived. It was time to stand up. It was time to stop asking white folks for freedom, time to take control of their own lives. It was time for Black Power. Carmichael led the crowd in a responsive chant that would become the rallying cry for the remainder of the march. "What do you want?" he shouted again and again, and each time the crowd responded more loudly "Black Power!" It was not the first time those words had been spoken. Carmichael had talked before of the need for Black people to have power over their own destinies, as had Frederick Douglass, W.E.B. Du Bois and Richard Wright. But in the charged context of the urban unrest and rising militancy of the mid-1960s, the slogan suddenly took on new meaning, signaling a change in the course of the civil rights revolution.

Many white Americans heard the call to Black Power as "Black racism" or, worse, a declaration of race war. Julius Lester, a former SNCC field secretary, wrote, "All the whites wanted to know was if Black Power was antiwhite and if it meant killing white folks."[5] In words that uncannily presaged today's anti–affirmative action rhetoric, Vice President Hubert Humphrey, long a civil rights supporter, called Black Power "reverse racism." "There is no room for racism of any color," he said. "We must reject calls for racism whether they come from a throat that is white or one that is black."[6] *Time* magazine called Black Power "the new racism," and accused SNCC and CORE (Congress of Racial Equality) of moving "dangerously toward a philosophy of black separatism and perhaps ultimately of black Jacobinism," evoking images of the guillotine and the bloody French Revolution.[7]

Many Blacks were also dismayed and frightened by the new slogan. The NAACP's Roy Wilkins called it "the father of hate and the mother of violence,"[8] and Whitney Young, executive director of the Urban League, warned that his organization would renounce ties with SNCC or any other group that "formally adopted black power."[9] But most Blacks, even those who shared a continued commitment to integration, heard the call for Black Power as a clear and forceful articulation of what the boycotts, sit-ins, marches, and voter-registration drives had always been about: the conditions produced by three hundred years of slavery and segregation must change, and, as Rosa Parks had said, we must take it on ourselves to "determine when and how we would gain our full rights as human beings."

The words of a statement published in the *New York Times* by a group of influential Black churchmen best expressed the sentiments that made Black Power a rallying cry that resonated throughout Black America. The churchmen deplored the overt violence of riots, but said it was "more important to focus on the real sources of these eruptions." Their basic cause lay "in the silent and covert violence which white middle-class America inflicts upon the victims of the inner city." The real problem, in short, was not "the anguished cry for black power, [but] the failure of American leaders to use American power to create equal opportunity in *life* as well as *law*" for all its citizens.[10]

Just as the initial fearful reactions by whites to the call for Black Power foretold the rhetoric of "reverse discrimination," there was in the Black churchmen's statement an early indication of the divide that exists today between many people of color and most whites. People of color are likely to judge the presence of the economic and social conditions of segregation, discrimination, and poverty as the clearest measure of whether we have achieved equality. Experience tells us that if the conditions have not changed, the racism that produced them is still alive and well. In contrast, many whites want to believe that the goals of the civil rights movement were achieved when we made formal discrimination illegal and that equality of opportunity can be accomplished without significant redistribution of resources.

In 1967 Stokely Carmichael and Charles Hamilton, a political scientist teaching at Columbia, sought to clarify any continuing confusion about what Black Power meant. In a small, plainspeaking book, *Black Power: The Politics of Liberation*, they presented a political framework that they called "the last reasonable opportunity for this society to work out its racial problems short of prolonged destructive guerrilla warfare."

In setting out its central tenets, they said that Black Power strove for "the creation of power bases, of strength, from which Black people can press to change local or nationwide patterns of oppression — instead of from weakness." It did not mean merely putting Black faces into office. "Black visibility is not Black Power." The goal of Black Power was self-determination and "full participation in the decision-making process affecting the lives of Black people." They argued that Black Power was also concerned with shaping a new Black consciousness:

> Black people must lead and run their own organizations. Only black people can convey the revolutionary idea — and it is a revolutionary idea — that black people are able to do things themselves. Only they can help create in the community an aroused and continuing black consciousness that will provide the basis for political strength. In the past white allies have often furthered white supremacy without the whites involved realizing it, or even wanting to do so. Black people must come together and do things for themselves. They must achieve self-identity and self-determination in order to have their daily needs met.[11]

Proponents of Black Power believed that institutionalized racism, rather than the racism of individual whites, constituted the major barrier to human equality. In 1963, when unidentified terrorists bombed a Black church in Birmingham, Alabama, and killed five little girls, that act of individual racism was widely deplored. But Carmichael pointed out the irony that, in the same city, "five hundred black babies died each year and thousands more were physically, intellectually, and emotionally maimed because of conditions of poverty," while the larger society seemed to know nothing of this institutionalized terrorism and therefore did nothing about it. In order to defeat institutionalized racism it was necessary to move beyond appeals to individual conscience and gain control of institutions.

"A riot is the voice of the unheard," said Martin Luther King in explaining the unprecedented urban violence that erupted across America in the late 1960s. What may have been most frightening to white society about the politics of Black Power was its adherence to Aldous Huxley's admonition that "liberties are not given, they are taken," and Malcolm X's counsel that freedom must be achieved "by any means necessary." In a speech in 1964 Malcolm X told a group of students: "You'll get your freedom by letting your enemy know that you'll do anything to get your freedom; then you'll get it. It's the only way you'll get it . . . When you stay radical long enough and get enough people to be like you, you'll get your freedom."[12]

The year 1967 saw the greatest outbreak of urban uprisings in American history. The National Advisory Commission on Civil Disorders, better known as the Kerner Commission, reported eight major uprisings, thirty-three "serious but not major" outbreaks, and 123 "minor" disorders. The report blamed "white racism" for the disorders, noting in particular "pervasive discrimination in employment, education, and housing . . . growing concentrations of impoverished Negroes in our major cities, creating a growing crisis of deteriorating facilities and services and unmet human needs." The commission said that "a new mood had sprung up among Negroes" who had directed their anger toward "local symbols of white American society."[13]

New urban rebellions erupted in 1968, after the assassination of Dr. Martin Luther King, Jr. King had planned the Poor People's March and encampment in Washington, D.C., to call attention to the problems left untouched by the civil rights laws. Committed to nonviolence, he nonetheless recognized that the feelings of anger expressed in the riots could not be ignored. He hoped that a massive, militant, and disruptive protest could express this anger and force Congress to confront the problems that produced the rage. In fact, a year before his death King had spoken of the unmet goals of the civil rights movement and the need for new, more confrontational tactics in the next phase of the struggle. "Negroes must fashion new tactics which do not count on government good will but serve, instead, to compel unwilling authorities to yield to the mandates of justice," he proclaimed. "Nonviolent protest must now mature to a new level to correspond to heightened black impatience and stiffened white resistance. This higher level is mass civil disobedience. There must be more than a statement to the larger society; there must be a force that interrupts its functioning at some key point."[14]

There was indeed a disruptive force that had interrupted business as usual in America, but that force was hardly nonviolent. The combined human and property costs of the urban rebellions from 1964 to 1972 were enormous: over 250 deaths, 10,000 serious injuries, and 60,000 arrests, and a cost in police, troops, and losses to business in the billions of dollars.[15]

Affirmative action was forged in the fire of urban rebellion. The students and community activists who demanded that government agencies, universities, and businesses open the doors of white institutions to a significant nonwhite presence were graduates of and heirs to the militant civil rights movement of the early sixties. They were advocates of the politics of Black Power that had grown out of that movement. They insisted on community control of institutions within communities of color and representation within all institutions that affected the welfare of those communities.

Across the nation, community activists ran candidates for office at every level, from unions to school boards to city councils to Congress. Black mayors were elected in Cleveland, Ohio, in Gary, Indiana, and in Newark, New Jersey. Black farming cooperatives were established in Georgia, Mississippi, and Louisiana. From Oakland, California, to Boston, to Jackson, Mississippi, chapters of the Black Panthers, the Southern Christian Leadership Conference (SCLC), the Congress of Racial Equality and a host of other community-based organizations established breakfast programs for children, housing cooperatives, health clinics, freedom schools, and art institutes. In New York in 1967, Black and Puerto Rican parents in Brooklyn and Harlem demanded community control of neighborhood public schools, and for a brief period community school districts were established, with local school boards composed of parents and representatives from community organizations. In Oakland, the Black Panthers monitored the activities of the police department with armed patrols, and in cities across the country, communities of color, long the victims of police brutality, sought increased control of police and greater representation on the police force.

While many of these initiatives were short-lived, their political impact was often long-lasting. Community organizations quickly learned that the inclusion politics of Black Power was more than slogan and bravado. When Blacks were represented within the institutions where they lived, worked, and learned, it made a significant difference. Moreover, the individuals who participated in these struggles — the students, parents, and community residents who took part in election campaigns and the building of community institutions — would continue their involvement in later campaigns for community power.

The Minority Student Program at the Rutgers Law School in Newark, for instance, came into being even as buildings continued to burn in the Newark uprising of 1967. Rutgers had graduated only twelve Blacks since 1960, and the rage expressed in the streets made it apparent to the law faculty that it was neither morally nor politically tenable for their school to continue as a publicly funded enclave of white privilege in the midst of Black poverty. The faculty voted through an emergency plan to admit twenty Blacks with the entering class that fall and forty more in each of the next two years. Wade Henderson, a member of that first cohort of affirmative action entrants, who went on to become Washington bureau director of the NAACP and national director of the Leadership Council for Civil Rights, recalls that "the atmosphere of urgency was palpable." When he arrived on campus "the air still smelled of char from burned-out buildings." In 1970, out of ten thousand lawyers in the State of New Jersey, fewer than 1 percent were nonwhite. By 1990, two thousand Blacks, Hispanics, and Asians practiced law in the state, and 40 percent of those had come through the Rutgers minority admissions program.[16]

The underlying ideology of Black Power extended well beyond Blacks to other disenfranchised groups, spurring a movement of new ideas and activism. By the late sixties, in the West and Southwest, Chicano activists were reading Stokely and Malcolm and studying Chicano history to construct a politics that demanded voices and places for Mexican Americans in venues of power. Chicano students in California looked to Cesar Chavez's Farmworkers Union for a model of bottom-up social change. Workers and students of working-class origin were key to this movement's success. Like the advocates of Black Power, the proponents of "Chicanismo" were concerned with understanding and resisting the class exploitation and racism that shaped their experience as Mexican Americans, and like their Black brothers and sisters, they developed a politics that was rooted in their culture and communities.

By the early 1970s, they had "organized tutorial programs, sparked cultural events, sponsored colloquiums and conferences, pressured for larger enrollments of Mexicans in college, inspired and fought for major curricular changes, the establishment of college-university study centers, departments, and degree programs, and the hiring of staff and faculty."[17] And in the larger community, "students directed voter registration and voter education drives, worked in social rehabilitation, opened centers for community action, organized barrio schools, participated in mass protest, and faced serious confrontation with the authorities."[18] According to Juan Gomez-Quinones, a Chicano historian, the Chicano movement was "a continuation and acceleration of the historical struggle against national and class oppression by the Mexican people . . . As students they were privileged *vis à vis* their community and as Mexicans and offspring of a working-class community they were in an antagonist relation to the constituency and purpose of the university."[19]

Likewise, young Japanese Americans in California organized during the mid-1970s to demand redress for the losses experienced by their parents when they were interned in concentration camps during World War II. They, too, were children of the sixties who had watched the police dogs in Birmingham and the fires of Watts and Detroit. Fully aware that the racism behind the internment was not an aberration in

American history, they helped organize a movement to demand that the nation apologize and pay reparations to the internees.[20] The same culture that had lynched over four thousand Black men, invented Jim Crow, and written the Chinese Exclusion Acts had imprisoned Japanese Americans in the sand-blown hills and deserts of America's concentration camps. The young Japanese Americans now organized with other Asian students for Asian American studies programs and for university admissions programs that recruited Asian students from poor communities who were committed to returning to those communities.

Asian American students suffered a significant setback in the fall of 1975 at the University of California at Berkeley, when the faculty at the law school voted to eliminate Japanese and Chinese Americans from the minority admissions program, arguing that a sufficient number of Asian Americans were being admitted through the regular admissions process.[21] This move presaged a national trend toward excluding Asian Americans from affirmative action programs. The Asian American Law Students organization, opposing the Berkeley decision, submitted a position paper that documented the way in which the regular admissions criteria selected those members of their communities who were least disadvantaged and most assimilated, while excluding those who came from immigrant, working-class communities and were most likely to return to those communities. They argued that "the thrust of [minority admissions] programs should not be to simply increase the number of minority attorneys, but rather to insure that disadvantaged people and people who have the skills and commitment to work in low income Asian American communities are given access to a legal education."[22]

Indigenous peoples in the Americas, in the Pacific, and elsewhere were also reading Malcolm's words as they reconstructed a politics of self-determination and fought to reclaim stolen land and sovereignty.[23] Steven Biko, the martyred leader of South Africa's Black Consciousness movement, for instance, often cited the Black Power movement in the United States as a primary source of inspiration and political theory for young black South Africans.

And, in 1969, nearly six hundred American Indians, representing more than fifty tribes, took up their own cause in the civil rights renaissance. They occupied Alcatraz Island in San Francisco Bay and issued a Proclamation to the Great White Father and All His People. The document offered to purchase the island for "twenty-four dollars in glass beads and red cloth," and set out a plan to develop on it several Indian institutions, including a center for Native American studies, an American Indian spiritual center, an Indian center of ecology, a great Indian training school, and an American Indian museum. The proclamation closed with a reaffirmation of their claim to this island as a symbol of their claim to all the lands that had been taken from them and their commitment to self-determination.

In the same year that American Indians occupied Alcatraz, Black and Latino construction workers staged demonstrations in New York, Pittsburgh, Chicago, and Seattle that halted work at major construction projects, including Seattle's King Dome and Pittsburgh's Three Rivers Stadium. Most construction unions remained segregated; in 1969 African Americans held only 2 percent of the nation's higher paying construction jobs and only 7.2 percent of lower paying craft jobs.[24] Chicago's Black Coalition demanded ten thousand building jobs and closed down construction projects for over two weeks.[25] Pittsburgh demonstrators shut down some $200 million worth of construction projects and carried signs reading IF BLACKS DON'T WORK, NO ONE WORKS.[26] Unions began, often grudgingly, to implement training and outreach programs to integrate the trades.

After demonstrations at the construction site of a new state office building on 125 Street in New York City, New York's Governor Nelson Rockefeller signed an agreement for the hiring and training of Black and Puerto Rican workers. The agreement set up an advisory committee comprising representatives from the Harlem community and, as a result, of the five hundred workers employed on the construction project, a third were hired from the community and half of those were trained for skilled crafts.[27]

Though inspired by the activist spirit of these transformative movements, many of today's affirmative action programs do not reflect the radical ideal of community control. This is the outcome of a strategy of compromise and co-optation by institutions that sought to appease the anger of the excluded without relinquishing significant power. The students and community activists who demanded affirmative action and embraced the politics of community empowerment would have had little impact if their communities had not been ablaze. Students, labor activists, and community organizers who called for minority admissions, ethnic studies programs, set-asides for government construction contracts, and fully integrated police and fire departments, for instance, seemed moderate when their voices were accompanied by the flames of urban rebellion in Detroit, Newark, and Watts. The rage of the young people who were burning and looting was not mindless violence uninformed by political ideology. On the contrary, the Report of the National Advisory Commission on Civil Disorders found that those who participated in the riots tended to be somewhat *better* educated than those who did not, and that the burning and looting were usually directed "against symbols of white American society — authority and property — rather than against white persons."[28]

When the Panthers carried guns to the state capitol in California they carried as well a ten-point political platform. When Black high school students walked out of classes and marched against the Board of Education in Philadelphia, they quoted Malcolm X and Franz Fanon in their demands. Militant rage was not mindless. It was political.

It was no coincidence that the period marking the height of urban unrest was the period in which both government and private corporations began affirmative action programs in earnest. In September of 1965, President Johnson issued Executive Order 11246, regarded as the originating document of federal affirmative action. It was aimed at "the full realization of equal employment opportunity" and required firms conducting business with the federal government to "take affirmative action" to ensure such opportunity.[29] Firms across the country were to set "good faith goals and timetables" for employing "underutilized" minority group members available and qualified for hire.

In 1967, the Department of Health, Education, and Welfare began requiring colleges and universities receiving federal funds to establish affirmative action goals for hiring female and minority faculty members. By the early 1970s the Equal Employment Opportunity Commission had taken the position that all employers within its jurisdiction, not just those receiving federal funds, must institute result-oriented affirmative action programs.[30]

Local governments and private businesses soon followed the federal government's lead. For example, in 1966, the City of New York, the Roman Catholic Church in Michigan, and the Texas-based retailer Neiman Marcus announced plans requiring their suppliers and contractors

to take affirmative steps toward hiring African Americans.[31] Some businesses resisted affirmative action efforts in the 1960s, but by the early
1970s others, like Dow Chemical, were making voluntary efforts to
diversify their workforce, having found that affirmative action could
help raise profits.[32] By the 1980s so many companies had found affirmative action beneficial that the National Association of Manufacturers
adopted a policy statement supporting affirmative action as "good
business policy,"[33] and some companies filed amicus briefs and sent
telegrams to the White House opposing the Reagan administration's
effort to curtail affirmative action.[34] CEOs of Time and Pillsbury publicly stated that they would retain their affirmative action programs
even if the government did not require them to do so.[35]

When a tangible threat of mass insurrection loomed, making room
for a few more folks from the nation's ghettos seemed to those in the
seat of power but a small price to pay. If the chief complaint of protestors was that the Civil Rights Act had produced no real change, then
perhaps it was time to show some results.

While there were many white individuals and even some white
institutions who were moved, at least in part, by moral purpose, what
was seen as morally necessary was often influenced by the perceived
threat of prolonged disruption to business-as-usual. Against this back-
drop of moral claim and threat to civil stability, President Johnson, in
a 1966 speech at Howard University, acknowledged that the formal
equality written into the civil rights laws was not enough.

> You do not take a person who, for years, has been hobbled by chains
> and liberate him, bring him up to the starting line of a race, and then
> say, "You are free to compete with all others," and still justly believe
> that you have been completely fair.
>
> Thus it is not enough to open the gates of opportunity. All our
> citizens must have the ability to walk through those gates.
>
> This is the next and more profound stage of the battle for civil
> rights. We seek not just freedom but opportunity — not just legal
> equity but human ability — not just equality as a right and a theory
> but equality as a fact and equality as a result.[36]

Johnson's words, which made a strong and simple case for affirmative action, were a compelling expression of the nation's moral commitment to justice, issued from the highest level. Johnson, the ultimate

political pragmatist, understood that until we achieved more than formal equality, there would be no justice. More important, he understood that without something more closely resembling justice, there would be no peace.

Affirmative action as we know it today is the product of this era of rebellion and compromise. Powerful institutions made token concessions, partial payments on the demands for full equality, in an effort to purchase peace. But in the face of rebellion, as history reveals time and again, power rarely yields more than is necessary to bring about a temporary cease-fire. The programs that came into being in the 1960s and 1970s were not all that community activists had sought. Invariably, they were limited in both scope and number. When student activists demanded open admissions, university administrators typically established small minority admissions programs that used substantially the same admissions standards as before. When community activists demanded community participation in the hiring and firing of police, governments established police practice review boards with little actual power. When ghetto organizers sought control over the award of contracts for services in their neighborhoods, they got small set-aside programs, typically requiring the major white businesses who monopolized lucrative government contracts to offer between 5 and 15 percent of their subcontracts to minority-owned companies.

Not only were these programs more limited than what activists had demanded, but the political goals that motivated and shaped them often differed from those of the activists. The affirmative action programs put in place met the needs of the institutions that created them: the students of color who were admitted to universities were typically those whom faculty and administrators determined would fit most easily into the dominant campus culture, not those most likely to advance the interests of the communities that had demanded shared access. SAT scores continued to be the primary determining factor in college admissions, and minority students from middle-class families were far more likely to gain admission to top schools than those from economically disadvantaged communities. Likewise, the minority contractors who benefited from set-asides were most often those who already had close ties with influential whites, not those most likely to bring new resources back to the minority community.

This transformation of the ideal of affirmative action as a vehicle for community power to a mechanism for co-optation gave rise to the phenomenon of the affirmative action beneficiary who turns against the very people who opened the door for him. Consider the sad irony in the story of Ward Connerly, the Black appointed by Governor Pete Wilson to the University of California Board of Regents. An affirmative action appointment if ever there was one, Connerly, who had made a small fortune as a real estate developer, and who himself benefited from set-asides, sponsored the resolution ending affirmative action in the entire University of California system.

Those of us who are affirmative action's strongest supporters know that, in their current incarnations, many affirmative action programs have serious weaknesses. Although there is a continuing need for affirmative action that addresses the effects of past and continuing discrimination based on race and gender, we are nonetheless concerned when the programs fail to address directly the problems of the most needy. When we hear the complaint that affirmative action "only helps the privileged" from the very people who are demolishing programs for the poor, we hear hypocrisy. The limitations this complaint identifies are not inherent in affirmative action. Compromises to power during the turbulent shaping of affirmative action have made it a very different animal from that envisioned by the original proponents.

The same understandings of the struggle against racism and for human liberation that guided the civil rights movement inform affirmative action in its truest form. The first of these beliefs is that the entrenched inequalities that are the legacy of two centuries of slavery and one century of Jim Crow laws will not disappear of their own accord, or by the mere enactment of laws that prohibit segregation and discrimination. Social systems three centuries in the making can be dismantled only through affirmative action; it requires affirmative efforts to tear down the walls that white supremacy took centuries to build.

The second is the understanding that white supremacy injures us as groups and communities. When Rosa Parks refused to get up from her seat, she understood that it was not just her own tired feet that were at stake. Every Black person in Montgomery was made less human when she was forced to give up her seat to a white man. The four young men who sat down at the Woolworth lunch counter in Greensboro were not concerned just for their own self-respect and dignity. They represented all of us who are discriminated against. When the WHITE and COL-ORED signs came down, the stigma they symbolized was removed from African Americans as a group.

The third is that freedom is something fought for. The privileged do not give away privilege unless they must. The civil rights movement, whether nonviolent or violent, has made significant advances only when it has been militant. This was Frederick Douglass's meaning when he said, "Those who profess freedom, and yet deprecate agitation, are men who want crops without plowing up the ground. They want rain without thunder and lightning. They want the ocean without the awful roar of its many waters." He recognized that "power concedes nothing without demand. It never did, and it never will."[37]

This is the lesson of the anonymous New York City poet who authored the subway graffito "If someone gives you your freedom, you still haven't got it." These understandings, which have come out of the long struggle against white supremacy, remain important for all of us engaged in the fight for affirmative action. Affirmative action can have a shallow or a deep meaning. The shallow meaning goes something like this: there were once laws and practices that denied people of color access to schools, jobs, and housing. There was a need to make sure that these explicit practices of segregation and discrimination ended. The practices were mistakes or things done by a few bad people. We regret them and we will invite a few token persons from minority communities into our institutions to make up for that mistake. We also recognize that it would help the children of the powerful to learn more about the nonwhite world if a few nonwhites were around, but we will decide whom to invite. We will decide who is qualified to serve our purpose of creating an environment where we can learn what we need to know about them.

The deep meaning of affirmative action, however, is radically different and recognizes that the only remedy for racial subordination based on the systemic establishment of structures, institutions, and ideologies is the systemic disestablishment of those structures, institutions, and ideologies. Radical affirmative action goes beyond the remedy of simply declaring that discrimination is illegal and pretending that our culture is colorblind. It says that it is not enough for the discriminator to remove his boot from the victim's throat and call it equal opportunity.

The student and community activists of the 1960s and 1970s who fought for affirmative action shared this understanding of what was required. They knew that racism operated not primarily through the acts of prejudiced individuals against individuals of color but through the subordination and exploitation of their communities. They understood that institutional racism operated by denying economic resources, education, political power, and self-determination to communities of people defined by race. When these freedom fighters demanded affirmative action — when they sat in and sued and took over buildings and went on hunger strikes and closed down universities — they demanded redress for their communities. They demanded a stop to university expansion that forced poor people out of housing. They sought courses and research that addressed community needs. They vowed that unless the walls that kept their communities out were opened, those walls would come tumbling down.

They demanded the admission of students and the hiring of faculty who identified with their excluded communities — not just people who shared their skin color or language, but individuals who would represent and give voice to the oppressed. Under this version of affirmative action people of color, women, and other historically excluded groups come to the universities, to fire and police departments, to law firms and corporate boards, so that they can serve the interests of their communities; their purpose is not to educate elite white folks and serve elite white interests. This deep version of affirmative action recognizes that racist institutions remain racist as long as they serve the exploiters of oppressed communities. It recognizes that those who are privileged by race and gender cannot judge who is best qualified to engage in the struggle against that privilege.

Under this version of affirmative action President Bush and the U.S. Senate could not have decided that Clarence Thomas was the African American best qualified to serve on the Supreme Court. Under this version of affirmative action the Harvard Law School could not decide that there is no woman of color in the entire world who is qualified to be on their faculty. Under this version faculty and students of color would not first ask whether their white colleagues think their work is important but whether the work will serve the cause of liberation.

There is another critical component of the deep meaning of affirmative action: a demand for substantive justice. Civil rights activists fought for inclusion, for an end to privilege based on race, gender, *and* wealth. The shallow version of affirmative action is an attempt by those with privilege to buy their way out cheap, to create an illusion of justice overlaying growing divisions between have and have-not.

We all want to believe in our individuality and agency: if our hearts bear malice toward none, we hope others will recognize this and allow us to live in peace. Although racial division and racial hierarchy exist out there, we want to define ourselves apart from where we are placed in the division and hierarchy. The sad truth is that individual good will and self-definition mean little without structural change. Until substantive justice is attained for all, there will inevitably come days when the structures jump out from hidden places, revealing the contradiction in our existence: there is no place to hide from the instability that race and class hierarchy plants at the heart of our lives. Yet every day we wake up and pretend this is not so.

I was not surprised by the Rodney King verdict. The brothers at the South-Central barbershop where I got my hair cut had predicted this result when the trial was first moved to Simi Valley, and I had learned to trust their wisdom in such matters. Still, I was stunned. It was the inevitability, the predictability, of the verdict that left me speechless. It was the realization that the violent, videotaped assault on Rodney King in the name of law was not a horrific aberration but the unspoken rule. The fact that black and brown men are daily subjected to police brutality, that every thirty-nine seconds an infant is born into poverty, that we will spend $40,000 a year to imprison an adolescent while refusing to spend a tenth of that to educate a child — all of this violence was embodied in the in-your-face gesture of the acquittal of the assaulting police officers. The whole world had seen the videotape; now the whole world would witness the final insult. It doesn't matter — a crime against a Black man by agents of the state, no matter how blatant, just doesn't matter. Though these jurors were not the self-proclaimed bigots that served on Southern juries thirty years earlier, their verdict could have stemmed only from the racism that infects all of America. They could not be easily dismissed as representatives of an unfortunate but isolated lunatic fringe. Incapable of seeing themselves in Rodney King, incapable of imagining that he was their father or brother or son, they could watch a videotape of a helpless man curled on the ground, savagely beaten by four armed police officers, and see only a "massive black man" who was "in control" and who must have deserved this beating by innocent cops who were just doing their job.

It was the inevitability of the verdict and its business-as-usual quality that lit the spark and made the victims of America's everyday violence recognize their rage and erupt with violence of their own. I remember fearing for my people as I drove home that evening, knowing that those who suffered most from the violence of oppression would suffer first in the uprising against it. I also knew that rage finds its outlet, that pain must be expressed. I heard Mayor Bradley, on my car radio, asking his brothers and sisters to express their outrage "with words," to work within the system. But I knew that my brothers and sisters had heard the system's verdict the way I had: NOT GUILTY. Not guilty of unemployment, impoverished schools, and substandard housing. Not guilty of no health care, of watching eight hundred of our young people die in Los Angeles that year in gang-related homicides, of seeing our suffering yet passing by on the other side of the road.

The last time our words were really heard was when Watts and Newark and Detroit burned. I knew that I had no adequate expression for my rage and that once again those in our community least able to protect themselves from the power of the state were taking up positions on the front lines. The words our young people were crying in the streets, "No justice, no peace," reminded me of how we had lost touch with the original meaning of affirmative action. The rebellion revealed how we had allowed a shallow version of affirmative action to replace the original deep meaning that was so clear when the fires of the 1960s were all around us. I sensed that we had come full circle.

A theologian once said, "The public expression of pain summons God into our presence." When we acknowledge the suffering that comes from oppression or racism or alienation or violence, there is a moment of epiphany when we can see that our pain is shared. In this moment we have a chance to breach the barriers that divide us. The pain expressed by the young people who looted and burned in L.A. is the pain of all of us.

Those who fear the loss of privilege have always tried to stop the expression of pain. They pass laws to forbid talking about it, and they imprison the poets and the prophets. As soon as the fires began, as soon as the young prophets started to express their rage and pain, the powerful set about silencing their truth. The eyewitness news reporters stood on corners before burning buildings and told us that this was the work of hoodlums and hooligans, engaged in senseless violence. Politicians soon joined the chorus. Senate candidate Tom Campbell called the looters "evil people, [a] criminal element."[38] Even as pundits cited the prophetic findings of the Kerner Commission and a dozen commissions before it, they felt compelled to say, "Of course the violence cannot be condoned." When Byron Scott, a star guard for the Los Angeles Lakers basketball team who had grown up in South-Central, said of those who were rioting, "I know how they feel," he was castigated on radio talk shows and editorial pages for "advocating, if not inciting, additional violence" and for abusing his position as a public figure.[39]

All of us were frightened, horrified, and saddened by the human suffering we witnessed, but the politicians and the press spoke of this suffering in words of condemnation and moral judgment for "those people," for the "hoodlum," for the "animal," who, even as he waved at the TV camera, was faceless, was someone we could neither know nor care for. The guardians of privilege spoke in words that drowned out the voices raging against the everyday violence of hopelessness and humiliation. Their words tried to obliterate the raging poets' truth of our collective suffering.

Each of us knows the pain of living in a society divided against itself. We have tried to put the pain back where it was before young people in Los Angeles lit the fires that made it visible once again. In the weeks and months that followed the Los Angeles uprising, we pushed to the back of our consciousness the knowledge that we cannot go on like this. Now, when we drive to work or pick our children up from school, we have forgotten Los Angeles, just as we have repressed the memory of the burning cities of the 1960s. We tell ourselves that there will not be another conflagration, although there certainly will. We want to believe that if we push down the pain, if we tell ourselves enough times "we're not guilty," it will go away. But the day will come again, when we are sitting at a desk or at the kitchen table, when we will hear sirens, hear the phone ring. "Get out of there!" someone will say. "The city's about to blow."

In Los Angeles those in charge did what they always do when things start to look bad. They sent in the troops, as they had done in Newark and Detroit and Watts thirty years before. But if the uprising in Los Angeles taught us anything, it confirmed that there is no police force, no army, big enough to keep the peace when there is no justice; that authority cannot replace community. The young people we are raising to despise themselves, to have no experience with reward for work or joy in contribution to the polity, to have no fear because they have nothing to lose, can tear down half a city, at least, before the state can bring in enough tanks and troops to stop them.

We must build a community that reclaims those angry young people. We must recognize that America's poor, its sick, its unemployed, its homeless, are us. We need to end the war against the poor and join forces to wage a new war on poverty. When our politicians appeal to our greed, our selfishness, and our fear, we have the power to say to them, "We are better than that."

This is the deepest meaning of affirmative action: racism, sexism, homophobia, and poverty injure us all, and this knowledge calls us to active, affirmative battle. This is what Rosa Parks and Martin King and Malcolm X and the young people of SNCC understood about freedom. This is knowledge out of the ashes of burned cities; this is the meaning that informs our defense of affirmative action. None of us is free until all of us are free. And because we are not all free, we won't go back.

ANTHONY ROMERO

Adding the verbs

ANTHONY ROMERO has spent the morning shepherding potential philanthropists through a Manhattan housing court. He wants them to see the scene: children crying in the halls, benches full of poor people waiting, a mother telling a judge about backed-up sewage in her apartment, one eviction case after another. Here are the individual faces of poverty in the city, revealing obvious human need coupled with the stark inability of the judicial system to meet that need. Romero explains his analysis of what would make life better for those tired mothers and their children; what interventions could make a difference. It takes money, he concludes. Not just charity, but funding for the kinds of programs that enable people to help themselves.

By the end of his talk, his listeners are not only convinced of the efficacy of well-placed philanthropy; they are also filled with curiosity about their guide, a charming young Latino whose pale gray, European-cut suit hangs with casual elegance from his thin frame. He looks white, but his second-generation New York Puerto Rican accent, which he also wears with casual elegance, marks him unmistakably as the other. He seems to know much about how poor people live, yet he seems to his audience so different from them — so articulate, so accomplished, so dynamic. "What about you, Anthony?" one woman finally asks. "How did you make it to where you are?"

Anthony Romero smiles his wide, generous smile and replies, "Two words: affirmative action."

"Oh, no," the woman replies quickly. "Not you, Anthony. You're so smart, so special . . ." as though she wishes to redeem him from a negative label.

"And," he replies, still smiling, "I needed affirmative action."

Anthony Romero is one of the highest-ranking Latino foundation officers in America. Currently the director of the Human Rights and International Cooperation Program at the Ford Foundation, he supervises a large staff and numerous grants with budgets totaling millions of dollars. How did he get there from his childhood in a Spanish-speaking home in a Bronx housing project?

His parents were immigrants. His father, Demetrio Romero, grew up working on a sugar plantation in Puerto Rico, attending school only until the fourth grade. As a consequence, he was never comfortable with writing. His son describes the strained hand with which he signed his children's financial aid applications. "Ironically, in his shirt pocket — he always wore a proper dress shirt — he would always have a gold Cross pen and an Ace comb," Anthony recalls. Demetrio Romero was gregariously friendly to all, never afraid to approach someone simply because of his limited English or perceived lower social status.

Shortly after coming to America, Romero went to work as a "houseman" at the Warwick Hotel. He stayed for thirty-nine years, loyal to the union, and waited for a promotion to banquet waiter, a higher-paying position. He knew his long wait was a result of discrimination. He was known to all as a good worker, but Latinos were rarely promoted. The excuse of limited English made little sense, since many waiters were European immigrants — Greek and Italian — for whom English was a second language. Furthermore, speaking perfect English was hardly a central requirement for banquet servers, who had little or no need to converse with customers at large hotel functions where everyone was served the same meal. After many years, the banquet job was made available to Demetrio Romero, and he took pride in doing that job well.

Anthony describes his mother, Coralie Romero, as "the brains in the family." Her own mother was a widowed factory worker, struggling to support her four children. Coralie dropped out of school to help support her family, abandoning her chance for betterment through education and leaving behind embarrassing schooldays when her shabby clothes marked her as a child of poverty. Determined that her children would have more, she told her son he must study: "That's the way people make it in America." When she noticed his early interest in reading, she encouraged him, all the while planning and scheming to make a better life for her children.

The Romero family lived in a low-income housing project, walking up and down twelve flights of stairs because the elevator never worked. It seemed that nothing worked. Anthony recalls winters with no hot water or heat, going to bed at night wearing a knit hat and gloves. Crime was out of control. An entire family was murdered in the apartment next door, and young Anthony and his sister were not allowed outside to play. Spending long hours in the apartment alone, they developed a special closeness, which has lasted into their adulthood.

Every night Demetrio Romero would ride the subway back home to the Bronx and call from the station to announce that he was beginning the walk home. The family would wait anxiously until he came through the door. The reality of crime meant they were never sure that he would make it. Years later Anthony recalls this ritual with the sense of humor and pathos that mark much of his commentary on the state of human affairs. "What were we going to do if something happened? But I think it made him feel better to call."

When asked how the *New York Times* would describe the neighborhood he grew up in, he replies, "The same as I do — horrible social problems, crime-ridden. But the *Times* would fail to understand that there were many families like mine that lived in such places."

In a family like the Romeros', "people were venerated [and] there was never fear of laughter." Frequent visits from friends and family, his mother's quiet passion for books and prayer, his father's aggressive embrace of humanity — all created a rich and festive environment that eclipsed the squalor of the high-rise project.

By the time he reached high school, the family — mostly as a result of his mother's persistence — had managed to move to a working-class neighborhood in New Jersey. They exchanged the crime and poor schools of their exclusively Black and Latino Bronx neighborhood for the explicit racism of a nearly all-white environment. Anthony and his sister were called racist epithets for the first time, and classmates shared an endless litany of racist jokes and stereotypes, sometimes adding that the cruelty was not meant to include the Romeros, who were "not like the rest of them."

The Romero kids chose the classic response to this kind of marginalization: excellence. Anthony was salutatorian of his high school class, and his test scores, along with the checkmark in the "Puerto Rican" box on the PSAT application, brought recruiting letters from many of the top universities in the country. No guidance counselor or teacher knew or cared about the opportunities available to him; no one in his family had had any experience with American higher education. The recruiting letters would have gone into the trash if the older brother of a friend had not explained patiently to Anthony that these schools would offer financial aid as well as admission because they were embarrassed that they had no Puerto Rican students; he didn't have to turn them down because his family was poor.

Some of the Ivy League schools wanted to send interviewers to the Romero home as part of their affirmative action outreach efforts. Although these efforts made it possible for Anthony to learn about the best schools in the country, he does not recall them positively. The visits seemed like inspections. It felt as though, Anthony recalls, they couldn't believe that someone with his background could really have those grades and test scores. The Yale recruiter was obnoxious to his family, he remembers, so, on the basis of some pretty pictures of Princeton and that school's proximity to home, he accepted admission there. He had little sense of what Princeton represented in the world of power — nor of how bereft he would feel once there.

When he and his family arrived on campus the first day, all the Romeros were dressed in their Sunday best. He remembers his roommate's family arriving in Bermuda shorts and T-shirts. "His father was a Yale-educated lawyer. We were obviously visiting; this was obviously their home." Across vast gulfs of class and culture, Anthony and his roommate, "the Baltimore preppy," became lifelong friends.

Worried that he didn't really belong at Princeton, Romero worked with what he now sees as unhealthy desperation. He earned straight A's that first semester. Looking back, he says with regret that he was driven by a sense of shame over his family's humble roots.

He worked summers at the Warwick Hotel, in service jobs that seemed at the time "below" his status as a college boy. He bristled when the managers called his father Chico, a made-up generic name for a Latino worker. "This the family never knew until I worked there . . . To friends and family he was Mecho, never Chico. When I went to the hotel and was known as 'Chico's son,' I had an incredible argument with my dad. I gave him my 'race analysis' of this naming, and he told me to keep my university education out of his job."

Many years later, Anthony describes his father as a man whose dignity "came from within," who could let the bumbling prejudices of others roll off his back while he did what he had to do to earn a living. Having grown beyond the vulnerability that plagued him at Princeton, having lost to an early death the father he adored, Anthony now says he learned more by working at the hotel than he did in Princeton classrooms.

From Princeton he went on to get a law degree at Stanford and then took an entry-level job as a junior staff person at the Rockefeller Foundation. He quickly developed a reputation for excellence, and moved on to Ford, where he was soon promoted to the supervisory position he now holds. "I feel I represent organizations and issues like a lawyer with a client," he says of the matters he specializes in: the rights of racial minorities and other oppressed groups. Unlike most of his colleagues in the elegant foundation offices, Romero feels a strong identity with the racial minorities, the poor, the "target populations" the grants are intended to uplift. He works in places where people wear suits that would take the better part of a hotel worker's yearly wage to buy; where grants are discussed over restaurant dinners that cost what a family in the projects is expected to eat on for a month.

In the beginning, this atmosphere made him lose his grounding. He remembers one sunny day early in his career when he was on the way to a meeting to make a critical presentation urging top foundation officials to issue a public statement in favor of minority scholarships. Up ahead, he saw picket lines from Local 6 of the Hotel and Restaurant Workers Union — his father's old union. The group he was supposed to meet with had picked as a lunch spot a hotel where workers were on strike, and he had to decide whether to cross the picket line of a union that had made it possible for his father to earn a wage that would feed his family, or to abandon a meeting at which he would be the key advocate for the kind of scholarship that had made it possible for him to go to college. "The scene was spinning like a sixties' movie, where the camera goes all around the room." He made a split-second decision to join his superiors inside the hotel and to decline to order a meal as his concession to the strike.

It is a decision he reports with painful regret. As a newcomer to a world that was not his, fighting what felt like a losing battle to save affirmative action scholarships at a time when judges, politicians, and key foundation insiders were willing to abandon them, he believed he couldn't start out with a disruptive move.

There is no affirmative action beneficiary who doesn't know that dilemma. It is a function of trying to work within institutions that have never had anyone like yourself; sometimes your survival instincts trump your principles. There are few like Anthony Romero, willing to talk about that feeling in an open way. "I am much more secure now in my career, and would like to think that I could get the entire group to not enter," he says with quiet reflection.

Anthony Romero has grown from tentative outsider to insider critic. He has risen in the foundation world because of multiple talents that superiors quickly recognized. On any given night, the light is on in the window of the high-rise office he occupies. Here, as at Princeton, he works harder than anyone else. He also uses charm; co-workers report that he is liked and admired by everyone from the janitors to the board of trustees. A former professor recalls, "People don't just like Anthony. They meet him and they fall in love."

His humor and his obvious devotion to the human family draw others to him. He knows all the workers behind the cafeteria counter at the Ford Foundation by name. They call out to him in Spanish, teasing him about his vegetarianism. "Antonio! Arroz con pollo today. What kind of Latino are you, anyway?"

He now heads several programs, grouped under the title Human Rights and International Cooperation, within the Peace and Social Justice division of the foundation. His goal, he says, is to "put the verbs in — to *secure* human rights, to *ensure* peace, to *establish* international cooperation, to *achieve* social justice. We could spend the rest of our lives identifying issues. I want to *do* something." Then he adds, "How you do it is as important as what you do." He wants his division members to work with a "zealotry that doesn't know any bounds, and in doing that to have a great deal of fun. We should enjoy it, be gnawed, irritated, angered — a total obsession."

This sense of urgency has also drawn Romero to volunteer work. "I was losing my soul," he said. Administering large grants from the lofty plateau of foundation offices distanced him from the community he came from. He joined a mentoring project, hoping to make an immediate difference in one person's life, and took on a Puerto Rican high school student. Over mild resistance on her part, he went with her to museums and cultural events, and he conceded to her quid pro quo demand: an outing to a hip-hop roller skating joint. He laughs a characteristic, self-deprecating laugh. "There I was, this pale, skinny guy, rolling along with the homeboys and homegirls."

He helped her with college applications, using his position to get more information about the admissions process. Unlike his own college applications, typed on a manual typewriter his father had brought home from the hotel, Laura's went out laser-printed on cotton bond paper. Yet even with his help, she ran into barriers. A financial aid package collapsed over the school's demand for her father's income tax returns, documents impossible to obtain from an absentee parent. By the time the explanations for the missing returns were submitted, the scholarship money was gone.

Anthony Romero was angry. He had worked hard to help this bright young woman overcome barriers and slog through the complicated college application process. Now her first-choice college, which had already accepted her for admission, was beyond her grasp. He knew there were hundreds like her out there — gifted, ambitious, with no one to tell them what they needed to do to get into college and out of the projects. He wrote an angry but judicious letter to the Hampshire College financial aid office, suggesting that they re-evaluate their procedures. How many students in need of financial aid are able to provide tax returns from absent fathers? Often they are poor precisely because their fathers are gone. In his characteristic manner of treating every problem as a mutual problem, he explained how Laura's aid application had fallen through the cracks, how extra effort is called for on behalf of minority students who are unfamiliar with the process: "There are many things I wish you — and we — had done differently. Next time, we both need to try a little harder."

There is in all his work a sense of urgency, as though he sees in Laura and in the clients his grants are supposed to serve someone who is family, someone who is the defenseless teenager he was, arriving by grace on a campus where everyone seemed rich, competent, and comfortable with privilege, surviving challenges to his sense of self, leaving bruised but nonetheless a *gran hombre*, the honorific his father used on his deathbed to describe his precious son.

A woman waits on a bench in housing court. The heat is off again, and her baby is recovering from pneumonia. When Anthony Romero pushes through a grant for a tenant's rights project, he knows the immediacy of that mother's need. There are things we must secure, today, putting the verbs in, making justice real. For her, for the grant makers who will understand her need through his translation, Anthony Romero is the *gran hombre*, brought by affirmative action to a place where he can make a difference in people's lives.

[2]

"We Won't Go Back":
The First and the Second Assaults
on Affirmative Action

ON OCTOBER 12, 1995, thousands of students across California boycotted classes, marched, sat in, and held rallies to protest the California Board of Regents' decision to end affirmative action for minorities and women in the University of California system. Students and teachers from all nine UC campuses participated in the day of protest. At UC Berkeley, ten thousand took part. At UCLA, students held a demonstration that culminated in a march and sit-in shutting down the busiest intersection in Los Angeles. Several student organizers were arrested. Students and faculty held teach-ins on affirmative action at UC Davis, UC Santa Barbara, and UC Irvine. The regents, dominated by hand-picked appointees of Governor Pete Wilson, had voted the previous July to adopt the anti–affirmative action resolution. Wilson was then a candidate for the Republican presidential nomination and hoped to make the hot-button issue of affirmative action central to a campaign that would also feature the race-baiting rhetoric of xenophobia, attacks on welfare, and an assault on bilingualism. In a symbolic gesture, filled with cruel irony, Wilson announced his candidacy while standing in front of the Statue of Liberty.

The Board of Regents' conservative majority hoped that by passing this politically volatile resolution when school was not in session, they could avoid student demonstrations and the inevitable attention and sympathy that protestors would attract. But the young people who took to the streets when they returned to school thwarted this plan. They understood enough of their university's history to know that the UC campuses were closed to many in their grandparents' and parents' generations and that the door that had opened for them had never opened wide. By rights, the university belonged to them: it was a public institution supported disproportionately by working people's taxes. Confident that they belonged, that they were important and valued members of their scholarly communities, that their presence was critical to the university's character and identity, the protestors knew that the educational enterprise would suffer in their absence. Moreover, the well-being of the communities from which they came — the state's black, brown, and yellow ghettos, the barrios and migrant worker camps — depended on the students' access to institutions of power. Their fight would keep the doors open for those who would follow them.

When I heard on my car radio that students at Berkeley and UCLA were in the streets again, I smiled and felt tears welling in my eyes. "Good for them," I said to no one in particular as I waited for the light to change and listened to a young leader from a student group called Diversity in Action interviewed on National Public Radio. "We plan to pay a personal visit to each one of the regents who voted for this resolution," she was saying. "We're holding them accountable for the assault on affirmative action."

"It's been too long," I was thinking. Too many years of sitting by while people like Pete Wilson defined the terms of the debate. "Good for them," I said again. I was proud of these young people for standing against the power of the regents and standing for the justice and humanity of inclusion and integration. I felt *nachas,* a word my father borrowed from his Jewish colleagues and would use when he was most proud of me, a feeling that parents experience when their children put into practice the ideals their parents have preached. These students were willing to cut through the cant of "reverse discrimination." They were talking back against the lie that said they did not belong at these fine universities among the young people we were educating to lead our nation.

These brave students were following in the footsteps of an earlier generation that had taken to the streets to defend affirmative action, those who organized what became known as the National Coalition to Overturn the Bakke Decision. The coalition, first organized by students in California, mounted a nationwide protest following the California Supreme Court's 1976 anti–affirmative action decision in *Regents of the University of California v. Bakke. Bakke,* decided in 1979, was the first case in which the U.S. Supreme Court confronted affirmative action head-on; it became symbolic of the assault on affirmative action and the political struggle that responded to it.

In 1976, I was a young assistant professor at the University of San Francisco Law School, where I had just begun my teaching career as USF's first and only Black law professor. My academic and professional credentials were the equal of my most accomplished colleagues, but I knew that I owed my job to affirmative action and to the community activists who demanded that the academy include people of color on its faculties.

When I first met some of those who were organizing the coalition, it was one of those wonderful San Francisco days. The morning fog had lifted, and a brilliant afternoon sun bathed the hills of Haight Ashbury as I looked across Golden Gate Park from my office window. A group of students knocked on my office door; there were six or seven men and women, African American, Asian, Latino, and white, all of them law or medical students at Berkeley, Hastings, and the University of California at San Francisco (UCSF). The coalition, which was organizing a demonstration at the State Supreme Court building in San Francisco and a teach-in at the UCSF medical school, wondered whether I would speak at both events. There were very few faculty of color for them to call on and fewer still who could explain the legal issues and speak with a law professor's authoritative voice. They needed me to make the constitutional arguments for affirmative action and to explain in everyday language why the legal arguments claiming "reverse discrimination" were wrong.

"Of course I'll come," I told them, but I wanted them to know that, ultimately, it would be their voices and not my legal arguments that would make a difference. The most important message I would have for these young people, as I traveled across the state in the following months to speak at demonstrations and debates, was one of encouragement, reassurance, and support: "Keep organizing. Trust yourselves.

You're right to be in the streets, speaking for your communities and answering the lies that call you 'unqualified' or 'inferior.' Be proud that you're on the front lines of the struggle. We cannot thank you enough for that."

In 1973 and again in 1974, Allan Bakke, a white, thirty-seven-year-old civil engineer, had applied for admission to the medical school at the Davis campus of the University of California. He was rejected on both occasions. In 1970 the medical school had initiated a special admissions procedure under which "disadvantaged" applicants were evaluated by criteria that placed less emphasis on entrance test scores and more emphasis on subjective measures. This procedure enabled about sixteen minority applicants to join Davis's freshman class of a hundred students. Bakke went to court in 1975, complaining that the special procedure admitted students who were less qualified than he and that he was denied admission solely because he was white. This, he argued, violated the Equal Protection Clause of the Fourteenth Amendment. The trial court agreed with Bakke and held the special admissions procedure unconstitutional. In 1976, the California Supreme Court, by a six-to-one majority, affirmed the trial court's judgment, and the university appealed to the U.S. Supreme Court.

In 1976, the University of California regents were defending affirmative action. Unlike the majority of the 1995 regents, who were openly committed to ending affirmative action, the 1978 board recognized that without affirmative action, the state university would remain a virtually segregated institution, despite a pledge to open its campuses to historically excluded communities. The university's defense of the Davis admissions program was sadly lacking, however, and many members of California's minority communities believed that the university had colluded with Bakke to rid itself of a program it never really wanted. At the trial in the state court there was no expert testimony explaining why traditional admissions criteria were inadequate to judge the true potential of the minority candidates. No statistics were presented to demonstrate the compelling need for doctors in California's minority communities or to show that the numbers of minority doctors could not be increased without the special admissions program. Nor did the university question Bakke's dubious assertion that he was indeed "better qualified" than minority applicants who were accepted. Needless to say, university lawyers made no mention of the medical school dean's "special admissions program," under which white children of politically well-connected university supporters or substantial financial contributors were admitted in spite of being less qualified than other applicants.[1]

Perhaps the most glaring inadequacy of the trial record in the *Bakke* case was the complete omission of any evidence of past discrimination by the university. Such evidence was abundant in the university's history. Between 1866 and World War II, there was only one black graduate from the university's medical school. Blacks were once forbidden to live on the Davis campus. In hundreds of school desegregation cases, dating from the 1950s until the very year Bakke sued, federal and state courts found that California had unlawfully deprived minority students of equal educational opportunity at every level of public education. Moreover, most of the applicants to medical school in 1974, when Bakke was applying, had entered elementary school in 1954, when the Supreme Court declared segregated schooling illegal for the first time. As one of the briefs in the *Bakke* case pointed out, these children received "the promise and not the actuality of *Brown*."[2]

Allan Bakke himself had attended elementary school in Dade County, Florida, a school district that a federal court found had illegally segregated its students during the very years that Bakke was in attendance. While Bakke could not be blamed for the injury done to the Black children who were denied the education he was given, his marginally superior scores on the medical school entrance exam may well have resulted from the educational advantages white children received in a segregated public school system. Because none of this evidence was made part of the trial court record, the California Supreme Court could simply declare that there was "no evidence of past discrimination" against minorities at UC Davis and that therefore affirmative action could not be used as a remedy for unproven wrongs. This judicial use of an inadequate trial record to ignore widely recognized past institutional discrimination would become a disturbing pattern in affirmative action cases.

By the time the *Bakke* case reached the U.S. Supreme Court, in 1978, many white Americans were ready to hear the argument that affirmative action was nothing more than discrimination in reverse.[3] A 1978 Gallup Poll found that whites ranked "the problems of black Americans" last on a list of thirty-one concerns.[4] In an analysis of several similar polls of racial attitudes, Stanford University professor Seymour Martin Lipset concluded that "most whites do not believe discrimination is the principal cause of Black inequality."[5] Bakke's "reverse discrimination" claim was appealing, because, for the first time in our history, many whites believed that equality had been achieved and that programs designed to improve the status of minorities resulted in an unfair advantage.

As late as 1970 a Louis Harris survey found that 76 percent of whites believed that Blacks experienced discrimination and had not yet achieved full equality, and a majority of whites believed that Blacks faced discrimination in housing, education, and employment.[6] By 1977, however, the Harris Poll found that only one in three whites believed that discrimination existed, and even fewer thought racism was a factor in housing, education, and employment. At the same time, 55 percent of whites believed Blacks were pushing "too fast" for equality.[7]

This view was exacerbated by a small but newly visible Black middle class. Black faces were increasingly prominent on television and in entertainment and sports, and when beer commercials showed construction workers or yuppie office workers at the neighborhood bar, one out of four was invariably a person of color. Things had changed for the better for many middle-class Blacks since the passage of the civil rights legislation of the 1960s, but things had become worse for the Black poor — and most Blacks remained poor. Black unemployment doubled between 1967 and 1977, from 638,000 to 1.5 million.[8] The Black unemployment rate went from 7.4 to 13.2 percent, and Black teenage unemployment soared from 26.5 to 38.6 percent.[9] The modest progress made by the Black middle class could not offset these declines among the poor. The median income for all Blacks in 1977 was 59 percent of white income — just one point higher than it had been in 1966. Ironically, the relatively small number of Blacks who achieved success was offered as proof that racism no longer existed. If most whites believed that race was no longer a factor in Black unemployment and poverty, it was only a small step to the belief that Blacks at the bottom were there because of their own shortcomings.

Black power and the radical nationalist and community-based movements among other people of color also served to turn many whites against affirmative action. These movements shifted the focus of protest toward the economic and social problems of the masses and gave the goal of equal justice an activist edge. Suddenly, those who believed they had a stake in the status quo felt threatened by new claims for rights and redistribution of power. That fear, combined with the visceral fear of fiery young black and brown activists, heightened the opposition to change and made it easier for whites to think of themselves as victims.

As has been the case throughout this country's history, the intensified racial antagonism that fostered the assault on affirmative action was not unrelated to other political and economic developments. The recession at the end of the Vietnam War brought with it a growing sense of economic insecurity among middle- and working-class Americans and a resurgence of political conservatism and distrust of government. The passage in 1978 of California's Proposition 13, a measure that placed strict limits on government spending in an attempt to relieve the tax burden of property owners, was a harbinger to a nationwide tax revolt and a reflection of the anxiety felt by Americans caught between a rising cost of living and decreasing real wages. Blacks and other groups who counted on government for employment and legal protection became scapegoats for fiscal problems they had not created.[10]

Bakke's legal argument — that he was the victim of reverse discrimination — was seductive because it resonated with the insecurities and fears of many white Americans. His argument, in fact, called on a well-established anti–affirmative action rhetoric that had come into use even before affirmative action was fully conceived.[11] In a 1964 article published in *Commentary* magazine, for example, the Harvard sociologist Nathan Glazer warned that Blacks were now demanding not just equality of opportunity but "equality of results or outcomes,"[12] and Daniel Patrick Moynihan denounced the beginnings of affirmative action as "a new racialism."[13]

Historically, the academic scholarship on race has shifted to reflect the political climate outside the university. The sociologist Stephen Steinberg has shown that in response to the 1960s politics of confrontation and crisis, academics produced a scholarship of confrontation, and that the shift to the right in the past two decades brought a corresponding scholarship of victim-blaming and backlash.[14] This scholarship of backlash had its beginnings in the 1960s, with Daniel Patrick Moynihan's "Report on the Negro Family"[15] and Nathan Glazer's *Commentary* article "Negroes and Jews: The New Challenge to Pluralism."[16] It came to full fruit in the 1990s with Richard Herrnstein and Charles Murray's *Bell Curve* and Dinesh D'Souza's *The End of Racism*,[17] books embracing the core thesis of American racism: Black inferiority.

The anti–affirmative action rhetoric was firmly in place by 1975, when Glazer's *Affirmative Discrimination* was published. In it, he argued that "rights attach to the individual, not the group," and positioned himself as the champion of a "colorblind society." He even accused proponents of affirmative action of engaging in racial classifications reminiscent of the Nuremberg Laws. In *Affirmative Discrimination*, Glazer first set forth the argument that would absolve most whites of any responsibility for the continuing legacy of slavery and segregation. Of white ethnics, he wrote:

> These groups were not particularly involved in the enslavement of the Negro or the creation of the Jim Crow pattern in the South, the conquest of part of Mexico, or the near extermination of the American Indian. They came to a country that provided them with [fewer] benefits than it now provides the protected groups. There is little reason for them to feel they should bear the burden of the redress of a past in which they had no or little part, or to assist those who receive more assistance than they did. We are indeed a nation of minorities; to enshrine some minorities as deserving of special benefits means not to defend minority rights against a discriminating majority but to favor some of these minorities over others.[18]

Glazer's version of history, quoted in an amicus brief submitted to the Supreme Court in support of *Bakke* and paraphrased in Justice Powell's opinion for the Court, neglected the role of ethnic whites in excluding Blacks from the labor movement and the patronage systems of city political machines, among other historical facts. More important, it espoused a narrow ethical view of human relations, one that holds we have no responsibility for righting wrongs that are not of our doing and that denies our connectedness as a human society.

The arguments against affirmative action that we hear today — that it is antimeritocratic, stigmatizing, anti-individual, engendering of race consciousness, racial resentment, and balkanization, and, above all, that it is just another form of racism — are so often repeated that many of us, including numbers of people who favor affirmative action, have come to hear them as observations of nature rather than rhetorical argument. The reasons these rhetorical arguments work are many and complex, but if we are to understand what makes them seductive, we need to address the complexity of the cultural narrative that gives them context and resonance.

One indication that they are rhetorical and not factual is that they were created at a particular time to achieve a particular political purpose. A pair of visual images separated in time by a decade reveals the racial scapegoating embedded in anti–affirmative action rhetoric. During the same week the Supreme Court would hear the appeal in the *Bakke* case, the cover of the *Saturday Review* featured a photograph of two hands, one black and one white, reaching out to clutch the same diploma as it falls through the air. The title of the cover story — "The Bakke Case: Are Racial Quotas Defensible?" — was the only other image on the page. The message was, Your white hands and their black hands, seeking the single prize, the opportunity that cannot be shared. Ten years later the conservative North Carolina senator Jesse Helms would use this same *us* versus *them* imagery in a political advertisement, made for television, that pictured the hands of a white man tearing up a job rejection letter while the voice-over said, "You needed that job, and you were best qualified. But it had to go to a minority because of a racial quota."[19]

On February 22, 1977, the U.S. Supreme Court agreed to consider *Regents of the University of California* v. *Allan Bakke,* and on October 12, 1977, beginning the first week of the new Supreme Court term, the justices heard oral arguments in what many believed was the most important case since the 1954 *Brown* decision outlawing segregated schooling.[20]

That day a long line wound its way up the marble staircase of the Supreme Court building and between the Corinthian columns at the entrance. The courtroom was filled to capacity. Some had camped out all night for a chance to hear the case argued, but most of the audience had secured scarce tickets through their connections to the Court or through the parties to the case. The men in the audience wore gray and blue vested suits. Many had been classmates at Ivy League schools, and they greeted each other in the familiar but hushed tones associated with the dark wood and leather chairs of upper-class men's clubs. The scarcity of women was vivid testimony to the many years of gender exclusion in this professional elite, and while some people of color could be spotted among the select gathering, it was a small number, considering the special interest this case held for them.

The demonstrators who marched across the street from the Court, and in cities across the country, were of a decidedly different complexion and comportment. From New York to Berkeley, multiracial crowds of young people raised placards and banners and chanted, putting the Court and the world on notice: whatever the outcome of the discussion among those inside the velvet-curtained courtroom, the struggle would continue in the streets. The protestors would not accept a return to the days when they and their communities were excluded from institutions of power and privilege.

"We won't go back. We won't go back," the demonstrators chanted outside, as Archibald Cox stepped to the courtroom's podium to begin the university's argument in his gentle and affable style. Cox, a Harvard law professor who had been retained to argue the university's appeal, had argued many cases before this Court, first as solicitor general during the Kennedy administration and later as the first Watergate special prosecutor.

Affirmative action was a logical, fair, and — most important — constitutional means of redressing discrimination, he argued. If the Court forbade affirmative action, our universities would become once again what they had been for over a century: all white. No one wanted this, his argument assumed, least of all the elite, who sent their children to school to learn how to succeed in this world of many races.

It was not a matter of whether the university could prefer less qualified minorities over better qualified whites, he said, but a question of whether the university could consider race in selecting from a large pool of qualified applicants. The university's choice in allocating its resources was a voluntary decision made by a responsible (white) policymaking body. The medical school faculty's decision to consider race, he reminded the Court, was made not in order to discriminate against whites but to remedy the effects of "generations of pervasive discrimination against minorities."

Bakke's lawyer, Reynold Colvin, responded by focusing on the facts of the case. By recounting the details of Bakke's struggle for admission, he hoped to make the justices see the case as the story of an individual fighting against the capricious power of government. He told them that Bakke had not come to court to represent a class or an organization, or to establish a new legal precedent. He merely wanted a chance to go to medical school. When the justices became impatient and pressed him to make his constitutional argument, he answered, "Allan Bakke's position is that he has a right, and that right is not to be discriminated against by reason of his race." Colvin argued that the Equal Protection Clause absolutely prohibited consideration of race under any and all circumstances, but the Court had already made clear in the school desegregation cases that the government could consider race, at least where it was necessary to remedy past discrimination. It was unlikely to buy Bakke's absolutist argument.

More than eight months would pass before the Supreme Court announced its decision. It was sharply divided. Four justices voted to strike down the Davis affirmative action program and order Allan Bakke's admission. They avoided the constitutional issue of whether a race-conscious affirmative action program violated the Equal Protection Clause and concluded that Bakke had been treated unlawfully, in violation of an antidiscrimination provision of the 1964 Civil Rights Act. Another four justices voted to uphold the Davis admissions program, finding that it violated neither the Civil Rights Act nor the Equal Protection Clause.

Justice Lewis F. Powell cast the deciding vote, in an opinion that straddled the two camps in the Court and struck a compromise between the forces for and against affirmative action. He agreed with four of his colleagues that Bakke had been wronged by the medical school, but he agreed with the other four that it was legitimate to use race as a factor in selecting applicants. Powell's opinion said that all racial classifications "are suspect" and can be justified only if they are necessary to achieve a "compelling state interest." Remedying past societal discrimination was not such a compelling interest, he said. Societal discrimination was "too amorphous," but a court, a legislature, or a government agency could consider race in order to remedy specifically identified past discriminatory acts that were in violation of the law.

Furthermore, a university could consider race in admissions if it was essential to the creation of a diverse student body. A university faculty, he argued, had a compelling interest in exercising its First Amendment right to academic freedom, and the freedom to select a student body of its choosing was part of that right. If a university faculty believed that a racially diverse student body was important to its students' education, and it could achieve such a student body only if it considered the race of applicants, then it was constitutional to consider race as one of many factors in the admissions process. By way of example, Powell referred to the admissions program at Harvard, where, he said, race or ethnic background was "deemed a 'plus' in a particular applicant's file," without insulating that individual from comparison with all other candidates.

Powell's penchant for compromise would make his opinion the "judgment of the Court" despite the fact that no other justice had joined his opinion. It was a decision that appeared to give half a loaf to each side. While ordering Bakke's admission and declaring even remedial classifications subject to strict judicial scrutiny, the Court made a significant concession to the young people who had filled the streets in front of the Supreme Court building and in every major city. Race-conscious affirmative action was still permissible, and any institution with the political will could easily identify the compelling interests that justified its use.

Universities with strong affirmative action programs followed Powell's middle course, using race as one factor among many to continue their efforts to build vibrant, multiracial educational communities. Schools that had always dragged their feet in integrating their campuses used the *Bakke* decision as an excuse to abandon token efforts at affirmative action. Federal and state affirmative action programs aimed at race and gender integration of the work site remained in place, and many businesses in the private sector found that affirmative action had positive bottom-line results. Nicholas Lehman, recounting this period in the history of affirmative action in a June 1995 article for the *New York Times* magazine, noted that all through the 1970s and 1980s a quiet but firm support for affirmative action was evident in the massive and largely voluntary programs instituted by big business. "All along, the overwhelmingly white establishment has supported affirmative action," wrote Lehman, "and that is what accounts for its durability."[21]

At the same time none of America's least advantaged citizens was a winner in the *Bakke* case. The Court had, by the slimmest of margins, declared that affirmative action was permissible in certain narrow circumstances, but there was no guarantee that those who ran America's universities and businesses would choose to continue these programs, which had only just begun to bring equal opportunity to minorities and women. Allan Bakke was admitted to medical school, but he was hardly representative of the poor and working-class whites who, the polls showed, identified with him so strongly. Few of them would benefit from his victory.

The real winners were the country's economically and educationally privileged. Archibald Cox had asked the Court to ensure the right of the elite to choose who would share their privilege. His request had been granted. At most schools, affirmative action programs provided only token access for minorities while maintaining admissions processes heavily weighted toward the children of the upper classes. The Court failed to address itself to the issues at the core of the national debate around affirmative action. The majority had not confronted America's continuing racism, nor had they answered the critical question of the meaning of the Equal Protection Clause: Does the Constitution require a neutral stance that will maintain existing inequities of opportunity, or does it require an active and fundamental reconstruction of a world shaped by race, gender, and class privilege?

Almost twenty years after the Supreme Court announced its decision in *Bakke,* another case challenging a university affirmative action program was headed its way. Many people were calling *Hopwood* v. *State of Texas*[22] "Bakke II," and indeed it had all the markings of a Hollywood sequel. Cheryl Hopwood and three other rejected white applicants had sued the University of Texas Law School, claiming that the school's affirmative action admissions program violated their constitutional right to equal protection of the laws. Like Bakke, they argued that the program amounted to reverse discrimination because their scores on traditional admissions criteria were higher than those of most Black and Mexican American applicants who were admitted.

A Federal District Court held that the law school's admissions program was constitutional because it was necessary to remedy the continuing effects of official discrimination in primary, secondary, and higher education in Texas. This discrimination was "well documented in history books, case law, and [in] the record of the trial," said the District Court, and it was "not a relic of the past." In 1994, desegregation lawsuits remained pending against over forty different Texas school districts, and although the public school population in Texas was approximately half white and half minority, the vast majority of both white and minority students attended schools that were segregated in fact if not by law. The high school graduation rate for whites was 81.5 percent, compared with 66.1 percent for Blacks and 44.6 percent for Hispanics.

At the university level, a United States Department of Education, Office of Civil Rights (OCR) investigation, conducted between 1978 and 1980, found that Texas had "failed to eliminate vestiges of its former de jure racially dual system . . . which segregated blacks and whites" and that there were strong indications of discrimination against Hispanics. In 1994 the OCR had still not determined that Texas had eliminated its segregated system of public higher education.[23]

Nevertheless Cheryl Hopwood and her co-plaintiffs appealed the District Court's ruling to the Fifth Circuit Court of Appeals. In the 1960s, this Deep South court was known for its fearless and heroic judges, white Southerners who dared to enforce the rights of Blacks despite ostracism by their own communities and threats from the Klan and the White Citizens Council. A federal judge in Louisiana, for instance, had ignored death threats against himself and his family and signed a midnight desegregation order. An Alabama judge threatened by the Klan refused FBI protection and slept with a pistol under his pillow. These men understood that the South they loved must face up to its racism before it could be healed of it. In contrast, the Fifth Circuit in the 1990s was dominated by conservative judges committed to turning back the clock to a time before the liberal Warren Court had set a racial revolution in motion. All three of the judges on the panel that heard the Hopwood appeal were Reagan and Bush appointees. Not surprisingly, they voted to reverse the District Court, and declared the Texas admissions program unconstitutional.

The opening sentences of the Fifth Circuit opinion, reversing the District Court, were typical of the upside-down rhetoric of reverse discrimination:

... in order to increase the enrollment of certain favored classes of minority students, the University of Texas School of Law discriminates in favor of those applicants by giving substantial racial preferences in its admissions program. The beneficiaries of this system are blacks and Mexican Americans, to the detriment of whites and non-preferred minorities.[24]

According to the three Circuit Court judges, Black and Mexican American beneficiaries of affirmative action were a "favored class [given] preference in its admissions program . . . to the detriment of whites." In fact, the University of Texas had instituted affirmative action precisely because these minority groups were disfavored by traditional university admissions practices and by historical and contemporary racial discrimination in the Texas educational system.

Texas is a state with an active Ku Klux Klan and regularly reported hate crimes against people of color; a state that admitted Blacks to its law school only when it was forced to do so by the United States Supreme Court in 1950; a state where a licensed attorney once said to one of us, without irony, "We like our dirt black and our people white"; where a sitting judge once joked, "How do you make a Mexican omelet? Well, first you steal three eggs."[25] As recently as 1960 the University of Texas segregated Mexican American students in campus housing and assigned them to a dormitory known as "the barracks," and until the mid-1960s, a Texas Board of Regents policy prohibited Blacks from living in or visiting white dorms.[26] This history was ignored by the Fifth Circuit Court, in willful disregard of the District Court's detailed findings of fact. By rhetorical transformation, Blacks and Mexican Americans became "favored minorities" and whites became victims of racial discrimination.

As *Hopwood* headed for the U.S. Supreme Court, there were dire predictions that the Court would affirm the Fifth Circuit's decision and thus sound the death knell for affirmative action on university campuses. The Court had demonstrated its hostility to affirmative action in several recent cases. The Fifth Circuit had rejected Justice Powell's compromise position that universities could use race as one factor in admissions in order to achieve the educational benefits of a diverse student body. For almost two decades colleges and professional schools had relied on Powell's *Bakke* opinion in shaping their minority admissions programs. Now, many feared, the Supreme Court was poised to end this settled practice. Other Court watchers were more optimistic. They were counting on the pragmatism of Justice Sandra Day O'Connor, the swing vote in the most recent affirmative action cases, each of which had been a five-to-four decision. In a brief asking the Supreme Court to take the case and overturn the Fifth Circuit ruling, the Clinton administration Justice Department echoed Archibald Cox's argument in *Bakke*, reminding the Court that the practical effect of the Fifth Circuit holding would be "to return the most prestigious institutions within the state university systems to their former 'white' status."[27]

But *Hopwood* was not destined to resolve the constitutional debate. Three months after the Fifth Circuit announced its shocking decision, the Supreme Court declined to hear the university's appeal, offering a technical procedural flaw as its reason: because the University of Texas had already revised its admission policy, the case did not present a "live controversy."[28]

Experts in intricacies of federal jurisdiction would be left to argue over the formal effect of the Court's order. It was apparent, however, that a Court sharply split on affirmative action was not prepared to confront the issue head-on when the nation was also deeply divided and the stakes were so great.

Justice Ruth Bader Ginsberg's one-paragraph opinion explaining the Court's decision appeared designed to advise the public not to interpret the Court's refusal to hear the case as an endorsement of the Fifth Circuit's analysis. At the same time the effect of the refusal was to leave the Fifth Circuit's order in place, and educational institutions in Texas, Louisiana, and Mississippi were left in a difficult position, obliged to conform to an appeals court ruling that might or might not ultimately prove to be the law.

The Supreme Court will not be able to sidestep forever the issues presented by *Hopwood*. Other "reverse discrimination" plaintiffs will surface, and eventually the Court will have to decide a *Bakke II*. Whatever the outcome of that case, the struggle over the meaning of racial justice will continue, just as it did after *Plessy* v. *Ferguson* in 1896, after *Brown* v. *Board of Education* in 1954, and after *Bakke*.

Ultimately, how we will reconcile the American ideal of equality with the continuing legacy of our nation's history of inequality will be determined not by nine men and women who sit on the Supreme Court, but by all of us. Through the politics of street demonstrations, teach-ins, community meetings, and dinner conversations with friends and family, we must all decide what actions best respond to the reality of inequality and the need to heal the wounds of our racism, sexism, and homophobia.

Those who would have us go back to the days when all institutions of power and privilege were the exclusive domain of a white male elite understand that the battle is, at bottom, political. By the spring of 1996 the second assault against affirmative action was in full force. Anti–affirmative action legislation had been introduced in both Houses of Congress; and in thirty-five states, governors, legislators, attorneys general, or the governing boards of public university systems had jumped aboard the bandwagon.

Once again, California was a bellwether. Anti–affirmative action forces launched an all-out attack, beginning with the university regents' recision of affirmative action in the nation's largest public university system, followed closely by a ballot measure, deceptively titled California Civil Rights Initiative, that would amend the California constitution to outlaw race- and gender-based affirmative action in all public agencies.

It was hardly surprising that politicians from Pete Wilson to Bob Dole to Pat Buchanan were bashing affirmative action. Twenty years after *Bakke*, America's working middle class was experiencing an anxiety about its economic well-being much like that which had fueled the first assault. Rather than face the vexing problems that growing concentration of wealth, new technologies, and globalized markets presented for the American economy, many politicians turned to the tried and tested diversion of racial scapegoating.

Ending affirmative action would cure neither the real economic problems faced by white middle-class workers nor their understandable anxiety. As Robert Reich, a Harvard economist and the secretary of labor, had noted, between 1975 and 1995 the American middle class, the largest in the world, had "quietly crumbled day by day." In that period, 98 percent of the increase in household incomes went to the top fifth of American households. Meanwhile, adjusting for inflation, the typical American family was living on less than it had fifteen years earlier. By 1992 the top 5 percent took home 20 percent of the nation's total income, and the growth in their share of the nation's wealth accelerated at a pace unprecedented in American history. At the bottom, America's poor, particularly in the inner cities, were almost completely cut off from participation in the economy. Meanwhile, what Reich called the "old American middle class" was at best standing still, staving off downward mobility, "pulled and stretched by the need to work two or more jobs to keep a family solvent, by uneasiness about health care, by the specter that today's job will disappear tomorrow, and by fears that their kids will be denied the opportunity for a better life."[29]

Is there a vision of affirmative action that can at once right the wrongs of racism and sexism and poverty while speaking to the very real anxieties of all of America's working people? To discover this vision is the challenge that faced the California students who organized in opposition to the California regents' rollback of affirmative action and the grassroots organizations that sprang up to oppose the so-called California Civil Rights Initiative. The task for all of us who live in a world cracking apart from economic stagnation and disregard of human need is to confront the legacies of oppression that are with us still — to know what makes us jointly human, overriding demagoguery and racial scapegoating.

The first assault on affirmative action resulted in the watered-down compromise of the *Bakke* decision. The present assault, whatever the outcome, will not signal the end of this struggle, for as long as the gap between have and have-not grows wider, any legal determination that affirmative action is or is not constitutional is rhetoric overlying a contradiction that no *Bakke II* can resolve. The various legislative and executive actions chipping away at affirmative action, as well as the reverse discrimination lawsuits, will continue, as will the chorus of those in the streets shouting, "We won't go back." We believe the new defenders of affirmative action will prevail. They will make the nation see the inevitable in their shining faces — black, white, yellow, brown — as they march through the streets of our cities.

ROBERT DEMMONS

"Even the guys who hated him most respected him"

"OUT OF CONTROL" was what Federal District Court Judge Marilyn Hall Patel called the San Francisco Fire Department in January 1988. She was speaking to a courtroom packed to overflowing with nearly a hundred mostly male and mostly white off-duty firefighters. For the last hour Patel had been grilling Fire Chief Edward Phipps, and she was exasperated. "The continuing incidents of racial harassment have not been dealt with expeditiously or firmly . . . there seems to be neither the commitment, interest, nor ability in the department to carry out the court order or carry out antidiscrimination laws," she said. "The department is clearly out of control. This is not a fraternity. It is a fire department here to serve all of San Francisco."

Judge Patel's exasperation reflected eighteen years during which she and other federal and state judges had concluded repeatedly that racial discrimination was rampant in the fire department. Each of them had faced delay, foot dragging, and even open defiance in response to their efforts to integrate the department and enforce the law. Patel had personally supervised the most recent four years of contentious litigation and issued several interim orders against the department when the city settled the suit in 1988, agreeing to end the discriminatory practices and to set long-term goals for the hiring and promotion of minorities and women.

During the course of the litigation, minorities and women, along with whites who joined the efforts to end discrimination, were subjected to vicious harassment. Black firefighters found feces in their beds. They were urinated on while they slept. Raw eggs were placed in their boots, and their equipment was sabotaged. The editors of the white firefighters' union newspaper "whited out" the faces of Blacks in group photographs of firefighters who had been recognized for meritorious duty. Patel had ordered the city to protect the plaintiffs and others who were working to integrate the department, but now, only months after the signing of the decree, she had learned of a new outbreak, including an assault on a white training officer, who was roughed up by several off-duty white firefighters because he had been helpful to Blacks and women, and an incident where two veteran fire inspectors, a Black and an Asian, found a swastika, mounted on a plaque, left on the desk they shared.

Patel put the department's top brass, sixty-one officers, on notice: they would face jail and fines if the incidents did not stop. But the resistance continued. Twice the white firefighters' union appealed the consent decree and Patel's order, each time unsuccessfully. In 1989 a group of seven white firefighters filed a reverse discrimination suit. In 1992 Barbara Phillips, the court-appointed monitor, issued a report: the department had failed to develop an adequate management plan, and sexual and racial harassment continued. The report told of female firefighters receiving threatening and obscene phone calls and enduring physical intimidation. Phillips recommended that the department be placed in receivership. Mayor Frank Jordan, a former policeman and a conservative, defended the fire department's record. In 1995 an angry Judge Patel extended the court's supervision for another two years, noting that the city had fallen short of its affirmative action hiring goals and that the department was still riddled with complaints of racial and sexual harassment. She directed the city to hire a management consult-ant and warned that this was the city's last chance.

In November 1995, eight years after Judge Patel's "out of control" declaration, Willie Brown, a longtime power in the state legislature and one of the city's most popular politicians, was elected San Francisco's first Black mayor. In his inaugural address the new mayor announced that he was appointing Robert Demmons as fire chief. Local papers called the appointment "a shocker" and "a bold and telling stroke on the part of the mayor." Demmons, San Francisco's first Black fire chief, was the president of the Black Firefighters Association and for over twelve years a driving force behind the legal battle to integrate the department. The department's number one pariah would now become its chief.

"Even the guys who hated him most respected him," says a friend. Why did they hate him? "I think it was insecurity," she says, "the insecurity that many white male working-class guys are feeling in these times. The firefighter's job is one of the last well-paid, well-respected blue-collar jobs around. This was their turf. They wanted to keep it for themselves, to pass it on to their sons. They didn't even want to give it to their daughters, much less some black guys."

Bob Demmons's fight for integration imperiled the security of the white firefighters' fragile world. He not only challenged the whiteness of that world; he also challenged the notion that you had to be a macho guy to be a firefighter. He said that all sorts of skills were important, that women and gays and smaller Asian guys could do the job. By saying this, he was upsetting the white firemen's sense of self. It was this that made him the object of their hate.

Robert Demmons was born in 1940 in Dallas, Texas. His parents moved to San Francisco when he was two. They came to work in the shipyards, as part of a great wartime migration of Blacks who traveled from Texas and Oklahoma to California's cities in search of jobs and a better life for their children. "I was the baby of the family. My brother and sister were ten and six years older, and I didn't have to compete with them for my parents' attention. I grew up like an only kid . . . I guess I was spoiled. There's no other way of putting it."

Demmons says this with a certain pride, as if he recognizes that the attention lavished on him by parents and older siblings is one of the sources of his quiet strength and self-confidence. "I always thought I was just as important as the next person," he says. He lived with his family in a segregated public housing project in Richmond, California, across the bay from San Francisco, until he was eight. After his parents divorced, he lived with his mother in San Francisco's Filmore district, and when his father remarried he moved to Oakland to live with him.

In San Francisco, Demmons attended Freemont, an integrated elementary school. He remembers that he was pretty good at math and that often he'd finish the assignment before anyone else and get all the answers right. When the white kids did well, the teachers made a big deal of it, but they never recognized his good work and didn't keep him challenged. One day his teacher asked the students what their fathers did. "We all had our hands up, but she just asked the white kids. She expressed a great deal of interest in each kid's father's job, but it was like the Black kids didn't exist or what our fathers did wasn't important. My father was a janitor, and I wasn't ashamed of what he did."

His mother recalls that he was a "mischievous boy who hung around with a lot of bad kids." She worried about his getting into trouble or being hurt. "He was very irreverent and absolutely fearless." Demmons admits that some of the guys he ran with "were pretty rough. I didn't recognize if someone was older or bigger. I'd stand my ground. It was almost as if I thought I was grown." An older boy who was one of his running partners later became a gangster and was killed. "A lot of people were afraid of him, but he treated me like a little brother."

When Demmons graduated from high school he joined the marines, a move he says saved his life. It took him away from the street life that destroyed many of his boyhood friends, and it taught him institutional survival skills that would serve him well in his battles with the San Francisco Fire Department. "When I first went in the marines I got into a lot of fights. In the marines they encourage you to fight, and I'd grown up in a culture where you didn't allow someone to insult you or one of your friends without fighting them. But I watched the guys who rose to positions of power and I learned how to fight back in other ways. Later, there were things that would happen to me in the firehouse that, if I'd had the attitude I had in high school, would have made me kill somebody."

Demmons joined the department in 1974. He did well at the fire college despite the double standard that some members of the department used to discourage minority recruits. Demmons recalls an assistant chief telling them, "The courts may have gotten you in here, but they aren't going to get you through the fire college." Not only did they grade the minority recruits harder, but they often looked the other way when the white recruits performed poorly. "The white guys would tell us about stuff they had screwed up on or failed to complete, and when the results were posted they'd have perfect scores." When Demmons graduated, he and another Black firefighter, who had also done extremely well, were assigned to the slowest station in the department. The white guys, who were slated for the fast track, were assigned to the busiest stations, where they would get the experience required for promotions.

Despite this early exposure to the department's racism, Demmons had little interest in fighting civil rights battles. "I came into the fire department to be a firefighter, not an advocate," he says. At the first opportunity he applied for assignment to one of the largest stations in the city, one with a truck, an engine, a rescue squad, a water rescue unit, a battalion chief, and an engine unit. "I put in for that station because it gave me the opportunity to work all those different units. I wanted to learn as much as I could about the job."

Demmons continued to encounter racism, but when he did, he dealt with it man to man. One night, while he was receiving calls at a firehouse with an alcoholic lieutenant, the station was called to a fire. Demmons could not rouse the dead-drunk lieutenant, but department policy required that a lieutenant be on the truck, and the driver refused to leave without him, so the company missed the run. Fortunately, it was a false alarm. That evening, when the battalion chief learned of the missed run, he called the station. Everyone knew the lieutenant had a drinking problem, including the battalion chief, but Demmons tried to cover for him. He sent some guys upstairs to rouse the lieutenant, who finally woke from his stupor and stumbled to the phone. As Demmons was hanging up the line, he heard the lieutenant explain the missed run. "Well, chief," the lieutenant said, "you know how it is. We have a new nigger here."

Demmons took the lieutenant aside and told him that he didn't appreciate being blamed for the missed run and didn't like it when people used racial epithets. "I just talked to him," he recalls. He says the lieutenant stopped using the *n* word, and "by the time I left that station, you would have thought we were best friends."

In 1978 Bob Demmons took the exam for promotion to lieutenant. He had been an engineering major at City College and had always done well on exams, and he studied especially hard for this one. As he was leaving the exam, a white guy turned to him and said, with a laugh, that he was relieved when he discovered how many repeat questions there were on the test. What did he mean by "repeat questions?" Demmons asked. "Questions that were on the last test," the man replied.

"Suddenly I realized that the white guys were getting copies of old exams and the department was repeating old test questions to give these guys an advantage." Later he discovered that 122 of the 144 multiple-choice questions on the 1978 lieutenants' exam were repeat questions.

Now he understood what was going on when he would walk into a room and a group of white firefighters would frantically hide sheets of paper. "I was hurt. These were people I considered friends, guys I'd fished with. It wasn't a good feeling. I hadn't aligned myself along racial lines, and here they were, making their decisions based on that."

Demmons and nine other Black firefighters who had taken the 1978 test filed an Equal Employment Opportunity complaint and eventually became plaintiffs in the federal suit. "It wasn't something I did willingly," he says. "I considered myself a pretty private person, but what I found out is that I was linked to other people."

Throughout the course of the litigation Demmons and the Black Firefighters Association held press conferences, sent representatives to speak at community meetings, and picketed firehouses where they believed racist acts had taken place. Shauna Marshall, one of the attorneys in the suit, remembers the first time she met Demmons. It was one of the first meetings between the women and Black plaintiffs, when the coalition between the two client groups was still fragile. "Bob was clearly in control of the meeting . . . Whenever things would start to fall apart, he'd remind people of why we were there. He was like a facilitator or translator, helping the client groups to understand the lawyers and one another and helping the lawyers to understand the clients."

Several qualities make Demmons an effective leader. He is a passionate advocate, driven by his cause. "He's tireless; he doesn't sleep," says Eva Patterson, another of the attorneys in the case, "and he's one of the brightest people I know. So much of the consent decree is a reflection of Bob's genius." Friends and colleagues who watched him live through what he always calls "the struggle" speak of his inner strength, his warmth, and his almost shy smile. He often speaks so quietly that you have to lean close to catch his words, but he speaks directly to you and with an animation that makes you listen.

In a city famous for its diversity and tolerance of differing lifestyles, one colleague calls him "truly one of the most open people I've ever met." Many of the other Black firefighters were not ready to accept fully the women who had joined them in the suit; they too were hanging on to the macho image and definition of firefighting. Demmons understood early on that women could not only do the job of firefighting; they could also bring valuable technical, interpersonal, and conceptual skills to it. It was his idea to open the Black Firefighters Association's physical training program to women. After the first fire college graduation that included women, the association held a party to celebrate the new graduates, and Demmons gave an emotional speech, saying what a great day it was to see our daughters become firefighters.

Demmons took a special interest in one of the women plaintiffs in the suit, helping her to train, showing her the ropes of department politics, and pushing her to take exams for promotions. An improbable father-daughter relationship developed between the older Black firefighter and the young lesbian, who, because she was white and Irish American, was treated like the ultimate traitor in a department dominated so long by Irish American men.

One of the department's most popular firefighters before the suit, Demmons took a genuine interest in the white guys he worked with and treated them with warmth and respect. Later, when he was drawn into a leadership position in the struggle to integrate the department, he drew on his past experiences and personal friendships in the firehouses. When he faced white firefighters across a picket line or in the courtroom, it was his natural way to remind them that he was the same guy. He refused to demonize the white firefighters. "Remember this is me telling you this," he'd say. Speaking to his white colleagues as people he knew and cared about, he forced them to treat him the same way.

"Sometimes the guys in the Black Firefighters Association would come to me and complain that 'they're doing this or that to us,'" recalls Demmons. "I'd tell them I didn't want to hear about 'they.' I'd ask them who it was, because I wanted to deal with the offender as an individual. I wanted to force him to deal with me when I could see him and he could see me and we could speak, one man to another."

Throughout the eighteen years that Bob Demmons fought discrimination in the department from the outside, he remained a highly respected firefighter and proved himself an outstanding administrator. He rose quickly through the ranks from lieutenant to captain to battalion chief to assistant chief for management. He knew that his promotions were a direct result of the court order, but he and the firefighters who served under him also knew that he deserved them.

On the wall behind Chief Demmons's desk is a print picturing South African President Nelson Mandela. THE STRUGGLE IS MY LIFE, reads the caption. It is not far-fetched to compare Bob Demmons with his hero, as one San Francisco newspaper did. Both have been insurgents fighting a closed, racist institution, leading a struggle that is larger than themselves. Both now must lead the institution that excluded them. But, most important, they share a vision: to build a new inclusive world where every person is valued and respected. There are some white firefighters who fear that a Black man as chief means "pay-back time," but Robert Demmons isn't interested in pay-backs.

Will the wounds heal? "Well, there's still a lot of racism and sexism in the world around us, and until that environment changes substantially, you'll see divisiveness in the department," says Demmons. "But we can work to make this a place where bigotry and abuse are not tolerated, where every individual knows that they will be respected and allowed to do the job.

"I'd like to see a fire department where we truly appreciate that we're privileged to be serving the citizens of this city. During the struggle I went to a lot of community meetings. Sometimes I'd feel embarrassed, talking about our problems in the department when I knew that the problems of the people who lived in many of those communities were so much greater — kids on drugs, poor housing, no health care. When I look around and see people whose life is so hard, I feel blessed. That's what I mean when I say that we're privileged to serve others."

One small step in pursuit of this vision of service is Demmons's plan to get firefighters more involved in the community by setting up blood-pressure testing centers in each fire station for neighbors. When a reporter asked, sarcastically, whether storytelling time for the kids would be next, he replied, "Not a bad idea."

It is graduation day for the class of 1996, and Robert Demmons is wearing his fancy-dress chief's uniform with the gold braid. This is his first time officiating at the commencement. He is proud of this class of young men and women, but he can't take his eyes off the graduates' families. The gathering of Asian, Black, white, Latino, gay, and straight San Franciscans was a sight unthinkable when he started his career. The proud faces of the parents, grandparents, husbands, wives, and lovers of these young firefighters are what make him certain that the struggle was worth it. He is looking at the faces of affirmative action.

[3]

The Big Lie:
Colorblindness and the Taboo
Against Honest Talk About Race

Under our constitution there can be no such thing as
either a creditor or a debtor race . . . We are just one
race here. It is American. — *Supreme Court Justice
Antonin Scalia*

In order to get beyond racism, we must first take
account of race. There is no other way. And in order to treat some persons equally, we must treat
them differently. We cannot — we dare not — let
the Equal Protection Clause perpetuate racial supremacy. — *Supreme Court Justice Harry Blackmun*

I T IS 1994. I am watching the Midwest regional final of the NCAA
basketball championship, fondly known as "the Dance." Michigan is
playing Arkansas. The winner will go to the Final Four, a sports event
drawing a larger audience than the Superbowl or the World Series. I am
rooting for the Razorbacks, my favorite team since the beginning of the
season. I love the way they play, but I know I'm really pulling for them
because of their coach, Nolan Richardson, who is Black.

No doubt my affinity for Richardson has its origins in my childhood.
I used to sit down to televised sports events and root for the team with
one Black player, if there was one. In those days schools like Arkansas,
Duke, Kentucky, and Louisville didn't even have Italian kids playing
for them, much less Black kids.

Now the racism in the NCAA and the symbols that signal racism's
presence are more subtle, more complex. Most of the players at this
year's Dance and a handful of coaches are Black. In the weeks leading
up to the tournament, the Black Coaches Association, led by coaches

like Richardson, threatened a boycott of the NCAA, calling attention to a number of association policies and practices that limited the opportunities of young Black athletes. These coaches are what my dad fondly used to call "race men." Being a "race man" has nothing to do with not liking white folks. It has a lot to do with loving Black folks and yourself. W.E.B. Du Bois, A. Philip Randolph, and Thurgood Marshall were "race men." Clarence Thomas is not.

I am rooting for Arkansas because when I look at Coach Richardson, he reminds me in many ways of my dad and Justice Marshall. Richardson is a serious, dignified man who has risen to the top of his profession by virtue of his talent and humanity. He cares deeply for the young men he teaches. He has high expectations and demands much of them. A brilliant coach, he has one of the best win-loss records of any coach in Division I basketball, but you don't hear his name mentioned when people talk about great basketball minds. Sports writers call him a "good recruiter" and a "motivator," while the kids on his teams are "great natural athletes." TV commentators don't use words like "discipline" and "execution" when they talk about Richardson's team. Arkansas plays "street ball." Rick Petino's Kentucky team plays "up tempo." Nolan Richardson must know that there is racial meaning in these words. This is why I'm rooting for Arkansas.

Bill Clinton is also watching the game. He's right there in the stands, and he too is screaming for the Razorbacks. When the final buzzer sounds, Arkansas has won. Pandemonium rules the arena in Dallas, and the nation's chief executive walks briskly to midcourt to meet Coach Nolan Richardson. He gives the coach a two-handed high five, bumping his chest in a moment of spontaneous, joyful exhilaration, and then, in full view of the Reunion Arena and millions of television viewers, the two men hug, a bear hug.

I am not exhilarated. I am strangely conflicted. I'm happy for the Hogs. Happy for their strong, dignified Black coach. But I don't feel happy for the country or the state of race relations. I am trying to understand why this is so. After all, isn't this the scene I dreamed of when I was a kid searching for that one Black ballplayer on the screen? Isn't it a scene that Charles Houston and Thurgood Marshall might have hoped for when they began the long line of cases that culminated in *Brown* v. *Board of Education* in 1954? Isn't this the scene that we imagined as we sat in and went to jail so that Black and white young people could play on the same basketball courts and cheer in the same stands in arenas in Dallas, Atlanta, and Charlotte?

But it's more complicated than that. I empathize with Nolan Richardson because I'm sure he knows it too. This scene *looks* like a colorblind world, and maybe in the brief moment of that two-handed high five Bill Clinton believes it really is. But my gut is telling me I know better, and so, no doubt, is Coach Richardson's.

What if Richardson were to ask the President to support the Black Coaches Association in the scholarship dispute? What if the Black players on both teams had emulated the Black athletes of the 1968 Olympic Games and raised black-gloved fists above their heads during the National Anthem, protesting that Blacks are unemployed at two and a half times the rate of whites, or that Blacks are three times more likely than whites to have incomes below the poverty level? Would it still look like a colorblind world, or is our silence on the issue of racism the price we pay for the good will that purports to know no color?

The assumption that Americans are no longer racist is central to the argument against race-based affirmative action. Opponents of affirmative action proclaim that we have won the war against bigotry and achieved a society that is essentially free of racial prejudice. Slavery, the genocide of native populations, segregation, the wartime incarceration of Japanese American citizens, are all distant memories, unfortunate blemishes on an otherwise glorious history. If there was a time when some significant number of us were bigots, the argument goes, that time is long past, and none of us is responsible for crimes committed before we were born. Certainly, critics concede, a small number of practicing racists remain, but they are social outlaws in a society committed to racial equality, outlaws subject to strong antidiscrimination laws as well as social sanction. In this book, we call this argument the Big Lie.

Some of our most influential political voices have eagerly promoted such notions. Robert Dole attacks affirmative action on the ground that slavery occurred "before we were born," and future generations ought not to have to continue "paying a price" for ancient wrongs. Newt Gingrich dismisses affirmative action by asserting that the long history of discrimination against African Americans is no different from that faced by white ethnic groups. "Virtually every American" has been subjected to discrimination, he argues.

The Big Lie is indispensable to the argument against affirmative action. If we believe that we have eradicated most of America's racism, there is no need for a remedy that takes racism into account. If there are no racist employers, then there is no need for government-mandated set-asides to ensure that those employers hire minorities. If the differences between whites and blacks in educational achievement and test scores are not reflective of continuing racial barriers to educational opportunity, then there is no need for minority admissions programs. If the playing field is already level, then affirmative action is no longer a remedy required by morality and justice. It becomes "reverse discrimination," "preferential treatment," and "racial entitlement." Only when such deceits are believed can affirmative action be turned on its head to become racism itself.

But evidence that the field is not yet level abounds. Consider, for instance, the story of Cynthia Wiggins. On a frigid December evening in upstate New York she stepped off the Number 6 bus. As she made her way across Walden Avenue, a busy seven-lane highway feeding into the New York State Thruway, she was crushed to death by a dump truck. Cynthia Wiggins was a Black teenage mother, on her way from an economically decimated neighborhood in central Buffalo to her job at the Walden Galleria Mall in the Buffalo suburb of Cheektowaga. Like the vast majority of young Black mothers, she was nothing like the "welfare queen" caricature that has come to represent her in the American psyche. She wanted work desperately. There were no jobs in inner-city Buffalo; even the McDonald's in her neighborhood was not hiring. So she made the trek each evening to this suburban mall.[1]

Her forced commute was part of a phenomenon that the Harvard sociologist William Julius Wilson has described in his influential work on the urban poor.[2] Wilson found that persistent inner-city poverty of the 1970s, 1980s, and 1990s is directly tied to the decline of urban manufacturing in the 1950s and 1960s. Poor people are largely unemployed, not because they can't hold jobs or are unwilling to work, but because working-class jobs have become exceedingly scarce, especially in urban communities. The fastest growing employment opportunities are in the suburbs, and white suburban communities have kept out affordable housing for poor folks.

But this young mother's death was caused by a more direct instance of racism. She was forced to cross this treacherous highway each night because the upscale mall where she worked would not allow the Number 6 bus on its property. From the day the Galleria opened in 1989, public buses from affluent white neighborhoods and charter buses from Canada were permitted to bring passengers right up to the store entrances, but not the Number 6, not the bus carrying poor Blacks from the city.

This is the face of American apartheid, 1990s style. Evan McKenzie, a political scientist at the University of Illinois, calls this phenomenon "suburban separatism,"[3] and describes how shopping malls have become privatized city streets designed to keep out Blacks and poor people. "You don't want to shop at Bonwit Teller downtown? Fine. We'll lock it up. Turn it outside in, and we'll keep out everyone you don't want . . . The way you deal with people who are different is that you never see them."[4]

Racism is alive and well in America, shaping our suburban geography and weaving through our private conversations. Recent polls confirm what we know from experience: racist attitudes persist in the 1990s. In a National Research Center survey conducted between February and April 1990, a majority of whites questioned said they believe Blacks and Hispanics are likely to prefer welfare to hard work and tend to be lazier than whites, more prone to violence, less intelligent, and less patriotic.[5]

A June 1993 Anti-Defamation League survey found similar disenchanting results. A significant number of whites reported their belief that Blacks are more prone to violence than other racial groups, prefer welfare over work, are less ambitious, are loud and pushy, and are not as hard-working as other groups. Somewhat smaller numbers of respondents said that Blacks do not take care of their children as well as people of other races, have less intelligence than people of other races, and have too much power in the United States. An especially disturbing revelation in this study was the finding that young people under thirty were more apt to hold racist attitudes than people between thirty and fifty.[6]

The sentiments reflected in these surveys were echoed by whites who participated in two focus groups sponsored by People for the American Way in December of 1991. The members of the groups were randomly selected young people between eighteen and twenty-four years old. They responded to questions and engaged one another in discussion while a professional pollster observed them through a one-way mirror. Promised anonymity, they criticized and ridiculed Blacks and frankly discussed feelings of revulsion toward them. While a few participants challenged the racial stereotypes offered by others, most went along with the group consensus. They believed Blacks do not have a work ethic, have too many children, and work less hard than whites. One man said that "blacks are fundamentally different" and he "does not like to associate with them." Another said, "They're just different. It's kind of bad to say, but I mean they do have an odor that's different from white people unless they cover it up with a deodorant or cologne or something of that nature. You know, their hair is different . . . It's just that I don't seek interest in these people and don't think I'm prejudiced because of that."

In a striking example of the cognitive dissonance that often accompanies racial prejudice, these same young people portrayed themselves as victims. They said that Blacks have a "chip on their shoulder," that "black people need to stop looking for discrimination." They were annoyed and nervous about expressions of what they perceived as Black separatism, such as the wearing of Malcolm X T-shirts or those that say IT'S A BLACK THING. YOU WOULDN'T UNDERSTAND.[7]

The most recent decade has also seen a significant rise in the number of hate crimes motivated by racial bias. In 1994 there were 1,637 Black victims of hate violence and 274 racially motivated offenses against Asian Americans. Racist hate groups such as the Ku Klux Klan have witnessed an alarming increase in membership; the KKK alone grew from 11,000 in 1981 to 22,000 in 1990. A recent poll showed that 68 percent of whites believe that 10 percent or more of all white Americans share the attitudes of the Ku Klux Klan toward Blacks. Sixty-two percent said they believe that antiblack feeling among whites has remained constant or increased in the last four or five years.[8]

In 1965 the Kerner Commission predicted, "Our nation is moving toward two societies, one black, one white — separate and unequal." Although evidence of overt bigotry is alarming, it is arguably less significant than the facts that show the stark material reality of two nations.

A 1991 study by the U.S. Department of Housing and Urban Development, for example, reported that Blacks had more than a 50 percent chance of being discriminated against when seeking housing and that African Americans were rejected for home loans at twice the rate of whites.[9] Study after study confirms that white and black "testers" are treated differently when they apply for housing or mortgages. We remain a largely segregated society.

According to another study, in the early 1990s more than a third of America's Blacks were living in urban ghettos, and Hispanics were similarly isolated. And while residential segregation decreases for most racial and ethnic groups with additional education, income, and occupational status, this does not hold true for African Americans.[10]

Forty years after the Supreme Court outlawed school segregation in *Brown* v. *Board of Education,* racial isolation in school is still the norm for most minority children. A 1993 National School Boards Association study found that 70 percent of Black and Hispanic students now study in classrooms with a predominantly minority enrollment and that schools are becoming more segregated than ever. In the Northeast region of the country, half of Black students and 46 percent of Hispanic students attend schools where more than 90 percent of the students are minorities.[11] These high concentrations of minority students are inevitably accompanied by the "savage inequality" of family and community poverty and sparse financial resources for the schools involved.

Stark disparities are evident when the incomes of African American and white households are compared. In 1990, for instance, the median income of African American households was 63 percent of the median income of white households. This figure was only 1 percent higher than the 62 percent in 1980, which in turn represented a 1 percent increase over the figure in 1970. In 1993 approximately 33 percent of the Black population lived in poverty, compared with 13 percent of the white population. Again, there has been little change for Blacks since 1969, when about 32 percent of the Black population lived in poverty, compared with approximately 9 percent of the white population.[12]

Disparities in incarceration and mortality rates between Blacks and whites also indicate the continuing impact of racism. Although whites are more than twice as likely as Blacks to be arrested and charged with a criminal offense, more Blacks than whites are incarcerated. Blacks below the age of seventy-five have a higher mortality rate than whites at every income level, and thirteen of the fifteen leading causes of death kill Blacks at a rate that is 10 to 54 percent higher than the rate for whites.[13]

What is particularly disturbing is that minority children suffer from the effects of American racism even more acutely than do their parents. The poverty rate for Black children is 45 percent; for whites it is 17 percent.[14] What's more, in 1990, 88.5 percent of all homicide victims in the United States were young African American males between the ages of fifteen and twenty-four, an increase of 10 percent over the 1980 figure.[15]

Despite the overwhelming evidence that race continues to matter in America, many of us continue to believe that our nation has overcome its racism. The Big Lie is seductive primarily because most Americans want to believe it is true. We want to believe that we are not racists. A racist is an evil person, and most of us know that we are not cruel-hearted bigots. Moreover, if we can believe there is no racism, or that there is very little, those Americans who benefit from white privilege can continue to reap the benefits of that privilege while denying any moral responsibility for the suffering of others. Because all of the arguments against affirmative action rely on our eagerness to believe that, as a society, we are essentially free of racism, it is especially important to understand how the Big Lie works and appreciate the source of its seductiveness.

The deception begins with a rhetorical ruse that elides the ideal with reality. The constitutional ideal of equality is invoked as if equality has been achieved, so now our only concern is to guard against some new inequality, such as discrimination against white males. "Our Constitution is colorblind" we are told, as if this means that most individuals and institutions are free of racial bias. To believe this we must accept a formal and extremely narrow definition of racial discrimination or racism, under which only self-professed bigots are racists and none of us is held responsible for perpetuating the white supremacy of even the very recent past.

Today's "colorblind" argument has its origin in the famous dissenting opinion of Justice Harlan in the 1896 case of *Plessy* v. *Ferguson*. "Our Constitution is colorblind, and neither knows nor tolerates classes among citizens,"[16] Harlan wrote, noting his disagreement with his fellow justices on the Supreme Court. The Court's majority had held that Louisiana's law segregating passengers on public transportation did not violate the Constitution, because separate accommodations for Blacks and whites did not constitute unequal accommodations. The majority maintained that the segregation law in no way demeaned Blacks or signaled a belief in their inferiority. In an argument often echoed in today's affirmative action debate, the Court's opinion accused Blacks of mass paranoia. If the enforced separation of the two races stamped the colored race with a badge of inferiority, "it is not by reason of anything found in the act, but solely because the colored race chooses to put that construction upon it,"[17] said the Court.

Harlan countered that the majority was willfully blinding itself to what everybody knew — that the segregation of the races was a declaration of white supremacy. The "real meaning" of segregation, he wrote, is "that colored citizens are so far inferior and degraded that they cannot be allowed to sit in public coaches occupied by white citizens."[18]

Harlan invoked the metaphor of "colorblindness" for a very different purpose, though, from that of today's opponents of affirmative action, who quote his words while ignoring his meaning. His intention was to declare an ideal, a mandate, and a standard against which the Constitution would judge the state of affairs in a racist world; it was not to deny the existence of racism. He was calling his colleagues' attention to the white supremacist meaning of segregation, which they sought to overlook. If slavery and segregation had legally institutionalized a racial caste system, then the Equal Protection Clause of the Fourteenth Amendment required the disestablishment of that caste system. In other words, he was forcing his colleagues to see the racism in the purportedly neutral practice of segregation. He was acknowledging racial reality in order to meet the constitutional ideal of equality, not denying it.

This element of Harlan's dissent became the central lesson of *Brown v. Board of Education,* the 1954 landmark case that declared segregation inherently unequal and overruled the "separate but equal" doctrine of *Plessy.* Separate could not be equal, the Court argued, because the purpose and effect of racial segregation were to maintain the caste system of which Justice Harlan had spoken. This caste system was composed of beliefs, practices, and institutions that functioned to deny Blacks full membership in the community of citizens. The Equal Protection Clause of the Constitution required the dismantling of those racist meanings, practices, and institutions, and that dismantling could not occur without attention to the reality of racism.

We cannot desegregate a segregated institution without giving attention to race. When federal courts implemented plans to desegregate schools after *Brown*, they were forced to acknowledge the race of the students they were assigning to each school. It also became clear that they could not dismantle segregation by simply taking off the books those laws which mandated segregation. Systems of white privilege in place for hundreds of years, in white universities, fire departments, businesses, and labor unions, would not dematerialize of their own inertia. Without attention to the race of those individuals who were being included and excluded, and without affirmative action to change the business-as-usual policies and practices, these institutions would remain all white. The dismantling of institutionalized privilege required affirmative action.

Of course, when it became apparent that equal opportunity could not be achieved without some redistribution of opportunity, the redistribution was resisted. There was mob violence in Little Rock, Selma, and Boston; there was white flight from cities when school desegregation threatened the status quo as whites had known it. Ultimately, the resistance to the redistribution of opportunity found voice in today's politics of anti–affirmative action. This politics argued quite forthrightly that opportunity should not be "equalized" or redistributed on the basis of race. In the words of Supreme Court Justice Scalia, "In my view, government can never have a 'compelling interest' in discriminating on the basis of race in order to make up for past racial discrimination in the opposite direction . . . [U]nder our Constitution there can be no such thing as either a creditor or a debtor race."[19] Justice Scalia, in effect, argues for a repeal of history. He simply presses the mute button on the messages of the past.

But antiredistribution and maintenance of white privilege cannot be squared with the *Brown* mandate to *de*segregate unless we assume that the playing fields are already level. Unfortunately, this assumption has held sway over the years, slowing progress toward full racial justice, even as America appears to adhere aggressively to the principle of racial equality. Just as his colleagues in *Plessy* turned the mandate of equal protection into the lie of "separate but equal," Justice Harlan's invocation of colorblindness has been transformed tragically from a constitutional mandate for a just society into a catch phrase for the denial of racism. Today his inspiring words "Our Constitution is colorblind" are quoted time and again to imply that the task of eradicating white supremacy is complete, leaving only the bogeyman of nonwhite supremacy.

To believe that we live in a colorblind society, free of the legacy of slavery and segregation, is to deny what we see and hear every day. During the last twenty years a Supreme Court increasingly dominated by conservative justices has touted a legal ideology of "formal equality," or equality as defined by law, that is committed to laws equal in theory but not necessarily equal in fact. The effect of this ideology of formal equality, is to make it possible to pretend that racism doesn't exist. Legal rules and doctrines that ignore much of what we know about human behavior and history define racism so narrowly that, for legal purposes, racism is rendered nearly nonexistent.

The first of these rules is the intent requirement. In the 1976 case of Washington v. Davis,[20] the Supreme Court found that Black job applicants to the District of Columbia police force, who had challenged the racially discriminatory effects of a civil service examination, had not been denied equal protection, since they could not prove the test was adopted with the specific intent of excluding Blacks from the job. Of course, it is almost impossible to prove intentional racism if the individuals involved are hiding their motives.

Moreover, much of modern-day American racism operates outside our consciousness. Americans share a historical and cultural heritage in which racism has played and still plays a dominant role. Because of this shared experience, we also inevitably share many ideas, attitudes, and beliefs that attach significance to an individual's race and often induce negative feelings and opinions about nonwhites. To the extent that these cultural beliefs have influenced all of us, we are all racists. At the same time most of us are unaware of our racism. We do not recognize the ways in which our cultural experience has influenced our beliefs about race or the occasions on which those beliefs affect our actions. In other words, a large part of the behavior that produces racial discrimination is influenced by unconscious racial motivation.

Traditional notions of intent do not reflect the fact that decisions about racial matters are influenced in large part by factors that can be characterized as neither intentional — in the sense that certain outcomes are self-consciously sought — nor unintentional — in the sense that the outcomes are random, fortuitous, and uninfluenced by the decision maker's beliefs, desires, and wishes.

The intent requirement also disregards how overtly racist practices and laws of the past have become entrenched in institutions of white privilege that do not require new racist intent for their maintenance. For example, in the *Davis* case, although the civil service exam had not been shown to be a valid measure of who was likely to make the best police officer, the Court held that it had been shown to measure verbal skills and that raising the verbal skills of police officers was a legitimate governmental purpose. The Court failed to acknowledge that most of the Black applicants who had lower scores than their white counterparts had attended public schools in the District of Columbia, schools that a federal court had already found denied Black children an equal chance to learn the very skills the civil service test was measuring. In other words, the test had in effect perpetuated an educational advantage gained by whites as a result of recent racism.

Acting as if there has been no racism in the past, or as if past racism is in no way connected to current white privilege, is another way that our courts define racism out of existence. The 1989 case of *City of Richmond* v. *Croson*,[21] the first of the Supreme Court's frontal attacks on affirmative action, is a prime example of how the Court employs historical amnesia to create a colorblind fantasy world. In *Croson*, the Court held that the rights of white contractors had been violated when the city of Richmond, Virginia, sought to help minority contractors break into what had been virtually an all-white business. Private contractors who received city-funded contracts were required to give 30 percent of their subcontracts to minority-owned businesses.

Race can be taken into account only when an affirmative action plan is a remedy for specific past discrimination engaged in or promoted by the city, the Court said. According to the Court's majority, Richmond had failed to prove that minority subcontractors had been discriminated against in the past, even though less than 1 percent of the city's contracting dollars had been awarded to minority contractors in a city with a 50 percent African American population. There is "no direct evidence of race discrimination [against minority contractors] on the part of the city . . . or any evidence that the city's prime contractors had discriminated against minority-owned [sub]contractors,"[22] argued Justice O'Connor, going on to suggest that the statistical disparity in hiring might have been caused by such nondiscriminatory factors as a preference by African Americans for jobs in other, lower-paying industries.

The historian Charles Hoffer summarizes the historical record of discrimination against African American contractors in Richmond as follows:

> . . . Non-minority contractors had for a century prevented African-American craftsmen from becoming businessmen, refusing them loans and finding other ways to keep them out of the larger marketplace (servicing the African-American market was permitted), while using their labor. The alliance that was to dominate city government and the awarding of city contracts was that between an old Virginia elite and a lily-white City Council. While some of this elite circle believed that African-Americans ought to be allowed equality in farming and trade pursuits (so long as they were willing to accept Jim Crow laws), there was no place for African-American businessmen outside of the African-American community. That attitude persisted through the end of a white-dominated City Council in 1978 and continues among the white minority of the Council and its supporters in the corporate business community.[23]

But the Court's majority blinded itself to Richmond's history of slavery and segregation, refusing to see the city's still segregated neighborhoods and segregated schools. The justices, moreover, denied their personal experiences in clubs, communities, and law firms where Blacks were once excluded and where, even today, Blacks are rarely seen.

When these realities are brought to its attention, the current Supreme Court majority employs legal technicalities to make racism disappear. Once the intent requirement is invoked to limit the existence of racism to only those cases where racist intent is proved, there is little discrimination to remedy. In the Richmond case, Justice O'Connor, writing for the Court's majority, disparaged the city's justification that affirmative action set-asides were a remedy for past and continuing discrimination in the construction industry; she called it an "amorphous" and "unsupported" assertion of "societal discrimination."[24] Whether O'Connor meant that she knew the evidence was there but the city failed to put it on the record, or that racism in which the entire society participates is "amorphous" and "unsupported," the reality of racial exclusion was denied either way.

O'Connor's opinion also suggests that the real problem in the construction industry is economic barriers, not racism, and that the culture of the Black community may have led Blacks to seek work in other places.

The latter explanation invokes the "culture of poverty" theories of conservative social scientists who argue that it is not discrimination but an aberrant, dysfunctional culture, existing independent of past or continuing racism, that keeps minorities trapped in poverty. This view, but a short step from theories of genetic inferiority, is advanced by one of affirmative action's most vociferous opponents, Dinesh D'Souza, in his book tellingly titled with the Big Lie itself, *The End of Racism*.[25]

Finally, in a clever twist, the Court and opponents of affirmative action often argue that the Equal Protection Clause protects individuals, not groups. Because the Constitution protects individual rights and not group rights, there can be no group injuries against a race. If there is no group injury, then there is no need for a group remedy such as affirmative action. It is a Catch-22.

Racism is an injury to a group. White supremacy defines Blacks and other nonwhite races as inferior as groups. Individual Blacks are discriminated against because of their membership in the group, and the entire group is injured by the beliefs and practices that define and treat them as inferior. By limiting constitutional rights to individuals, the Supreme Court acts as if there is no such thing as a group injury and denies the only kind of remedy that responds to the way in which racism operates. No group injury means no group remedy.

Of course the Court is not wrong when it says that the purpose of the Equal Protection Clause is to protect each and every individual without regard to his or her race. The ideology of formal equality is attractive and powerful because it starts out with a good idea: that of liberal individualism. Racial classifications are presumed invidious and are looked on with suspicion, because when we judge a person based on her race we disregard her human individuality and thereby deprive her of dignity and freedom of self-definition and self-actualization. The point here is that race should not limit our humanness or our status as citizens. This is the meaning of Justice Harlan's admonition "Our constitution is colorblind" and of Martin Luther King's challenge to us to judge one another by the "content of our character" rather than the color of our skin.

The Supreme Court relies on America's strong tradition of liberal individualism when it tells us that we can ensure human dignity and equality by promising each person fair governmental process. According to this line of reasoning, considering race in school admissions and employment decisions is suspect because it introduces a factor into the decision-making process that has nothing to do with who we are as individuals. Racial classification is wrong because if we distribute benefits based on an individual's membership in a racial group, we are likely to make erroneous assumptions about the attributes of that individual. Under this view, it matters not whether the purpose of the policy is the perpetuation of racial subordination or its demise. The classification injures each person whose individuality it ignores.

In an ideal world, where each individual is born into a community that respects and values her as much as any other person, fair individual process is all that is needed. In such a world, race consciousness and group-based decisions are necessarily in tension with equality and human dignity. But that is not the world we live in, and a legal theory that acts as if we already live in such a world perpetuates the Big Lie. When an individual's rights are denied because her group is subjugated, only remedies creating equality for the group can offer true equality for the individual.

There is still another way to think about promoting equality and human dignity that does not ignore our country's racism, one that derives from the point of view of human rights. Consider the constitutional command of equal protection as one requiring the elimination of society's racism rather than mandating equal protection as an individual right. Such a substantive approach assumes that ridding society of racial subordination is indispensable and a prerequisite to individual dignity and equality. It understands that white supremacy hurts us all. The recent transformations in South Africa are an inspiring example of this substantive approach to equality. There, the memory of legal apartheid is vivid, its wounds too fresh and its ravages too enormous for the Big Lie to prevail. When the white supremacist government was unseated in 1994 and its laws removed from the books, it was impossible for anyone to look at white wealth and black poverty and claim that such a disparity had nothing to do with racism. To suggest, for instance, that there were no Blacks in the construction industry because Blacks had chosen to pursue work as houseboys and maids, or that the dearth of Blacks in the universities and professional schools was unrelated to the inequalities of the apartheid school system, would be absurd. No one would dare tell the Black people crowded into Soweto slums that they must remain there while white people inhabit the plush suburbs of Johannesburg because that is the natural state of things, because Blacks are genetically inferior, because the welfare system has made them dependent, because Black culture is a "culture of poverty," because somehow in a free-market, merit-based competitive system they have fallen to the bottom.

In South Africa everyone, black and white, knows that white privilege is an inheritance from a regime of white supremacy and that equality requires the redistribution of that inheritance. Justice Albie Sachs, one of President Mandela's appointees to South Africa's new Constitutional Court, takes a very different view from that of our own Court. In an article in *The South African Journal of Human Rights,* Sachs says:

> From a human rights point of view, the starting point of constitutional affirmation in a post-apartheid democratic South Africa is that the country belongs to all who live in it, and not just to a small racial minority. If the development of human rights is the criterion, there must be a constitutional requirement that the land be redistributed in a fair and just way, and not a requirement that says there can be no redistribution . . .
>
> Affirmative action by its nature involves the distribution of inherited rights. It is distributory rather than conservative in character.[26]

Here in the United States, we too have had to confront the reality of our racism. When Governor George Wallace was standing in the doorway of the University of Alabama saying he would never submit to desegregation, when federal troops were required to escort Black children through mobs of angry whites in Little Rock, Arkansas, when television broadcast scenes of Black children being attacked by police dogs and fire hoses, federal judges could not pretend that we were a colorblind society. They issued orders requiring desegregation of all-white schools, police departments, and businesses. They understood that none of this could be accomplished without attention to race. Those first days are less than a generation ago. We have barely begun to dismantle the legacy of American apartheid. Justice Sachs is right: affirmative action is redistributive. It is resistance to that redistribution that makes so many want to believe the Big Lie.

While the Supreme Court and the laws it makes have provided the ideological framework that lends intellectual and moral legitimacy to the Big Lie, the justices are hardly the only ones guilty of denying the existence of racism. Most Americans claim that we live in a country where the color of our skin is no more significant than the color of our eyes.

In a 1969 article in *The International Journal of Psychiatry*, Dr. Calvin Butts called white racism an issue with "implications for professional mental health practitioners,"[27] and in 1974 Dr. Chester Pierce of the Harvard Medical School described racism as "a public health problem."[28] Much of our inability to recognize racial discrimination stems from a failure to recognize that racism functions much like a societal illness that infects almost everyone. If racism is indeed a societal disease, then our denial of its existence is a primary mechanism by which the disease resists cure.

As our culture has formally rejected overt racism as immoral and unproductive, hidden or unacknowledged prejudice has become the more prevalent, and in many ways more insidious, form of racism. Even when we admit to racially discriminatory practices, we rarely admit we are racist. This kind of massive denial is not possible without a strictly enforced taboo against speaking publicly about racism.

The taboo, like all social taboos, exists precisely because the forbidden thing is not eradicated. White supremacy as an ideology runs dangerously close to the surface as cross-burners enter the mainstream and books positing Black cultural or genetic inferiority-are reviewed favorably in the *New York Times*. Former Ku Klux Klan Wizard David

Duke commended 1994 Republican congressional candidates for having achieved much of what he had called for during his failed bids for the United States Senate, Louisiana governorship, and Republican presidential nomination in the early 1990s. "I'm happy to see the way things are going," he said, citing growing emphasis on welfare cutbacks, attacks on immigration, and the dismantling of affirmative action programs. After watching the Republican television spots, Duke said, "About 80 percent of them look like they were taken directly from my television spots. Imitation is the sincerest form of flattery."[29]

Since honest talk about our nation's racism is essentially off-limits, the old-time politics of race baiting has returned, disguised in the liberal rhetoric of colorblindness. Many of the same politicians who resisted integration and filibustered against the Voting Rights Act in the 1960s have eagerly jumped aboard the anti–affirmative action bandwagon of the 1990s, calling for an end to race-conscious remedies while disseminating malignant racially coded messages with a wink and a nod to old-fashioned racists.

Listen to the code words of the political campaigns that ushered in the so-called Newt Gingrich revolution: criminal, crime rate, inner city, welfare mother, illegal immigrant, alien hordes, social program participant, unqualified candidate, illegitimate children, racial preference, affirmative action. Is there any American voter who does not hear the racial subtext in these phrases? Is there any voter who cannot recognize the purposeful manipulation of white fears in the tough-on-crime, welfare reform, anti-immigrant rhetoric?

The same politicians who rely on these race-coded messages to polarize Americans call for an end to affirmative action programs that they say violate the principle of colorblind equality. The *coup de grâce* of the colorblind con game is to blame affirmative action itself for creating hostility, resentment, and racial divisiveness. The anti–affirmative action ballot measure deceptively titled the California Civil Rights Initiative is yet another example of how the ideology of formal equality is used to reinforce white supremacy. Its proponents sent the racist message "It's time to put them back in their place," while trumpeting the rhetoric of civil rights.

Cruelest of all are the insidious effects of our self-deception on our children. "The Stereotype Within: Why Students Don't Buy Black History Month" is the title of an article by a white sixth-grade teacher in the D.C. suburb of Montgomery County. The teacher writes about his experience with a class of twenty-nine students, of whom all but two were Black or Hispanic and all but three from poor families. The teacher had shown a film based on Langston Hughes's story "Thank You, Ma'am," about a young Black boy who attempts to steal the purse of an elderly Black woman. The boy fails, and the woman takes him into her home, where she proceeds to apply generous amounts of love and understanding to his wounds. The story's clear lesson is that love is powerful medicine and that all of us have it within us to be better people. The teacher described the discussion of the film as follows:

> I turned on the lights and asked if anyone wanted to share their reactions to the film. An "A" student, who is black, raised his hand and said, "You knew something bad was going to happen when it started. As soon as you see a black boy you know he's gonna do something bad."
> Me: Just because he's black, he's bad?
> Student: Everybody knows that black people are bad. That's the way we are.
> I was becoming a little horrified, both at the answer and that it would be coming from him of all students. I counted on the class to rebuke him. To provoke a class response, I restated his proposition that "Black people are bad" and asked who agreed with that. Twenty-four of 29 hands went up.
> Maybe I was misunderstanding the use of "bad." "Do you mean 'cool' or 'tough' or 'hot'? Or do you mean bad as in 'not good' or 'evil'? I asked. One of the best female students in the class assured me she meant the latter, as did everyone else.
> In her view, and in the view of most of my class, black people are determined inherently, genetically, naturally, to be bad people. To my students, it wasn't a matter of choice or upbringing, but simply a racial attribute. They had no doubt in this, nor was this their sole racial stereotype. As the discussion continued a disturbing picture of their self-image emerged. All of the following comments received a near consensus in the class.
> "Blacks are poor and stay poor because they're dumber than whites (and Asians)." "Black people don't like to work hard." "Black people have to be bad so they can fight and defend themselves from

other blacks." As students, they see their badness as natural. They don't mean any disrespect to me personally: It's "just how we are." "They don't need to work hard because it won't matter in the end." "Black men make women pregnant and leave." "Black boys expect to die young and unnaturally. White people are smart and have money." "Asians are smart and make money. Asians don't like blacks or Hispanics." "Hispanics are more like blacks than whites. They can't be white so they try to be black. Hispanics are poor and don't try hard because, like blacks, they know it doesn't matter. They will be like blacks because when you're poor you have to be bad to survive." "Black kids who do their school work and behave want to be white. White kids who do poorly or dress cool want to be blacks. Hispanic kids want to be black because they aren't smart (like whites)."[30]

This is the strange and awful fruit of segregation, 1990s style. These children experience the same injury identified in *Brown*. We don't need Dr. Kenneth Clark's doll tests, the psychological tests submitted to the Court in *Brown* as evidence of Black children's poor self-image, to see that the race-coded messages of American culture have, in the words of the *Brown* decision, "affected their hearts and minds in a way unlikely ever to be undone." And yet, if one of these children brought suit under the Equal Protection Clause, the Court would likely say, "There is no direct evidence before us that anyone has discriminated against these children."

Before *Brown*, signs on lunch counters, drinking fountains, and bathrooms read COLORED and WHITE. Before we declared ourselves color-blind, Black parents sat their children down and taught them an important lesson about what hurt them. They pointed to the signs, to the minstrel shows, and to the Little Black Sambos, and said to their children, "This is not about you. It is the white man's problem that he needs to think of you as less than he. This is the white man's way of keeping you in your place, of making sure you do not get your fair share. This is what he says you are, but you are not this person."

Now the WHITE ONLY signs are gone, but the color-coded messages remain. Children see them all around, but the Supreme Court, the Congress, the President, the academy, banks, and businesses claim they see no color there, and in doing so, they deny society's racism and shut down honest talk about it.

Remembering is a moral imperative. We must acknowledge the misdeeds of our past and confront their contemporary legacies. Out of the tragic history of American racism that we share, there is a way to universal human emancipation, if we will only see it. To see our racism and fight it is the only way to fashion a just world out of an unjust past. We are all Americans, and we are all racists. We owe it to our children to admit to our infection with the sickness of racism so that we can begin the work of finding a cure. We owe it to ourselves to stop telling the Big Lie.

[II]

EACH OTHER'S HARVEST

The Case for
Affirmative Action

[4]

On Meritocracy

We are each other's harvest . . . — *Gwendolyn Brooks,
from* Paul Robeson

I STAND BEFORE YOU as the proud product of affirmative action. By this I mean that closed doors were opened for me and opportunities were made available to me because of affirmative action. I specifically do not mean that I have ever had a job or educational opportunity I was unqualified for. I specifically do not mean that I benefited, ever, from quotas, or that I ever took a job away from a white man. In every job I have ever had since completing my legal education fifteen years ago, I have been the only Asian woman. The small space made available for me by affirmative action did not change the dominant culture or complexion of my profession.

"In fact, I've often sensed a quota of one. Once I'm there, they stop looking for others like me.

"I am stunned and assaulted by the attack on affirmative action. The message I hear is a familiar one: you are not supposed to be here. To this I can only respond: yes, I am. I am qualified to do the work I do. I never doubted my abilities to teach, but my own professors and those with the power to hire did. When I told a professor I wanted to teach law some day, he counseled me to drop that ambition. Another professor told me that the federal judge I was applying to never had hired and never would hire a woman or a nonwhite. When I later applied to teach, another professor, whose honesty I appreciated, took me to lunch to tell me he didn't vote to hire me because he didn't think I could maintain control in the classroom. Straight A's in law school did not change the presumptions working against me or change the repeated, well-meaning advice I got to limit my aspirations.

"I ignored this advice and knocked on doors, and affirmative action opened the doors. Pressure to diversify, to consider the talents of applicants like me, meant the professors who doubted my ability because they'd never seen an Asian woman in the front of the classroom decided to give me a chance. Given the chance, I performed.

"I would not deprive the next generation of what I have had: the privilege of working in places made diverse by affirmative action. When I started, I was the only Asian American woman teaching in a tenure-track position at any American law school. Affirmative action gave that to me, and I have worked diligently to deserve that honor. It is honor I feel, not stigma, that I live in a country that came through a great civil rights struggle with a renewed commitment to equality. It is an honor to benefit from affirmative action, and it is an honor that obligates me to fight so that future generations will benefit as well."

With those words, or some variation thereof, I spoke at universities, in testimony to the U.S. Senate, and at political gatherings, breaking silence on affirmative action. It was a subject I hated talking about, because it required suppression of rage, applying the etiquette of scholarly discourse to a substantive discussion about whether someone like me should be in the room at all. For years it was easier to remain silent, allowing the affirmative action debate to go on in someone else's venue. I listened passively and with a pounding headache. Then, in 1995, the assault on affirmative action intensified.

There are headaches that come from silence, as well as headaches that come from direct confrontation. Worse, there is a gnawing anxiety in the gut that comes when the body senses danger and chooses neither fight nor flight, but simple retreat into stillness. Finally, when I heard Newt Gingrich talking about my people on NPR, silence was no longer an option.

Affirmative action hurts the hard-working Asians, Gingrich said. They are the smartest, the best, and they are kept out in order to meet quotas for unqualified minorities. This kind of talk mines the deep tradition of meritocracy in order to drown out the facts: Asian Americans are underrepresented in every position of power in the United States, not because of affirmative action, but because of white male privilege.

The appeal to meritocracy is the most effective weapon in the anti–affirmative action arsenal because it taps shared beliefs and shared anxieties: we should reward talent and effort, and we fear that our own talents and effort will go unrecognized. This dilemma goes back to the birth of our nation.

Thomas Jefferson loved the manicured potagerie at Monticello. His innovative garden was filled with rare flora. The beds were tended to perfection, evenly spaced among the strips of lawn edged with small brick pavilions. This was the garden that logic made: science picked the most vigorous cultivars, engineering dictated the site plan, Jefferson's constant note-taking charted the planting schedules. This was the garden that merit made: a brilliant mind, an exploring spirit, a churning energy.

As many who read this description know, this was also the garden that slavery made. While Jefferson read Latin horticultural texts late into the night, others worked in the unpaid labor of running the great estate according to Jefferson's obsessive schedules and schemes.

Jefferson was the architect not only of Monticello, but also of the American dream of merit. Just as his heart raced with the thought of ever more produce from each season's scientifically managed garden, his soul leapt toward the dream of a nation where talent, not birthright, would govern life chances. This was the Enlightenment's son. Hard work, intelligence, and integrity would rule in his new nation. That was the promise of the new, and Jefferson, in bursts of evening passion, took out his quill to describe the nation that would live the promise.

The enslaved Africans toiled as he wrote, their lives making a mockery of Jefferson's dream. The sorrow of this man is that he knew it. He knew that what he wrote of merit, of reward for work, was not reflected in his own life, nor that of his new nation. Slavery is a failing, he wrote, that will haunt us for years to come.

This story is told not to condemn Jefferson, but to honor his longing for merit and to take on the conundrum he faced. The Enlightenment dream of reward for merit eludes us still and forms the basis of anti–affirmative action rhetoric. The dream is of each person judged by individual talent and effort, each person rewarded and encouraged to greatness by that creed. Not status, not accident of birth, not prejudice, not exploitation of others, not inheritance, simply individual talents and abilities. This American dream brings newcomers yearly in the stream that has not ended since the birth of the nation.

The case for affirmative action requires both a critique and a dream of merit. The first criticism of meritocracy is that its rhetoric masks privilege. The second is that the standards used to measure merit are both imprecise and narrow in ways that fail to identify the full range of talents we might justly consider meritorious. Finally, we must ask where, when, and to what end we should apply the principle that the best is reserved for the best. While many aspects of the pledge to meritocracy are humanistic, ethical, and wise, merit is not the only method of distribution possible in a completely just world.

We must take stock, first, of the real world, the one in which status and wealth too often determine outcomes. In this nation we purport to follow standards of merit when in fact we rely on practices of privilege. This is because the stated standards, whether for jobs, education, bank loans, or political appointments, are often not those applied in practice. Even when standards are applied uniformly, the stated ones often favor maintaining status rather than opening new opportunities to the talents of many. The myth of merit is used to obscure the lingering sway of nobility that our 1776 Revolution was intended to dismantle. By stating again and again that this is a nation of equal opportunity, we send a message that the existing distribution of wealth is fair. People deserve what they have because they amass wealth based on merit. Those who don't have don't deserve, the corollary goes.

Suematsu Takemoto, the father of Representative Patsy Mink, was a talented engineer who spent a lifetime making sugar grow on Hamakua plantation. From years of careful observation he knew the plantation: the machinery, the irrigation system, the soil, the cane. He could make all the components work in concert for ever higher yields, and his knowledge was respected by the workers below him and the managers above. They knew of his hard work, his educational attainment, his invaluable experience. And they knew that every few years the plantation would bring in some young *haole* boys from the mainland to learn what they could from Mr. Takemoto so that they could take the high-paying jobs above his. If you were Japanese, you could go only so high.[1] In many an immigrant family a similar tale is told. "You have to be twice as good, work twice as hard, to go half as far," the children grow up hearing.

Professor Lani Guinier speaks bitterly of her father's comparable experience: denied a scholarship at Harvard because another man had already taken the one set aside for Blacks. Dr. Ewart Guinier's intellectual brilliance, his stellar academic record, were ignored because a quota slammed the door in his dignified face. "That is a quota," Professor Guinier said, when right-wing propagandists labeled her the quota queen. "I have never supported quotas." African Americans everywhere feel that door shutting in a father's face. Who we are, our beautiful ebony skin, marks us as someone who cannot enter.

The dream of the door open to all is the dream of merit. We in communities of color are deeply attached, and rightly so, to the notion that ability, not identity, should determine life's chances. The attraction of athletics lies in that: we give thanks for Jesse Owens, Joe Louis, Jackie Robinson, and the bright lines that marked their victories in spite of all those who hoped they would fail. Our peoples have historically sought out and excelled in arenas where merit could not so easily collapse into privilege: sports, the military, small business enterprises. At several points in American military history, soldiers of color fought on suicide missions, knowing that they might die laying claim to the dream of judgment not by color, but by concrete contribution.[2] The race to the swiftest, the aria to the purest voice, the water to the deepest well. Those who marched for civil rights shared this dream.

Thomas Jefferson, author of the dream of merit in America's founding texts, fretted over the nonmeritocracy entrenched in the early Republic. He noticed that the energetic risk takers who amassed great fortunes in the New World raised their children in privilege and passed on wealth to a generation made lazy by largesse. Similarly, capitalist observers in today's America note sadly that most family businesses, no matter how successful in the first generation, decline in the second.[3] Merit, talent, effort fade when inherited wealth is assumed. Jefferson speculated that to truly reward the ablest, we should end inheritance: on a person's death, let his or her estate pass to the public trust. Encourage each individual to develop personal resources rather than wait for an inheritance. That is the way to keep the nation vibrant and end the lazymaking curse of aristocracy.

Jefferson found his ideas unwelcome among his wealthy counterparts. He himself struggled to impart the virtues of hard work and inventiveness to offspring whose talents never matched his, sending detailed instruction sheets to his daughter with schedules for study and self-improvement. There is a sense of tragedy in this man and in the legacy he left the nation: a belief in meritocracy and a practice of aristocracy.

At a well-known private university, there is a beautiful stable for horses, the gift of a benefactor who hinted genteelly that his daughter loved to ride, and if she were admitted, he would surely see that she, and others at the university, had adequate facilities. At every prestigious university in the country, a similar monument to privilege exists.

The opposite of merit is privilege, and in actual practice, merit is trumped by privilege as a matter of course, not exception. In the early 1980s Asian American university students began to notice that, while more highly qualified Asians were applying to the nation's best universities, the Asian admission rate was not increasing. At first they feared that affirmative action for other minorities did indeed have the effect of placing a quota on Asians. Instead, what they found was that the Asians were displaced not by other minorities, but by whites, including athletes and "legacy admits" — sons and daughters of alumni who were admitted to the Ivy Leagues with significantly lower test scores and GPAs than Asian Americans who were turned away. An Office of Civil Rights compliance review found that mean SAT scores of legacy acceptances at Harvard were thirty-five points below the scores for all admitted students.[4]

Even at some state universities, paid for by all citizens, admissions officers regularly accede to requests to admit an individual as a favor to a donor or politician. A recent scandal at the University of California revealed that affirmative action opponents on the UC board of regents, while they spoke of merit in voting to end affirmative action, were using their position to attempt to curry favor in the admissions process for their friends and relatives. Presumably, none of those admitted by this form of affirmative action for the well-connected are unqualified for university study, but they are certainly not the best qualified on traditional criteria, or they would not need to use their privilege.

Interestingly, the rich rarely feel their children are stigmatized by genteel bribes that determine the admissions outcome. If they did, they would make their donations anonymously. Along with the privilege brought by wealth and connections is the unconscious arrogance of such power, and perhaps the conscious design to ensure royal treatment. *"Of course* this is how I get things in life. I buy them. I am rich. That is not cause for shame, and may I remind you, there is more for me to spend if I am kept in a good mood." The rest of us seem to go along. Those disappointed anti–affirmative action applicants who complain bitterly that "their" right to admission was taken by a person of color never seem to think that they lost a seat to the donor's daughter or the regent's friend's son.

For every story of reward for ability, there are two stories of reward for privilege. Those who reject this unprovable math can turn to the statistics compiled by the Glass Ceiling Commission, established in 1991 during a Republican administration and supported by conservatives like Elizabeth Dole. The commission found a landscape of privilege handing out jobs in corporate America from top to bottom: Ninety-five to 97 percent of senior managers of Fortune 500 and Fortune 1000 companies are men; 95 percent of news media managers, and 85 percent of tenured professors are white and male; women consistently earn less than men of comparable educational attainment, and white men's median weekly earnings in 1993 were 33 percent higher than those of any other group; women M.B.A.s and J.D.s from the top schools in the country earn less than male classmates on graduation, and their wage gap grows over time. As for leadership positions — seats in the Senate, university presidencies, partnerships in law firms, editorial positions in the media, membership on corporate boards, mayors, governors — white men hold 95 percent of these jobs, although they represent only 43 percent of the workforce. Even in fields dominated by women, such as elementary education, it is men who more often than not serve as principals.[5]

President Clinton, in his 1996 speech defending affirmative action, noted these additional alarming facts: "The unemployment rate for African Americans remains about twice that of whites. The Hispanic rate is still much higher. Women have narrowed the earnings gap, but still make only 72 percent as much as men for comparable jobs. The average income for a Hispanic woman with a college degree is still less than the average income of a white man with a high school diploma."

The President went on to cite studies that showed "that black home-loan applicants are more than twice as likely to be denied credit as whites with the same qualifications; and that Hispanic applicants are more than one and a half times as likely to be denied loans as whites with the same qualifications."[6]

In one sense, the statistics the President cited are alarming. On the other hand, the fact that privilege, not merit, distributes opportunity is common knowledge, as illustrated in a conversation we overheard on a long plane ride. A charming young man, about seven years old, asked, "Dad, why are those people getting ice cream? I want ice cream." The father replied, "Son, those people are sitting in first class. We are in coach. They don't give you ice cream in coach. That's how it is in life; you get what you pay for."

"But, Dad," the observant child persisted, "how come *she* got ice cream? She's sitting in coach." The boy referred to a woman he had seen sitting in coach. She was, indeed, standing in the galley and eating an ice cream sundae provided by a flight attendant.

"Well, son," the patient father explained, "I heard her talking to the flight attendant. She's a flight attendant too, and she's off duty. In fact, she lives right next door to the guy who gave her ice cream. That's the second rule: it's who you know."

That short exchange makes clear the most basic lessons about an-timerit that young people learn in our culture: money talks, and so do connections. If you ask people how they got their first job, chances are they will tell you that they knew someone who knew a job was available.[7] The puzzle is how these facts are common knowledge even as we hold tenaciously to the myth of meritocracy. Perhaps we believe that money is merit, that the rich have more money because they are more meritorious. Certainly the rich have a psychological need to believe this. But do the 90 percent of Americans who call themselves "middle class" believe that they are also inherently "middling" in merit? Affirmative action becomes an easy scapegoat in a world in which we know but don't admit that privilege molds the distribution of everything from college admissions to ice cream sundaes with all the toppings.

The myth of merit masks privilege, in part through the belief that we can identify and reward the best without ambiguity. An agent who represents jazz musicians once said, "It's great to be white in America," referring to the runaway success of a good white singer. A good singer, but by his own acknowledgment no better than the hundreds of talented African American jazz singers who could never get a recording contract. In a foot race, crossing the finish line is what counts. In other endeavors, the qualities marking the best are subject to debate.

Downbeat magazine's annual poll asks readers for their views on the best musicians. The design of the poll is cunning, for there is rarely consensus on the "best" in jazz. What the editors know is that the jazz fans' commitment to their own subjectivity is the poll's seduction. Engagement in passionate arguments over who is the best drummer and why identifies the potential *Downbeat* subscriber. The subjectivity required to determine the best musicians is what allows racial and other politics to determine who gets a recording contract, a government grant for the arts, or a following in the markets created by fans.

Even when we sincerely endeavor to reward the best, we are clumsy and confused in our efforts. To avoid the vagaries of subjectivity, we seek quantitative measures, but the bias in standardized tests used in school and work settings is well known.[8] Tests like the SAT are notorious for bias in favor of those who come from educated white families. One study found that a child of a librarian had a 1120–times greater chance to win a National Merit Scholarship, selected by SAT scores, than did the child of a laborer.[9] Other studies have shown persistent bias against girls in such tests.[10] The corporate entities that prepare and administer the tests admit that what they measure is narrow; the scores tend to correlate with performance on future tests and therefore grades in school. Good test takers make good students, if the definition of good student is "one who does well on tests."

The intelligence and gifts of the A student are not something to deprecate. The point is simply that a test like the LSAT (Law School Admissions Test) predicts performance on law school exams, and law school exams reflect a narrow set of talents. The number of average law students who become excellent lawyers is enormous. Ask any practicing lawyer to name the lawyer she would choose to represent her if she was charged with a serious crime or was in an intricate corporate negotiation. Chances are she will name someone who was not an A student in law school. As Barbara Babcock, profiled later in this book, once said, "In our profession, qualities of character, judgment, empathy, and sense of craft make it impossible to quantify who is better qualified."[11]

In every profession, we see the application of entry-level standards that do not reflect the talents and abilities required for the job. Even as personnel experts admit the flaws in their predictive instruments, we cling to the notion that there is a best applicant, and that the job is that person's entitlement.

A notion of merit that asks us to line people up in order of ability assumes it is possible to determine the best with exactitude. Among the several flaws in this assumption is the reality that in almost all human endeavors there is a range of valuable talents. We live in a world of multiple bests. A good crew for a wilderness trip, for example, might include a seasoned guide, a good storyteller, a paramedic, and a talented cook. When several talents are valuable, it doesn't make sense to have a single notion of "the best." Second, something as complex as human talent is rarely measurable in arithmetic terms. Indeed, those who design rating systems for job applicants tell us there is no significant difference between 87 and 88 points, even though we act as though number 88 is somehow "more qualified" than number 87. Childish games, like rating potential sexual partners on a scale of 1 to 10, are laughable precisely because we know, from human experience, that the mix of intangibles and compatibility factors in human relationships cannot be distilled into numbers.

Getting at what we really mean by "merit" demands subjectivity. Consider, for instance, a professor writing an evaluation for a candidate for officer's training school. After answering a series of questions about intelligence and personal integrity, the professor is asked to pass judgment: "This individual will have the power to make decisions that will affect the lives of others. Would you be pleased if the safety and well-being of someone you cared about were dependent upon this person?" This is the kind of question that requires human subjectivity and reaches for information beyond what is revealed by test scores and grade point averages.

The problem with such an assessment, and the reason that immigrants and minorities have traditionally favored the civil service exam system, is that a subjective evaluation invites prejudice. At one law firm, the evaluation sheet for associates asked: "Is this our kind of person?" When insiders look for someone who "seems like the type of person who does well here," they tend to look for someone like themselves, missing the valuable talents of people who are different. Here is a double bind. To combat overwhelming forces of privilege and prejudice, we seek objective, quantifiable measures of talent such as civil service exams. Those measures, however, are inaccurate; they themselves reproduce privilege and ignore the subjective criteria that most of us find critical in evaluating our fellow human beings.

Jobs and economic advantage handed out as spoils for connections and social status form a hard reality, which leaves many Americans of average means with two choices: cling to the myth of merit, or accept that you are a perpetual chump. In any abusive situation, psychologists tell us, denial is a strong human defense. Abused children do this, women who are battered do this. Victims of race and class oppression do this as well. When we cannot change our circumstances, we make excuses for them: "Maybe I could have worked harder, studied harder in school. Or maybe I was born unlucky; that's why I can't win the lottery or find a decent job. There must be a reason why, in a world that rewards merit, I have so few rewards."

The obvious reason — that those with power are taking more than their fair share — is the hardest to accept. It requires either enraged action or total degradation: I'm a loser, and there is nothing I can do about it.

Affirmative action provides an answer: privilege should not trump merit, and merit should include the talents of those without privilege. Affirmative action responds to the evaluative challenges posed by inadequate numbers and possibly prejudiced subjective evaluation. A good affirmative action plan broadens the definition of qualification, expanding the pool of talent available for any given opportunity. New, wider measures of merit allow us to identify those persons with special talents for particular jobs.

Historically, the demand for affirmative action came from communities with unmet needs. Ghettos, left without basic services because of white flight, needed doctors, lawyers, merchants, and teachers who were unafraid to serve there. Ethnic communities found that, without community-based scholars, their history, their culture was ignored or misinterpreted by outsiders. Taxpayers in poor neighborhoods were tired of watching construction contracts allocated to incompetent insider cronies and racist contractors who hired only white men. If the working poor were paying for school construction, the community members decided, then the largesse of construction contracts ought to benefit their community. They wanted a share of the jobs and a say over how the projects were carried out so that their concerns, from environmental pollution to cultural sensitivity, were respected. In short, affirmative action meant sharing opportunity and control with those who never had it before. In this process a new definition of "qualified" arose.

The community-based definition of "qualified" asked different questions: Can this individual or firm meet the needs of those who are presently excluded from social advantage? Can this teacher successfully teach children for whom English is a second language? Does this teacher live in the community? Is she familiar with cultural strengths as well as cultural barriers to learning, and is she capable of devising strategies to address both? Serving the community well, as a police officer, teacher, building contractor, or university scholar, requires redefining the notion of "qualified."

In the antisubordination model, the goal of ending oppression is foremost. "Qualified" in that model means able to and motivated to work against oppression.

Law-enforcement officials, desperate to deal with the lethal mix of poverty and crack cocaine that brought chaos to our cities, have turned to the community-based model. This form recognizes that police officers who understand the culture of a community, who walk the streets, live, and work in impoverished neighborhoods, are more effective than officers from the outside who sit in cruisers without interacting with those whom they are supposed to serve. True community-based policing would also include the key element of community control, so that hiring, firing, and management of the police would be the prerogative of community representatives. This is the only way simultaneously to fight crime and to end police violence.

Again, asking "Who can best get crack off the streets?" might yield answers quite different from those to "Who scored the highest on the civil service exam?" Or "Who got the highest grades in the police academy?" True affirmative action demands adherence to community-based standards of qualification — expanded standards that go beyond the narrow traditional criteria.

In addition to expanding our conception of merit, we ask for critical evaluation of the premise that merit should always determine the distribution of public goods. Dr. Margaret Morgan Lawrence, for example, made a point of taking each of her three children out for special excursions, leaving the siblings at home. A highlight of such a trip was the special treat. "Let's have some ice cream," she would say. "It's a special treat for us; we don't have to tell the others." She raised her children to consider always the needs of others. She also taught them that sometimes you got a special treat, not because you were a hard worker, not because you were brilliant, not because you were beautiful — although her three darlings were all of those things in her eyes — but simply because you were.

As we reach for utopia, we wonder about a world in which neither status nor merit distributes life's goods. We wonder about a world in which each is entitled to share life's treats because he or she belongs, by birthright, to the human family.

The notion that the best should prevail is part of our culture. From an early age, children learn to sort themselves according to who is good, better, and best: choosing sides for pick-up basketball, bringing home "honor roll" bumper stickers for the family car, pursuing blue ribbons for raising the biggest cow in 4H competition. Conscientious parents seek to instill a positive self-concept in their children by emphasizing merits. "You are so good at fingerpainting; you pick the best colors."

At the same time, we teach lessons that are beyond the notion of merit: empathy, sharing, love. There are things we do in life, gifts we give, that are not about who is the best, the strongest, or the smartest. We teach our children to treat animals with care, to feel sadness at stories of human loss, to share with friends and siblings. The values reflected in these teachings are, in a sense, antimerit.

Consider a world of merit turned on its head. What if the best schooling went to the children with the worst test scores? Would our collective productivity rise or fall? Would the prison population grow or shrink? Certainly a general rule that the least qualified would get the best, always — in jobs, health care, education — is unworkable. Some jobs require minimal competence, and competence is a legitimate test of access to those jobs. Nonetheless, the immediate assumption that merit is always the best criterion for distribution is as ludicrous as the opposite assumption.

This is not an argument to make lightly. When we broached it with students, we found passionate resistance, particularly among working-class students of color who knew that the only reason they had made it to law school was that they were selected at an early age for magnet schools or prep school outreach programs. Their test score, their merit, was a ticket out of the ghetto, not something they would give up for the sake of some idealistic premise that the best should go to the least.

We are not about to take a lifeline away from students like those who have sat in our classes, yet we raise the question because we must think about ideals and principles even as we are pragmatists. There are plausible ways to distribute goods and opportunities other than relying on merit. For free theater in the park, many communities use first-come-first-served or random drawings. The logic is that taxpayers deserve an equal chance to partake of the benefits their tax dollars support. A merit-based distribution — perhaps a test of theater knowledge or a performing arts degree — would raise criticisms of exclusivity. The fact that wealthy lawyers sometimes hire messengers to stand in line all day for tickets is, interestingly, not subject to such complaint. At any rate, for a range of public goods — from starting times at public golf courses to townhouses in moderate-income housing developments — non-merit-based distribution is expected and accepted as just.

On the other hand, merit is often seen as a legitimate basis for distributing educational opportunities. Publicly supported magnet schools, for example, often use entrance examinations, auditions, interviews, and other screening devices to identify the most talented students. Public universities are often explicit about reserving their limited enrollment for the most talented students. Open admissions — the idea that all who want an education are welcome — is a rarity in American higher education. Similarly, the civil service examination systems, used at the federal, state, and local levels, typically rely on written examinations and scored interviews in order to distribute jobs to the most meritorious.

The commonsense appeal in the notion that the smartest students deserve the best schooling is undergirded by a certain illogic. First of all, we confuse and conflate different kinds of merit in this formulation: the merit of pure talent and the merit of effort. If merit means we reward hard work, is the student who scores high on standardized tests because of innate intelligence, but who is lazy in study habits, as meritorious as the student who works hard and consistently gets higher grades than test scores would predict? If intelligence is largely determined by either genes or environment, aren't we rewarding accident of birth rather than hard work and commitment to excellence when we say that intelligence is meritorious? The strongest argument for meritocracy, that it creates incentives for higher performance, does not support a meritocracy that focuses on talents that are gifts.

What's more, if the goal of public education is to produce the best-educated populace, using talent as the criterion for access to education might have the opposite effect. Academic talent is more likely to bloom in a family that has already had access to education. The best predictor of performance on standardized tests, for example, is whether your parents went to college. Giving places in public universities and magnet schools to the children of the educated means giving the slots to the students most likely to succeed without extra educational benefits. Excluding the children of the undereducated means barring those least likely to find the means to educate themselves. The result is less learning and lowered productivity.

The argument against random distribution of educational benefits is that we must reward excellence, and create environments where excellence reigns, in order to maximize learning and knowledge. In fact, a random distribution, or need-based distribution, might also achieve this goal. Rewarding talent, as opposed to effort, rewards people for something they did not work for, which may develop complacency as much as the pursuit of excellence. Furthermore, the assumption that a grouping of the most talented heightens educational attainment is unproven pedagogically. Many educational theorists suggest that the opposite is true: learning is enhanced where talent levels are mixed, when math whizzes learn how to explain complex equations to those averse to math, and where the assumption is that all children, not just the gifted, can learn math skills.

In the workplace, employers demand the prerogative to hire the most talented, and co-workers complain that they don't want to work with incompetents. Anyone who has had the experience of pulling more than their share on the job (it is interesting to note how many people claim to have had this experience, since by definition it cannot be universal) knows how embittering that is. The workplace is probably where merit is most accepted as the standard for hiring, firing, and promotion.

From the perspective of both management and worker, however, there are problems with purely merit-based systems. First, as we have already noted, merit and ability are elusive concepts. There is more than one way to succeed on the job, and what appears successful in the short run isn't always good for the long haul. For example, some law firms found that when they adopted the system of rewarding attorneys purely on the basis of billings, important nonbillable functions — training junior associates, performing public relations work, considering long-range planning — were neglected. Rumors about more than one law firm breakup point to the loss of civility that comes when daily computer printouts focus strictly on how much each partner made that day.

For workers, historically, pure merit is pure hell. The struggle for unionization and for contracts that clarify job requirements is in part the struggle to stabilize expectations in the workplace so that employers cannot arbitrarily change performance demands. The notorious "speed-up," in which management demands rising levels of production from the assembly line to the point of endangering workers' lives and forcing the cover-up of shoddy work, is a major reason for collective bargaining.[12] Similarly, the meritocracy of sweatshop piecework, under which workers are paid a pittance for each item produced, is a form of exploitation that sets poor workers — often women and children — toiling long into the night, at close work, with every break for a meal or a bathroom trip a loss in wages. The toll on the health of such workers is a shameful chapter in the history of capitalism.[13]

Minimum wages, maximum hours, and union contracts — systems that temper outrageous performance pressure in the workplace — were achieved in bitter labor battles. Workers were willing to risk life and livelihood for these concessions, because they wanted more for themselves and their children than the curse of the speed-up and piecework wages.

In a union shop, all are paid equally for fulfilling the minimum contractual requirements of the job. This stabilizes expectations and makes worklife livable for the workers. It prevents the union-busting and hatefulness that come when one worker is pitted against another in a game of merit defined by the boss.

Antiunion propagandists claim that it also encourages laziness and reduces productivity. Not true. No amount of coercion could match the productivity attained when workers are decently treated, involved in management, and proud of their work. Worker satisfaction and participation are critical to high-quality production.

Aside from the truth that the escape from narrow forms of merit makes management sense, there is the stronger reasoning of justice. Those who argue that the best, the fastest, the most productive, should take all are those who secretly believe they themselves will never be slow. In fact, all of us have stages in our lives when we are not the best, and we should consider why it is fair to take into account the needs of the slow. The best office worker may suffer an illness or the loss of a loved one that makes them the least productive worker of the month. The best assembly line worker might slip on the job and have to move to the slower line. It is probable, not just possible, that in a given worklife, each of us will have similar experiences.

The Americans with Disabilities Act is a monument to this truth. The ADA recognizes that, through no fault of their own, millions of hard-working Americans are disabled and cannot always win the "best" worker sweepstakes under traditional criteria. They nonetheless have talents to contribute to the workplace. Disabled citizens want to work, to pay taxes, and to remain productive. The ADA requires that employers hire people with disabilities and provide them with reasonable accommodation in the workplace, which means changing the definition of merit, when necessary, to accommodate the disability. Stipulating rest breaks, altering the physical design of the workplace, or providing equipment that compensates for loss of strength are the kinds of accommodations employers make to increase contributions from people with disabilities. Encouraged by laws that prohibit discrimination against the disabled, employers have made such accommodations and are often pleased with the results. People who work in spite of disabilities often are the most dedicated and reliable employees. The desire to overcome physical barriers often reflects a belief in the work ethic and an optimistic character that is a welcome morale booster for co-workers.

Our experience with disability law teaches us that our original notions of "the best" are often false. The best worker is not always the strongest or the fastest. While many employers fought against the ADA, claiming the requirement of reasonable accommodation would shut down business, no such dire consequences followed the passage of the ADA in 1991. Significantly, the ADA was passed precisely at the moment when the latest round of anti–affirmative action backlash was launched. Jesse Helms's notorious race-baiting anti–affirmative action TV ads were running at the same time that Congress was moving the ADA to passage.

How is it that the American public could accept affirmative action for the disabled, even given the significant expenditures that reasonable accommodation requires, but could not accept affirmative action for those burdened with racial discrimination? The answer is racism. Many members of Congress had personal experiences with illness and disability. Many spoke openly of their own disabilities, or those of family members, in explaining their support for the act.[14] The Americans with Disabilities Act is the most radical affirmative action program in the nation's history. It goes well beyond the principle of nondiscrimination, requiring businesses to spend money and change their operations to accommodate the disabled. This was an affirmative command: change business as usual, alter old concepts of merit, to include and welcome those who were previously kept out. That this affirmative action program met with virtually no opposition from the public reveals our divergent attitudes toward race and disability.

Physical disability is seen as "not your fault." Like getting struck by lightning, ending up in a wheelchair could happen to anyone. Race and the effects of racism are less clear in our social understanding. The Big Lie tells us that racism is a historical anachronism. Thus, the social dislocation in communities of color is attributed not to racism, but to choice. "Those people" have chosen to be poor or on crack or illiterate or in prison. If their burdens are self-imposed, there is no collective need for concern nor social justice in rendering aid.

No one chooses to live in degraded circumstances. Longing for a decent life is universal in a world of immense cultural diversity. This does not mean we should ignore individual responsibility for self-destructive choices. It simply means that once people are down, however they got there, it is not a good thing to leave them there. It is not a good thing for our material survival, because no amount of individual hard work and initiative can make us safe in a world that is falling apart. Nor is it a good thing for our spiritual survival, because we can look the other way only so many times when we pass the poor in the streets before we lose what is most important to us: our soul.

A world without merit is probably not a human world; the celebration of excellence, the appreciation of talent, and the admiration of hard work are part of the human experience.

Respecting excellence in human endeavors comports with both Darwinian science and religious traditions; whether evolution or God or both resulted in the talents human beings have, we were made to use those talents, and using them well responds to wisdom beyond us. Affirmative action is part of that dream. In breaking down barriers to the worlds of work, education, and governance, we welcome many talents to the table. Affirmative action is not a way to reward the unqualified, although an oft-told lie describes it as such. It is, in fact, exactly the opposite. It subjects job cartels to the rigor of competition. In more than one workplace, those former beneficiaries of discriminatory job protection have had to improve their skills and productivity in order to keep up with the affirmative action hires, all the while taking comfort in the myth that the newcomers are "unqualified."

There is nothing inherently wrong with hiring through a network that relies on friends and relations. Many of us, if we were in a position to hire, would think of turning to such a network. But cronyism is wrong when it results in discriminatory exclusion, and that is the inevitable result in a world marked by race and gender hierarchies. If we could eliminate those hierarchies, it might make sense to use friends-hiring-friends networks, allowing people to work with their buddies. Would we really want this? Anyone who has had the experience of making dear, lasting, and improbable friendships in the work world can tell you that the expanded horizons of that world are a benefit, one that might disappear if we worked only with our existing friends and relatives.

The world that affirmative action creates is richly diverse, with the strengths that diversity brings: alternative visions, new problem-solving skills, the bright dynamics and tensions of work across difference. While this chapter criticizes the notion of merit as it is presently applied, support for affirmative action is, in the end, support for the concept of merit. Affirmative action brought us, among other things, more effective fire and police departments. It created universities where minds are expanded at the crossroads of multiple world views. The charge that affirmative action stifles human striving is a lie. Affirmative action promises exactly the opposite: never again will talent and effort count for nothing while "who you know" rules.

In an ideal world, we would reward excellence and figure out a way to do so that is inclusive rather than exclusive. We would celebrate and support athletic achievement, for example, both in competitions that identify "the best" and in recreation programs that allow the millions who are "not the best" to participate in sporting endeavors. We might devise music concerts that both showcase "the best" musicians and allow audiences of less-than-best music fans to play along. We could welcome gifted mathematicians and nuclear physicists to premier institutions that support their research, and invite interested nonexperts to come to the same institutions to study and contribute to research at their own level. A world in which every citizen has a chance to pursue learning and excellence is the true dream of merit. It is a world enriched by many hands put to task, a world free of the plague of wasted lives. In the world of parsimonious merit, only the best, the fastest, the smartest, get the bulk of life's opportunities. The rest can live on the edges of life's possibilities, resigned to mediocrity and filled with smoldering resentment.

Rewarding excellence is not the same as using excellence to exclude and degrade. Human dignity requires that laborers have the right to reject the demand for outrageous production levels, that jobs are made available for all who can work, and that the means for a decent life are provided to all who can't work. These are basic human rights, and they are consistent with the dream of merit. To reward excellence while providing for all leaves us in the world of righteous merit. Whether in winning an Olympic gold medal, writing the breakthrough novel, or discovering a cure for AIDS, the recognition and glory of high achievers in a just meritocracy would never be at the expense of exploiting or ignoring the needs of others, or of excluding anyone from the game. Merit awarded in that context is the only true merit there is: the sweet reward of success in a humane world, where talent shines in the pure light of its own generosity.

My father, Don Matsuda, discounts Babe Ruth's records because

Ruth didn't have to hit against the best pitchers of his time: the stunningly skilled athletes of the Negro leagues. No doubt Babe Ruth was a great ballplayer, and it is a shame his record is tarnished by the exclusions of his day. He was not the architect of segregated baseball. Like many who unthinkingly benefit from today's segregations, he held no exceptional animus toward ballplayers of color, nor did he make any special effort to gain advantage over them. The price of his privilege is that some, in spite of the postage stamps and memorials commemorating his greatness, will always doubt that he was the best.

In baseball, and some but not all other endeavors, there really is a best. When everyone plays — Every One — the best is the best, and the rest lose nothing from that fact. That is the meritocracy that is true to Thomas Jefferson's dream and to ours.

LADORIS HAZZARD CORDELL

"I am ever hopeful"

"NO ONE, I REPEAT, NO ONE — not Mr. Gingrich, not Mr. Dole, not Mr. Gramm — should be permitted to deny those who happen to be poor or of low income access to our court system."

LaDoris Cordell is standing on the steps of the courthouse in Santa Clara County, California. This is where she comes to work each day as Santa Clara County's first and only Black woman Superior Court judge. But today Judge Cordell is not in her accustomed black robe, dispensing justice from behind a high mahogany bench. She is addressing a rally in support of the Legal Services Corporation, a federally funded program established in the 1960s as part of the War on Poverty. A Republican Congress is threatening to eliminate this program, whose lawyers represent millions of poor Americans each year.

"There are those in Congress who seem to have a problem with the concept of equal justice for all — who would change that mandate to equal justice only for those who can afford it. By eliminating the Legal Services Corporation," she says pointing to the building behind her, "they are slamming these courthouse doors in the faces of the needy and callously throwing away the key."

Judge Cordell is an attractive, elegant woman with a slim athletic build. A short stylish haircut has replaced the Angela Davis afro that she wore when she graduated from Stanford Law School, but her voice has an urgency and cadence that call to mind both the radical Professor Davis and the late Representative Barbara Jordan. Cordell reminds her audience that the work of Legal Services is not "frivolous"; it is "about life and death, about survival . . . If Legal Services is abolished, who will represent families facing evictions? Who will be there to argue on behalf of poor women seeking protection from batterers? The answer is, no one."

Sitting judges, especially those who must stand for election, do not often speak out about injustice in the legal system. It is risky business, likely to alienate powerful politicians as well as colleagues. But LaDoris Cordell is not like most other judges. "I believe in risk taking," she says. "There were no other judges who were willing to be there, and if those of us who are entrusted to be the guardians of our legal system do not speak out on these issues, how can we expect that anyone else will."

Judge Cordell was first appointed to the bench in 1982 when Governor Jerry Brown, as part of an effort to bring diversity to the state's judiciary, appointed her to the Municipal Court, the lowest court in the California system. She recalls her first day on the bench. "I was scared to death. The courtroom was packed. Somebody said, 'All rise,' and I walked in. One white woman's jaw just dropped when she saw me. Then, at the back of the courtroom, a group of young Latino men raised their fists and shouted, 'Right on!'" In her six years on the Municipal Court bench Cordell earned a reputation as a bright, dedicated, innovative, compassionate, no-nonsense judge, respected by colleagues, police officers, bailiffs, and law professors alike.

After she was passed over several times for promotion to the Superior Court by the Republican governor, George Deukmajian, she chose another option available in California: she ran for the position, in 1988. The conservative county prosecutor who opposed her in the election sought to label her a "soft-on-crime liberal" and an "activist," citing her innovative use of sentencing alternatives. Cordell ran on her experience and her reputation and won by a wide margin in a predominantly white district. "Our role as judges does not and should not end when we doff our robes," she said at her swearing-in ceremony. "If decrying oppression and bigotry constitute the 'judicial activism' of which I was so frequently accused throughout the campaign, then I must plead guilty."

LaDoris Hazzard Cordell was born and raised in Ardmore, Pennsylvania, the second of Lewis and Clara Hazzard's three daughters. Ardmore, a neighborhood in the suburbs of Philadelphia, is part of what is known as the Main Line. The small Black community where the Hazzards lived was one of the tiny pockets of poor Blacks established at the turn of the century among the estates where Philadelphia's "old wealth" made their homes. The wealthy required staff — to cook their food, clean their houses, tend their gardens, and look after their children. Before there were bus and train lines that carried servants from the city to what was then the countryside, the Main Line's maids, cooks, and drivers, along with their families, lived in close-by communities like Ardmore. "There weren't more than ten or fifteen streets of two- and three-story row houses in Ardmore," recalls Cordell. "Most of the folks who lived there were working poor. My family had more than most people, although we did not have much. My mother always dressed us well. It was important to her how we presented ourselves, and the Hazzard girls had a reputation for always looking good."

There were three churches in the small Black community, one African Methodist Episcopal and two Baptist. The community's activities revolved around the churches — vacation Bible school, deacon board, choir, church picnics and outings. Families were identified by the church they belonged to. The Hazzards attended Calvary Baptist. "The choir from our church would visit the other churches to give concerts. It seemed like a big deal, even though, looking back on it, the churches were only five minutes apart.

"I look like my dad. I have the Hazzard nose," says Cordell. "We're also alike in personality. He is very hyper." Lewis Hazzard moved to Ardmore from Virginia as a child, when his mother came to the Main Line to find work as a domestic. Because Ida Hazzard worked as a "live in" her only child was not allowed to live with her. He lived with relatives in Ardmore and saw her only on weekends. Lewis attended North Carolina A & T, where he learned the trades of tailoring and dry cleaning, but when he came home with the intention of opening a dry cleaning shop, he did not have the money for a building or equipment. Lewis Hazzard began his business by walking from door to door in the Black community, collecting people's clothes and taking them to a dry cleaner in Philadelphia. Through great effort and sacrifice, he saved enough to buy the machinery and rent a space on Spring Avenue, the main street in Ardmore, where he opened a shop that he owned for forty years.

"My father was a workaholic," says Cordell. "He worked day and night." Throughout her childhood he got up at 3 A.M. for his side job, delivering newspapers. At 6 A.M. he came home, only to go out again after breakfast, staying at the shop until 11 P.M. Cordell, the earliest riser among the rest of the family, remembers meeting her dad at the door each day and eating breakfast with him before he left for the shop. "He was the world's best dry cleaner," she recalls with undisguised pride. In time he earned a reputation on the Main Line beyond the Black community and had a large white clientele willing to pay well to have their cleaning done to perfection.

"I look nothing like my mother and I adore her." There is pure admiration in the daughter's voice. "My mom was very, very bright, but she had no opportunity to go to college. She had to work to help support the family." Clara Jenkins Hazzard also came to the Main Line when her family relocated in search of work. Roxanne and Earlie Jenkins moved from North Carolina to Bryn Mawr, a short distance from Ardmore, where Clara's mother worked as a domestic while her father worked as a cook at a local school. Judge Cordell tells of why her mother's family moved to Ardmore. A wealthy white man in Bryn Mawr couldn't stand the sight of Black people in his town, so he bought all of the buildings in the small Black neighborhood and evicted the occupants. The house her mother's family moved to after the eviction is the three-story row house where LaDoris grew up. "My parents moved in with my mother's parents when my father returned from college, and later they bought the house from my grandparents."

"What did I get from my mom? Her good judgment, I'd like to think, and her wisdom. She had tremendous judgment and common sense; so many people in the community would come to her with their problems. And she would stand up for what she believed in." LaDoris remembers her mother as an organizer. "When the schools were blowing up back in the sixties, my mother set up and ran the picket lines. We had to call every night to make sure the folks were out there each day. I had a little checklist and would do the calling. Everything was always immaculate and well ordered around my mother."

LaDoris and her sisters attended the Haverford public schools. County Line Road divided Haverford Township from Lower Merion Township. The Hazzards lived on the Haverford side of the road, most of Ardmore on the other side. "Our shop, our church, our friends were all on the other side of the road," says Cordell. This meant that from elementary school through high school LaDoris was often the only Black child in her class. She was an athlete, a musician, an outstanding student, and a leader — elected president of her class in her junior year and then vice president of the school. "I've always had the need to be part of the decision making wherever I was — to move things along and help shape them. I think I got this from my mother. It's hard to know what the white kids thought of me, but I felt like an alien. I felt I didn't belong."

During the entire twelve years she attended the Haverford schools, not one white person visited her home. Cordell remembers being invited to a classmate's house only once, a huge house, where she felt uncomfortable and out of place. "That was the only occasion that I had any contact with a white schoolmate outside of school. I think I developed a thick skin. I felt like a freak."

In 1967 Cordell left home for Antioch College in Ohio, a prestigious college noted for its innovative curriculum. During her freshman year she spent three months in the Mississippi Delta, where she directed a tutoring program for preschool children and adults. She was drawn inevitably into the struggles of the courageous people with whom she worked and today counts this experience as one that shaped her work and her politics. She believes that she would probably have been admitted to Antioch without affirmative action — "My high school grades and SAT scores were comparable to those of my white classmates" — but she credits affirmative action for the quality of her education. "It was the first time I was in school with a significant number of students of color, many of whom would not have been there if there had been no affirmative action. These were bright Black students with brains to match my own and with an experiential and political sophistication that forced me to reflect on who I was and my place in the world. I'm sure that they influenced my decision to do my work-study project in Mississippi."

Her admission to the small and elite Stanford Law School was a different story. "I know I wouldn't have been admitted to Stanford without affirmative action," she says. Cordell was the only Black woman graduate in 1974. The school had graduated its first Black student only six years earlier, in 1968, and was still almost exclusively white, male, and upper class. "I worked at Macy's and rode a bike to school while my classmates were driving Mercedes. The fact is, I got the grades, I did what I needed to do, earned that degree, and moved on. But it was affirmative action that allowed me to be there. I'm an affirmative action baby and proud of it and thankful for it too."

Most Stanford Law graduates go on to jobs in tony corporate law firms, but Cordell decided to practice in East Palo Alto, a poor Black and Latino community separated only by a freeway from the rest of Palo Alto, site of Stanford and some of the priciest real estate in the country. She began with the support of an Earl Warren Fellowship, working as a cooperating attorney with the NAACP Legal Defense Fund. In 1976 she set up her own office, the first person to open a professional law practice in East Palo Alto.

In 1978 Stanford Law School offered Cordell a position as assistant dean for student affairs. Continuing her practice part time, she took the job and set up the most successful minority recruitment program the school has ever had. During a period when the *Bakke* case was being litigated and affirmative action was under attack, Cordell changed the minority enrollment at Stanford from one of the lowest in the country to one of the highest, at almost 30 percent of the entering class. When asked how she did it, Cordell responds, "The institution said to me, 'Just make it happen.' They gave me a free hand. They wanted the best, the cream of the crop, but I got to define what the best meant. I went to recruit people at schools where Stanford had never gone, to historically Black schools like Fisk and Spelman, not just the Ivy League, because I knew the best were also there." Cordell's vision of affirmative action was shaped by her own experience. The law school did not need to lower its goal of admitting only the best, but it did need to expand its vision of what it meant to be the best, and only someone like LaDoris Cordell could help it do this.

Judge Cordell is speaking to a group of students at a local college. A young, serious-looking Black man in the front of the room raises his hand and says that he is concerned that affirmative action programs may cause his teachers, classmates, and potential employers to believe that he was admitted to the university under lower standards and that he is less intelligent, less qualified than his white classmates. Judge

Cordell listens quietly and then, with unaccustomed abruptness, says, "Get over it." Her tone is cross. She has answered this question too often before, and she is impatient with the young people who ask it. The student seems stunned. Cordell pauses, looks directly at the young man, and smiles, as much at her own temper as at him. "I don't mean to sound callous," she says. "What I mean is that all our lives we are stigmatized by the melanin in our skin. I was a licensed attorney with a Stanford Law degree when I was routed out of my car by the police and held at gunpoint. I still get followed by security guards in stores when I go shopping. This is the stigma that we deal with every day, and it has nothing to do with the existence of affirmative action. There's just too much to be done for us to spend our time focused on whether other people think we shouldn't be here."

Steady Hands is a charcoal drawing in which several hands of different shades and strengths grasp one another in support. "It represents the steady hands that a victim of domestic violence meets when she goes to a shelter," says Cordell, who is the artist. The drawing, part of a collection that Cordell has donated to support a crisis center for battered women and their children, was inspired on a Christmas Eve and Christmas Day when Judge Cordell was the duty judge at the Superior Court, fielding emergency requests for search warrants and restraining orders. In an editorial, she described that sleepless night and the calls at 2 A.M., 4 A.M., 6 A.M., every one about domestic violence: women battered by husbands, boyfriends, or ex-boyfriends; women battered with coat hangers, baseball bats, fists, and guns.

The editorial in the paper, the donation to the good cause, are part of the public life of this judge, her habit of acting when wrongs need righting. The chiaroscuro drawing is a reflection of her private self — of soul and heart. The themes of her art are the same as those that drive her work, the struggles against racism, sexism, poverty, and violence, but here there is a peaceful strength that contrasts with her energetic public self. A close friend says of Cordell's art, "It fits her time of reflection and quiet introspection. And while inspired by the external, it is embellished by some kind of collective memory."

Judge LaDoris Cordell's great-great-grandmother was a slave. "When I think of her — seeing me sitting here in my robes, deciding cases that affect people's lives — that to me is a wonderful statement of what indeed can happen in this country.

"People are slow to recognize the need to make changes within themselves, and then make change only with great trepidation," says Cordell, reflecting on the continuing resistance to affirmative action. "But my expectations of others are high. I believe there is good somewhere in everyone that I can reach — that if I speak the truth to them and make them listen to common sense, they will do the right thing. I am ever hopeful; not an idealist, but ever hopeful."

[5]

Tokens and Traitors:
On Stigma and Self-Hate

> There were two kinds of slaves, the house Negro and the field Negro. The house Negroes — they lived in the house with the master . . . and they loved the master more than the master loved himself. They would give their life to save the master's house — quicker than the master would . . . If the master got sick, the house Negro would say, "What's the matter, boss, *we* sick?" We sick! He identified himself with his master, more than the master identified with himself.[1] — *Malcolm X*

I SUPPOSE IT WAS inevitable that when Clarence Thomas was nominated to the Supreme Court I would spend the better part of the next three weeks hearing friends and colleagues ask for my opinion. "So, Chuck, what do you think about the new nominee?" All of the questioners were white. My Black friends knew what I was thinking and feeling. We nodded at one another silently, with wan smiles of commiseration. The looks conveyed, better than any words could, the complex mix of anger, frustration, hurt, and weariness invoked by this latest assault on our sensibilities. "White folks still ahead, Chuck Lawrence," my friend and mentor, the late C. B. King, would have said to me. He said this each time we exited a southwest Georgia courthouse in the 1960s, a venue where he and his student interns were then the entire civil rights bar. Whether we'd won or lost our case, he'd say these words with an irony that conveyed both resignation to the reality of America's racism and a determination to go to his grave fighting to change that reality.

Perhaps I should not have been so irritated by these questions from my white friends, receiving them instead as recognition that, as a Black scholar and professor, I might have some special insight about the nomination. Certainly I responded in that spirit, with a detached analysis of how I was not surprised that President Bush had made the appointment; how Clarence Thomas was particularly well suited to the Bush agenda; why it was not likely, once confirmed, that Thomas would radically change his outlook on a range of legal issues. Yet even as I made these professorial observations, I was experiencing resistance and anger. I was angry not just about the circumstances of the appointment itself but at the questions and the questioners.

My white colleagues were asking more of me than of one another: I felt I was being asked to own or disown Clarence Thomas or do both at the same time. I heard the same subtext, the same implication, that I often hear when people ask what I think of Louis Farrakhan or Colin Powell or the Reverend Al Sharpton or Shelby Steele. It is an implication of responsibility for the race. "He's one of you, isn't he?" is the unspoken challenge. Because I am a Black man, I am held responsible for Thomas's antichoice position, his lack of compassion for the elderly and the poor, his anti–affirmative action views, as well as the fact that he was the beneficiary of an affirmative action program at Yale Law School and the beneficiary of a much more insidious kind of affirmative action in receiving his appointment to the Court.

I would gladly disown him, but race in America being what it is, I cannot. I can disagree with his positions, I can decry his actions, but I will still hear the rhetorical question: "Isn't he one of you?"

When it was reported that Judge Thomas had received mediocre grades at Yale and that he had had little judicial experience, it was as though people turned to me with an accusation. It fell on me to point out that this time meritocracy had been abandoned in favor of politics, not race; to note that the political exception to meritocracy is the rule. But what infuriated me most about Thomas's nomination was the way in which the ideology of race allowed President Bush to select who would "represent" me while advancing his own political agenda. By nominating a Black with conservative beliefs and marginal qualifications, Bush simultaneously placed my ideological enemy on the Court and gave more ammunition to the opponents of affirmative action, who would count this appointment as yet another job for an undeserving Black.

While I cannot disown Justice Thomas, he has advanced his own career by his denial of any kinship with me. Of course he does not say, "I am not an African American." Aside from the physical impossibility of his passing for white, his racial identity is essential to his career-making disavowal of kinship. It is his acknowledgment of our kinship of ancestry that gives meaning to his rejection of our kinship of common experience and culture, of shared pain and triumph, of political commitment to one another and to our universal freedom. Thomas has repudiated this kinship as only a family member can. When he campaigned for Reagan and Bush, presidential candidates who made racist appeals central to their election strategy, and when, as head of the EEOC, he carried out the administration's policy of nonenforcement of the Equal Employment Opportunity Act, he did so as a Black man selected to publicly rebuke his kin. And each day that he sits on the Court, he rejects us with his votes to restrict remedies in desegregation cases, to eviscerate the Voting Rights Act, and to allow the physical abuse of prisoners.

Thomas insists that he has made his way to his present lofty status by dint of personal effort, that he has fought his way out of poverty on his own, and that his success is proof that every other Black can do the same. If there are those who remain poor, who have not so rapidly climbed the ladder of success, they ought to look to themselves for the reasons underlying their failure and not blame America's racism.

I experience a strong ambivalence as I listen to Clarence Thomas's story, an ambivalence born of a similar tale of individual striving. I grew up, as did many African Americans, hearing a strangely paradoxical story about equality in America, one that I saw play out in my parents' lives. We were told we lived in a racist world in which Blacks were seldom given a fair shake, but it was also a world where individuals from our community overcame discriminatory obstacles by a combination of God-given talent and superhuman effort and perseverance. Frederick Douglass, Sojourner Truth, Ida B. Wells, George Washington Carver, Booker T. Washington, W.E.B. Du Bois, Paul Robeson, Marian Anderson, Ralph Bunche, Jackie Robinson, and Thurgood Marshall — all of these men and women my parents held out to me as people whom I should emulate.

The Black community shared in the triumphs of each of these individuals because they proved to the white world and to us that we could be brilliant and talented and successful. They represented our capacity for humanness and extraordinary achievement in a world where we were thought to be and were treated as subhuman. We believed that each time those exemplars opened a door, the door would open further for the rest of us, and that each time these people proved themselves worthy, whites would learn of our worth as a race.

While the success of these heroes was symbolic of our race's capacity, it was success individually earned. We knew that it was success achieved in the face of discrimination, but we also believed that it proved the possibility for individual achievement in America. When Clarence Thomas told his "up from Southern poverty" story to the Senate Judiciary Committee, he relied on the seeming similarity between his story and the heroic lives my parents hoped I would emulate. In his opening statement before the Senate Judiciary Committee the nominee Clarence Thomas invoked the proud legacy of Justice Thurgood Marshall. "Justice Marshall, whose seat I have been nominated to fill, is one of those who had the courage and the intellect . . . to knock down barriers that seemed so insurmountable,"[2] he said.

To assume Marshall's mantle was the height of hypocrisy. Only months before, when Justice Marshall retired, he had expressed his opposition to Thomas's appointment as his successor in cryptic but clear terms: "There's no difference between a white snake and a black snake," he said. "They'll both bite."[3]

Thomas's life story is radically different from Justice Marshall's, and in that difference lies the divergence in their judicial philosophies and their views on affirmative action. During the confirmation hearings, Thomas recalled again and again his humble beginnings and his experiences with the humiliation of segregation and racial defamation. Doubtless, he has not forgotten those experiences. No Black person can escape them in America. What separates him from Marshall is what he makes of that humiliation and defamation, what he has done with that experience, and what it has done to him.

Marshall came to the Supreme Court by a very different route from Thomas's. Marshall chose the path of leadership within his community, of legal advocacy on behalf of those who were least powerful, of constant challenge to the institutions and politicians who exploited racism and poverty. His way was to speak truth to power, and that path was reflected in his role on the Court, where he was the Black community's voice. In the judicial conference room, on the pages of the Supreme Court Reports, and in his public discourse, disenfranchised groups counted on Marshall to make their story heard. On a Court increasingly insensitive to the plight of those denied the full fruits of citizenship, his was a voice for women, for gays and lesbians, for the poor, and for other minorities. Lyndon Johnson appointed Marshall in 1967 in large part because he was Black. Because the politics and the morality of a monumental civil rights struggle demanded Black representation on the Court, it never occurred to Marshall that this should stigmatize him or prove him less able or worthy than his colleagues. He knew he was a Supreme Court justice because the politics of Black liberation required it, and he was proud of those politics.

By contrast, Justice Thomas has chosen to serve those most powerful in society. A loyal foot soldier in the Reagan and Bush administrations, he was an eager spokesperson for the agenda of the radical right. His nomination to the Supreme Court resulted from his proven willingness to advance the ideology of his patrons without dissent. When Justice Thomas says that the "patronizing indulgence [of] racial paternalism" stigmatizes minorities, he knows whereof he speaks.[4] He has made his career parroting the master's words and doing the master's bidding. The stigma he bears comes with making oneself in the master's image; that is to say, as the master imagines you. This is the most demeaning stigma of all.

Opponents of affirmative action often argue that it actually harms those it is intended to help by stigmatizing its beneficiaries. The message is: "You're not good enough to make it on your own, not good enough to compete on a playing field with whites." Affirmative action, the argument goes, undermines the achievements of minorities and women by making it look as if those achievements were handouts from white male benefactors. "Racial preferences imply that whites are superior, just as they imply that blacks are inferior," they say.[5] What client wants to be represented by an inferior affirmative action lawyer? What patient wants a substandard affirmative action doctor? And as long as affirmative action programs remain in place, it will be assumed that every minority member received a "racial preference," that none has made it on his or her own.

This argument is a special favorite of colored critics of affirmative action, who have found a large and admiring audience among weary whites eager to have the support of a Black, Latino, or Asian voice. The minority critics of affirmative action range from the self-proclaimed conservatives, such as Clarence Thomas, Thomas Sowell, Glenn Loury, Dinesh D'Souza, and Linda Chavez, to self-described liberals, such as Shelby Steele and Stephen Carter.

The stigma argument gains a legitimacy coming from the mouth of Justice Thomas that it does not carry coming from, for instance, Justices O'Connor and Scalia. Because Clarence Thomas is Black, when he speaks of the "poisonous and pernicious . . . patronizing indulgence"[6] of affirmative action, he assumes the mantle and authority of the injured victim. Even when he speaks in the third person of "programs that stamp minorities with a badge of inferiority,"[7] he is heard as someone who speaks of his own degradation and humiliation. By calling his book *Reflections of an Affirmative Action Baby*, Stephen Carter similarly reminds us that he addresses the evils of affirmative action with both candor and special authority. The colored critics of affirmative action assume the authority of spokespersons for their race. And white opponents of affirmative action seem especially fond of quoting people of color who speak from their own experience of how they and other minorities are demeaned and made to feel inferior by programs designed to benefit them.

For example, in an anti–affirmative action op-ed piece in the *Washington Post*, a white writer claimed that he was prepared to "sacrifice principle" and support affirmative action if it could be "justified on pragmatic grounds . . . But if affirmative action actually harmed blacks, it would then be entirely indefensible," the writer argued, and "some black intellectuals are saying exactly that . . . that affirmative action harms blacks [because] preference implies inferiority. The implied inferiority not only is demoralizing for blacks, it actually aggravates the white racism that affirmative action is supposed to counteract."

The writer went on to quote Shelby Steele, one of the most favored of affirmative action's Black critics: "The effect of preferential treatment . . . puts blacks at war with an expanding realm of debilitating [self-] doubt." The column closed by saying "Steele is right. AFFIRMATIVE ACTION costs more than it is worth."[8]

Since a Black critic presumably speaks not just for himself, but for other Blacks as well, his voice has a unique authority. His race is offered as proof that this is the way Blacks must feel, or that at least the Black community is sharply divided on the issue. Somehow these minority critics of affirmative action see no contradiction in being made the "Black expert" on how color consciousness produces stigma.

Nonetheless, the stigma argument against affirmative action should be taken seriously. Many people of color who are otherwise supportive of affirmative action are honestly troubled by a remedy for discrimination that seems to replicate the demeaning message of white supremacy. Even if affirmative action is not the cause of self-doubt among minorities, we must be concerned if it perpetuates the myth of racial inferiority in the society at large. How should we respond to this dilemma?

A good place to start is to acknowledge that the stigma argument on its face is true. Many whites and many minorities still believe that nonwhites are inferior. When minorities are present in settings where they have not traditionally been included, the typical assumption is made that they must be less qualified, not as smart, that standards have been lowered. As Shelby Steele has written, "Even when the black sees no implication of inferiority in racial preferences, he knows that whites do."[9] But where does this stigma come from? Does affirmative action promote assumptions of inferiority, or have the critics of affirmative action incorrectly placed the blame?

It is a rare Black male lawyer or doctor who has not had the experience of being mistaken for a waiter at a fancy party or for a janitor when he shows up at the office in a sweatsuit. Black women professionals report similar cases of mistaken identity, of being confused with everyone from secretaries to prostitutes. Black faculty members are regularly stopped and questioned by campus security officers at universities where they have taught for years.

Stephen Carter, a Black Yale law professor, tells of attending an academic conference where a young white colleague from another law school glanced at his name tag and said, "If you're at Yale, you must know this Carter fellow who wrote the article about thus-and-so." Carter admitted that he did know this Carter fellow slightly, and then the young man, realizing his error, said, "Oh, you're Carter." Carter notes that because the young man admired his article, he could not, in his initial evaluation, imagine that its author was a person of color. "He had not even conceived of that possibility, or he would have glanced twice at my name tag. No, if the work were of high quality, the author had to be white — there was no room for doubt!"[10]

The stigmatizing beliefs about people of color, the assumptions of incompetence and inferiority, have their origin not in affirmative action programs, but in the cultural belief system of white supremacy. When we assume that a tenured Yale Law professor who is Black is less intellectually gifted and competent than his white colleagues, it is racism, not the existence of affirmative action, that leads us to that assumption. We may not be aware of the racist beliefs that shape our thought processes. We may not even be conscious that we have thought of race at all, but it is surely racism that caused a young white colleague to assume that a prominent professor whose work he so admired was white, even as he stared at the black face above the tag bearing that professor's name.

Race and racial categories are not natural. They are social constructions created by culture, politics, and ideology. In other words, race has no meaning except for the one it is given by a particular historical and political context. The meaning of race in America derives from a history and culture dominated by white supremacy. The particular meanings or beliefs associated with specific nonwhite groups are different, and they change over time. The image of Blacks portrayed in minstrel shows, for instance, is not exactly the same as that depicted in today's most popular Black television shows, but the stereotypes are still with us. The central premise of white supremacy persists: there are whole, complete, entitled human beings (read *white*), and there are "others," who are fundamentally inferior and less completely human.

It is this ideology, this meaning, that made segregation stigmatizing. To provide separate facilities for different groups does not necessarily demean one of those groups. Segregated men's and women's bathrooms do not mean the same thing as segregated white and colored bathrooms did. The meaning of racially segregated bathrooms was Black inferiority, Black untouchability. Likewise, affirmative action as special, different, or preferred treatment is not inherently stigmatizing. It is the meaning that we give to the different treatment that carries the stigma.

Were this not so, every daughter or son of a university alumnus who received a legacy preference would be assumed inferior, as would every boss's son. The students who are given special consideration because they are gifted athletes or musicians, the brilliant blind student who is given extra time to take an exam, the older student, whose experience and maturity have given her an edge in the admissions process over the twenty-one-year-old, and the student from Alaska or North Dakota whose scarcity makes him more valued than one of the hundreds of excellent applicants from New York, would all be stigmatized if special and preferred treatment alone were a cause for shame.

A former colleague of mine at the Stanford Law School used to brag, only half in jest, that with his law school record he would never have been hired by Stanford had his specialty not been tax, an area highly valued in a profession that makes much of its living advising the rich on how to keep their money. There is a shortage of tax teachers because it is such a lucrative specialty outside academia. My colleague was obviously in no way ashamed of this preferred treatment.

Most of us attribute the different treatment afforded the tax professor or the applicant from Alaska to good, if not important, motives. We certainly do not assume that all students from Alaska or all tax professors are less able than their colleagues. But that is our assumption when racial minorities are given extra points in the competition for scarce places. We dismiss the many valid reasons for treating members of the group differently and make the assumption that all the individuals who have been given added points are undeserving and inferior. More than that, we attribute inferiority to members of the racial group without knowing which are the beneficiaries of affirmative action. We simply assume that they are, believing implicitly that "they" could not have made it "on their own."

Affirmative action programs have identified highly qualified minority individuals and given them opportunities to prove their worth. Many of them have outperformed whites who were supposedly better qualified. This evidence should lead us to question the validity, or at least the neutrality, of a selection process that wrongly predicts performance. But it doesn't. Instead, we assume the validity of the pre–affirmative action evaluative process and the inferiority of all minorities, including those who have proven the original criteria wrong.

Ask our parents about life before affirmative action. Ask the people of color who broke racial barriers long before affirmative action was ever thought of, and each of them will tell scores of stories of insult and humiliation that long preceded affirmative action.

That the stigma of racial inferiority predates affirmative action is not news to the more insightful critics of affirmative action. It certainly is not news to Stephen Carter, whose *Reflections of an Affirmative Action Baby* is often cited to prove that affirmative action harms people of color at least as much as it harms whites. "Affirmative Action, to be sure, did not create this particular box into which black people are routinely stuffed," Carter writes. "Black people have always been the target of openly racist assumptions, perhaps the worst of these being that we are stupid, primitive people."[11]

Why, then, does Carter oppose the very affirmative action of which he is an admitted beneficiary? His answer is that, while affirmative action may not be the origin of the perceived inferiority of people of color, it "will not alter this perception [and] white Americans will not change it simply because it is unjust."[12] Carter's solution is for Blacks and other people of color to "commit ourselves to battle for excellence, to show ourselves able to meet any standard, to pass any test that looms before us, in short to form a vanguard of black professionals who are simply too good to ignore."[13]

This solution — that each of us disprove the racist myth of our collective inferiority by the evidence of our individual excellence — is not a new one. Carter, no doubt, first heard the instruction "you must be twice as good as white folks" from his parents. It is a powerful lesson that Black children have grown up with for generations. It taught us that we were bright and capable, that we could surmount the very real barriers of racism, and that each of us was "responsible for representing our people."

It is easy to empathize with Carter's longing for recognition of his talents and achievements. Every person of color who has broken the barriers of racial exclusion has felt, if not spoken, his sentiments: I want to be the best, not the best Black. How else can I disprove the myth of my inferiority and that of my people? But when whites and others define affirmative action as a gift or compensation to those who are otherwise unqualified, they reinforce notions of the inferiority of minorities. The token Black who seeks to disprove belief in Black inferiority through his intelligence and industry finds himself in a double-bind. Being the best results in the label "exceptional Black individual," while being less than the best translates "recipient of racial preference." Neither of these options destroys racial stereotypes.

How does a person of color confront this dilemma? One way is to separate himself as far as possible from affirmative action, criticizing it as unneeded and unfair in his case. His explanation is that he would have achieved his position on his own, by virtue of his merits, and been spared the stigma of affirmative action.

The high-achieving person of color who wants recognition of individual achievement often feels the need to disavow affirmative action, because in the minds of most Americans it connotes inferiority. But would a white student with high SATs who received a scholarship based on financial need be stigmatized because other poor white recipients had lower scores? Would an alumnus's son at Yale be stigmatized by the admission of other sons of alumni who had lower SAT scores than his? The inadequacies of second-rate white colleagues are viewed as individual failings and are unlikely to be attributed to whites as a group, but the failure of any Black is a failure imputed to the race. The subtext, the unspoken but clearly heard meaning, of the "I got here on my own" story is "Not like those others." Affirmative action stigmatizes the assimilated token minority because the recipients of affirmative action are other minorities, and they are thought of as inferior.

There is an alternative to escaping the stigma of inferiority by distancing oneself from other minorities. This is to recognize the real source of the stigma and confront it directly. If the assumptions of Black inferiority have their origin in the symbols, stories, meanings, and beliefs created by the ideology of white supremacy, we can address those beliefs head-on. When a colleague assumes the Black author of an erudite law review article is white, for instance, he has internalized society's racist beliefs. He is probably not a bigot; he should not be singled out as more blameworthy than the rest of us. But we should point out to him and others that his beliefs are the legacy of our shared history of racism and evidence of the continued vitality of our racist beliefs. The blame for his error should not be placed on affirmative action.

When the token person of color in a white institution finds himself longing for colorblind recognition as "the best" rather than "the best Black," he has, perhaps unwittingly, defined "the best" by asking only whether his work is highly valued by his white colleagues. It is easy for the Black, Native American, Latino, or Asian professional to fall into the trap of looking only to whites for approval and esteem. Many people of color have spent the greater part of their academic and professional careers within institutions where the primary reference group was white. When they attended elite colleges and graduate schools, the professors who were mentors and passed out grades, who handed out the laurels and anointed their successors among the elite, were white. Colleagues in the universities where minorities teach and the corporations where they work, the people they look to for recognition and respect, are also mostly white. The powerful and famous of the most prestigious universities, newspapers, political and financial institutions are the people who decide who is "best," and almost all of them are white. In such settings it is easy for the token person of color to begin to equate what powerful whites think valuable with "the best."

This is not to say that there is a "Black way of thinking" or that the work of people of color should be evaluated only by people of color. Rather, it is an observation that, in these settings, the judgment of what is "best" is quite naturally informed by the experience and legacy of white supremacy. Those in power are most comfortable with individuals who think and act much as they do, and, perhaps more important, they value individuals whose work serves their interests. The student who reminds the professor of himself as a young man will be considered very bright. The scholar whose work is sufficiently original to be noticed, but who is still deferential and nonthreatening to her colleagues and to the institution, will be highly valued.

When I was teaching at Stanford, each year the faculty considered some of the top graduates from the top schools for teaching positions. Invariably we would receive a letter of reference from a particular highly respected Yale Law School professor who each year recommended a candidate as the "brightest young person" he had ever taught. We chuckled about the predictability of this assessment of ever-greater genius, but in the end the professor's evaluation always carried great weight.

When Stephen Carter learned he had been admitted to the Harvard

Law School under an affirmative action program for Blacks, he experienced the stigmatizing judgment of powerful whites firsthand: "The insult I felt came from the pain of being reminded so forcefully that *in the judgment of those with power to dispose,* I was good enough for a top law school only because I happened to be black"[14] (emphasis added). The judgment by which Carter determined whether he was the "best" or merely the "best Black" was made by whites. Carter's argument that Blacks should strive for excellence by a neutral standard of superiority inevitably plays out against reference to the white elite.

When the group that minority professionals refer to for validation is almost exclusively white, perhaps we are engaging in a form of unconscious self-denial. Only the elite whites, those with power to dispose, can bestow the distinction "best" or even "best Black." We do not see our own communities, other people of color, as worthy or capable of judging us.

It is revealing that Black parents admonish their children to prove their worth by outshining their white peers. Members of powerful groups worry only about being the best among their own. The valedictorian at Harvard or Princeton is unlikely to complain about being called the brightest in his or her class. It is sufficient that the powerful group to which he or she belongs has recognized his or her excellence.

People of color who wish to confront and resist directly the stigma that comes not from affirmative action but from white supremacy must learn to look to our own for criticism, recognition, respect, and acknowledgment of the high quality of our work.

My father, Charles Lawrence II, was of a generation of Black professionals who knew the meaning of looking to other Black scholars for an authentic assessment of their work. My sister, the sociologist Sara Lawrence Lightfoot, recalls listening to Sunday afternoon conversations among my father's friends and colleagues:

> On one of these Sundays, our guests included several of my father's black male colleagues and their wives (all of whom had their own careers). These brainy black brothers had known each other for years. Like my father, who was a professor of sociology at Brooklyn College of the City University of New York, this handful of scholars — who represented a substantial portion of "our black intelligentsia" — had been reared in segregated schools, attended Negro colleges, and received their Ph.D.s from white universities, such as

Harvard, Columbia, and the University of Chicago. There was John Hope Franklin, the historian; Kenneth Clark, the psychologist; Hylan Lewis, the sociologist; and Hobart Jarret, in English literature. All of them were pioneers, lonely travelers whose intellects and achievements were often judged through a discriminatory lens, whose careers were checked by the heavy hand of prejudice . . .

To my seventeen-year-old eyes these men were "the brotherhood," with bonds that were deep, language that was fascinating, laughter that was infectious, and conversation that I only half-understood. I could feel how much they needed and loved one another in their charged and fiery dialogues, in their sibling-like rivalries, in the ways their ideas danced in and out of one another. Coming to our table, they looked forward to a comfort and camaraderie that they could never fully achieve in the university settings where each was usually the token Negro and often the first of his race to set foot in the place.[15]

These conversations meant much more to those men than a chance to relax among friends. They looked to one another for the honest and rigorous analysis and criticism they knew were necessary for their best work. As comrades who shared both the experience of being Black pioneers and a commitment to the advancement of the race, they relied on the others to judge their work with neither a hostile nor a patronizing eye. Scholars who had begun their academic careers in segregated institutions, as students of the best Black minds, they were accustomed to being judged by their own. W.E.B. Du Bois had been my father's mentor at Atlanta University, and never had any other teacher been so exacting or demanded so much of him. Du Bois's measure of each student's work always took into account the value of the work to the liberation of Black folk, a question that was also central to my father and his peers in their Sunday discussions.

Today, academics of color still, too often, find themselves tokens in predominantly white institutions, but we have found ways to create conversations like the ones my father and his colleagues knew. Each summer, since 1986, progressive Asian, Black, Latino, and Native American legal scholars have gathered for the Critical Race Theory Workshop; to be with each other, to study, eat, sing, and sit up late talking about what my father's generation used to call "the state of the race." We read and comment on each other's work, argue, and grapple with the hard questions of whether and how this work serves the larger political struggle.

During the school year, we meet in smaller study groups with colleagues who work and live close by. At conventions and conferences we find time for informal sessions at lunch or dinner. Whenever a "fellow traveler" comes to town, it is an occasion to talk about life and work. Scholars of color in other disciplines, feminists, gay and lesbian scholars, and progressive white male academics join us in some of these conversations. This is our reference group, as are our students and families and the communities from which we come. We look to them to hold us to the highest standards and to keep us honest even as we keep them honest. When people of color make powerful whites our only measure of excellence, we stigmatize ourselves. Only when people of color are among those who determine what is valued can we escape the injury done by an ideology that labels us inferior.

"I AM NOT AN UNCLE TOM," THOMAS SAYS AT MEETING, read the headline of a front-page article in the October 28, 1994, *Washington Post*.[16] The article described what the *Post* called an "extraordinary meeting" at Justice Clarence Thomas's chambers of about thirty Black journalists and other African Americans. Thomas's longtime friend and fellow Black conservative Armstrong Williams had arranged the meeting and invited the guests. Williams told the *Post* that he had hand-picked people "who would be open to seeing Thomas as a human being."[17] He said that most of those he chose were his own friends, and added that he intended to invite a select group of reporters to the Court every month.

It is indeed extraordinary for a sitting Supreme Court justice to hold a meeting for the purpose of refurbishing his public image with a particular constituency, but that was clearly the purpose of this meeting.

Fifty-seven percent of Blacks supported Thomas at the time of his confirmation in 1991, despite his dismal civil rights record as the chair of the Equal Employment Opportunity Commission and credible allegations that he had sexually harassed Professor Anita Hill. But now, even as he reminded critics of his lifetime appointment — "I'm going to be here for forty years. For those who don't like it, get over it"[18] — he was seeking to rebut what had become an all but unanimous indictment in the Black community that charged him with being a "race traitor," a "handkerchief head," and an "Uncle Tom."

The November 1993 issue of *Emerge,* a Black news magazine, featured a cover story entitled "Doubting Thomas." On the cover of the magazine was a picture of Justice Thomas in judicial robes with a white handkerchief tied around his head in the style of the stereotyped Aunt Jemima character. The article quoted none other than Royce Esters, president of the Compton, California, branch of the NAACP, which had broken ranks with the national NAACP to support Thomas. In retrospect, Esters said, "Clarence Thomas has turned out to be the house Negro. Here is a man we thought we could have some faith in because of his humble background, but now I feel foolish."[19] Others in the Black community expressed similar sentiments. A political science professor at Ohio State called Thomas "the worst kind of racist — a black man who hates himself."[20] The film director Spike Lee, in language that was predictably colorful but not inconsistent with the tone of the rest of the article, said, "Malcolm X, if he were alive, would have called Thomas a handkerchief head, a chicken-and-biscuit-eating Uncle Tom."[21]

These were cruel words and images, loaded with the pejorative imagery of betrayal, cowardice, and foolishness. They captured the peculiar injury that is done and the unique anger that is evoked when a Black man plays the minstrel, acting the part that racist whites have written. Black folk do not make such accusations lightly.

More often than not, Black Americans have been reluctant to publicly criticize other Blacks, especially figures who have risen to positions of influence and power. Black leaders are often exempted from public criticism in the name of racial solidarity or because of a belief that our brothers and sisters should be forgiven the sins that are a product of our shared suffering.

This was certainly the case when Judge Thomas was nominated to the Supreme Court. Many Blacks were reluctant to criticize him, arguing that a Black conservative on the Court would be better than a white one and that surely a Black man who had experienced both racism and poverty would demonstrate sensitivity to the plight of the oppressed once his position on the Court was secure.

Niara Sudarkasa, president of Lincoln, the historically Black university that Thurgood Marshall attended, testified on Thomas's behalf. "I feel we need to be very careful before we write him off as a person who would not be responsive to the concerns of the African American community," she said. "I don't think you can discount the fact that he grew up as a poor black in Georgia; I think that will have an impact on the cases that come before him."[22]

Maya Angelou challenged her brothers and sisters to keep the faith with Clarence Thomas as a lesson to young Black men and women that we would not give up on our own. With an eloquence and truth that are a poet's gifts to her people, Angelou wrote, in a *New York Times* op-ed piece, that "because Clarence Thomas has been poor, has been nearly suffocated by the acrid odor of racial discrimination, is intelligent, well trained, black and young enough to be won over again, I support him. The prophet in Lamentations cried, 'Although he put his mouth in the dust . . . there is still hope.'"[23]

Maya Angelou's words gave pause even to those of us who were Thomas's harshest critics. There is a strong tradition of forgiveness and redemption in the Black community, and we wanted to believe that, though Clarence Thomas had betrayed us, he would return to his people.

When Thomas was accused of sexual harassment, many in the Black community viewed the allegations and the subsequent hearings as an attack on a Black man who dared seek a position beyond his station. The hearings reminded Blacks of America's preoccupation with Black sexuality and of the sordid history of violence that went with that preoccupation. The reflexive emotional response was to close ranks, and Thomas played these deeply rooted emotions for all they were worth, calling the hearings a "high-tech lynching."[24] Some responded to this device by rallying around Thomas, hoping for his conversion to the cause of racial justice.

Whatever faith Black Americans might have placed in racial solidarity, whatever reasons we might have had to believe or hope that Clarence Thomas would be a voice for his people, the years subsequent to his appointment proved them baseless. At the end of Justice Thomas's third term, the record spoke for itself. In the ten major cases involving civil rights decided during Thomas's first three terms on the Court, he voted against minority rights every time: against voting rights, against prisoners' rights, against refugees' rights, against school desegregation orders, and against equal opportunity in employment.[25]

Even some of Thomas's strongest Black supporters during the confirmation process are dismayed at the consistency and cruelty of his anti-Black judicial agenda. At the end of his second term Niara Sudarkasa rescinded her prediction that Thomas's background would give him a special sensitivity to the plight of Blacks. "Two years is enough time to get a sense of the way people think, and I must say I have been very disappointed."[26]

It would appear that the very experience of deprivation, deprecation, and near suffocation by the "acrid odor of racial discrimination," which gave Maya Angelou reason to hope, has, in this man, produced a bitterness that has turned him against those who share the stigma and humiliation of blackness as white America has imagined us and as too many of us imagine ourselves.

In understanding Thomas's zealous embrace of right-wing ideology, in his chastisement of Blacks who "wallow in excuses" and refuse to "take responsibility of their own destiny," we might look to Stanley Elkins's essay "Slavery and Personality."[27] Elkins argued that oppression can cause its victims to seek the approval and love of their oppressors, to emulate them, and even to join them in persecuting friends and family.

The sociologist John Dollard wrote of a similar accommodation mechanism among some Blacks in his study *Caste and Class in a Southern Town*. "It may come to pass in the end that the unwelcome force is idealized, that one identifies with it and takes it into the personality; it sometimes even happens that what is at first resented and feared is finally loved."[28]

Though, of course, we can't pretend to know the workings of Thomas's mind, certainly many of his actions suggest to us that he subscribes to the attitudes and ideologies of his historical oppressors. His use of the racist rhetoric and code words of the Republican right against his own kin reflects this. In a 1980 speech to a Republican gathering, he portrayed his sister, Emma Mae Martin, as an example of the "welfare queen." "She gets mad when the mailman is late with her welfare check; that's how dependent she is. What's worse is that now her kids feel entitled to the check too. They have no motivation for doing better or getting out of that situation."[29]

Thomas caricatured his sister, distorting her life story to fit the white racist image of what she should be. As it turned out, Emma Mae Martin was only temporarily on welfare. For most of her adult life she had been a two-job-holding, minimum-wage-earning mother of four. She had gone on welfare to nurse Thomas's aunt, who had suffered a stroke. Before her stroke, the aunt had taken care of Martin's children while she worked her two jobs.[30]

Thomas's distancing himself from his sister, depriving her of self-respect and humanity, is typical of internalized racism and self-loathing. I believe that it can also explain his ability to distance and dehumanize the beaten prisoner, and his conviction that Black failure is explained not by the continuing legacy of slavery and contemporary racism but only by Black laziness and dependence.

Thomas claims that he does not worry about his critics in the Black community and feels no need to defend himself or his judicial record, but a man who is unconcerned about what Black people think of him would not arrange a meeting with sympathetic Blacks in the press and tell them, "I am not an uncle Tom."

When Thomas does speak in his own defense, he not surprisingly rejects the label "race traitor." In his estimation, he is simply a political and judicial conservative who disagrees with the civil rights establishment on how Blacks will best secure their freedom. He argues that his politics and jurisprudence are required by law and morality, that as a strict constructionist, his judicial decisions are guided by the text of the Constitution and the intent of the framers. He has also said that "God's law" requires him to oppose affirmative action.

Law does not operate in a vacuum, and even a "strict constructionist" cannot escape the political and moral consequences of his decisions. When Thomas gave the "God's law" defense of his record opposing affirmative action, a group of Black clergy held a prayer vigil outside his home and prayed that he find redemption. To their minds, Thomas's invoking God's name in support of a racist decision was blasphemy.[31]

Thomas has also cast his conservative views in the mold of the proud political tradition of Black self-help. He sees himself as an heir to Booker T. Washington, Marcus Garvey, and even Malcolm X. But unlike Washington and Garvey, who organized comprehensive, if flawed, programs to address the problems of impoverished African Americans, and Malcolm X, who engaged in constant and radical confrontation with white privilege, Thomas offers little more than platitudes. His self-help advice to the Black poor is small comfort in the face of a judicial philosophy that protects, above all else, the rights and privileges of the wealthy.

Ultimately, Thomas portrays himself as a beleaguered dissident from the orthodoxy of the civil rights establishment and Black leadership. Colored conservatives often employ this argument, that criticism of their politics is an attack on their free speech and independence of thought. To their minds, those who question their racial loyalty are simply imposing a form of racial political correctness. In a similar vein, colored conservatives often accuse their critics of essentialism, arguing that to malign people of color for racial disloyalty is to believe that all people of color think alike. To draw a connection between genetic inheritance and political philosophy, they say, is surely racist.

We are not saying that all Blacks must think alike, rather, the phenomenon of right-wing Blacks attacking their own has a political, social, and historical context. Certainly Justice Thomas has the right to his beliefs, but he also has considerable power to cause suffering when he acts on those beliefs. He should be accountable for his beliefs precisely because they are freely chosen and because he has been placed in a position to cause suffering in the lives of so many.

If he and other conservatives of color think that our society has purged itself of racism and there is no longer any need for racial remedies, then let them defend those positions. Let them account for our children who are ill-fed and uneducated, for our brothers warehoused in prisons, and for our absence in the halls of government and the corridors of power.

Despite the material and spiritual injuries that Clarence Thomas has inflicted on Blacks, he does us an important service. The extremity of his betrayal cautions each of us against our own complicity in America's racism. He is a vivid reminder of our own vulnerability to internalized racism and self-deprecation. The obvious impossibility of his assimilation among the whites he serves, and his painful isolation from his own community, are a warning that there is no freedom in dissociation from the suffering of our brothers and sisters. When those of us who are relatively privileged participate in society's defamation of people of color, we injure ourselves.

One of my most vivid childhood memories is of a classroom at the Dalton School, a fashionable and progressive New York City private

school. My parents had recently moved to New York to attend graduate and professional school, and they had enrolled me and my sisters
at Dalton so that we would escape the substandard schooling in our
neighborhood public school, where the vast majority of the students
were Black and poor.

It was circle time in the five-year-old group, and the teacher was
reading us a book. As she read, she passed the book around the circle so
that each of us could see the illustrations. The book was *Little Black
Sambo.* Looking back, I remember only one part of the story, one illustra-
tion: Little Black Sambo was running around a stack of pancakes with a
tiger chasing him. He was very black and had a minstrel's white mouth.
His hair was divided in many pigtails, each tied with a different color
ribbon. Even before the book reached my place in the circle, I had seen
the picture. The teacher had already read the "comical" text describing
Sambo's plight, and I had heard the laughter of my classmates. There
was a knot in the pit of my stomach. I felt panic and shame. I did not yet
have the words to articulate my feelings — words like "stereotype" and
"stigma" — that might have helped explain the shame and place it
outside me, where it belonged. But I did know, in a child's intuitive way,
that as the only Black child in the circle, I had some kinship with the
tragic and ugly hero of this story, that my classmates were laughing at
me as well as at him. I wished I could laugh along with my friends. I
wished I could disappear.

Today I still remember the humiliation of being the object of that
white laughter, but even more painful was the feeling that I had betrayed myself in my wish to deny my kinship with Sambo and laugh
along with my friends.

When Clarence Thomas was nominated to the Supreme Court, I
read in a *Time* magazine article that when he was a child growing up in
the 1950s, he was dubbed A.B.C. — short for America's Blackest Child
— by his playmates in Savannah, Georgia.[32] This disparaging nick-
name, hurled at the dark-skinned boy well before we discovered that
Black was beautiful, was a racial slur made all the more poisonous and
powerful because Clarence's taunting playmates were Black, because
even as they demeaned him they debased themselves. The taunted
child and the children who taunted him were all scarred by this ritual of
internalized racism. When I read this story the feelings from that day

at the Dalton School came flooding back, and I grieved for Clarence Thomas and for myself.

Justice Thomas's desertion of the Black community does more than warn us about the costs of betrayal or inspire us to examine our own sins before casting stones. It helps us to realize that we cannot fight the stigma of racism without understanding our participation in its perpetuation. That understanding requires empathy with Justice Thomas, but not without judgment. We must hold our brothers and sisters accountable precisely because we share their pain. If we do not hold Justice Thomas accountable, then we deny our own responsibility for that pain and for our freedom.

Ultimately what is most disturbing, and most sad, is the way in which Thomas's betrayal of African Americans' struggle brings us face to face with how we see ourselves and with the part of ourselves that internalizes the stigma white supremacy creates. Maya Angelou's call to keep alive the hope that Justice Thomas will see clearly the great injury he does is indeed a plea for us all to heal each other from the wounds of internalized racism. At the same time, we must also hold each other responsible for who we are and what we do today. When our brothers and sisters are shooting at us, whether with assault guns or Supreme Court opinions, we must speak forthrightly in condemnation of Black-on-Black crime and search for a way to end self-hatred. We betray ourselves if we choose only silence.

BERNADETTE GROSS

"I love the smell of wood"

"IF YOU CAN LAST until noon, you can stay," the supervisor told Bernadette Gross coldly. He gave her a job swinging roofing squares into a cart as they were cut. The pace was fast and at first the men cut squares that were as long as her reach. "I got into it," she recalls, "swinging 'em up on the cart. After noon, the pieces got smaller. I passed the test, and they didn't want me working so hard, because they had to work hard to keep up."

Bernadette Gross, journey-level carpenter, says of the construction work she loves, "It is nowhere near as hard as they make it out to be. They don't want that to get out." She is only half right. Many would find the work unbearably hard. But for Bernadette Gross, who once worked three low-paying jobs "day, night, and weekend" as a single mother of two young children, forty hours a week swinging tools is good work.

She wants women to know they can use tools. "I got women to put up a pyramid at the Women's Expo," she says. "We had a five-year-old, an eighty-year-old," she recalls, women from all over the country, using tools, putting up structures.

"Your toolbox is what you can do," she states, explaining how devastated she was when co-workers stole her tools. "You need the exact tool for each job. It took me six or seven years to accumulate them. It's expensive. You can't just replace things overnight. I think they were giving me a message: 'A woman shouldn't have these tools.' Guys would come and pick something up out of my box and say, 'You know what this is for? You know how to use this?'"

These days, Bernadette Gross has taken time off from the construction sites to do the other work she is gifted at: she teaches women how to survive in nontraditional jobs. As an instructor for Wider Opportunities for Women, she helps women get and keep jobs as carpenters, pipefitters, plumbers, mechanics — high-paying trades still largely reserved for men. Skills training is only part of it. Much of what she teaches is how to survive in a world that shuns women.

In comfortable middle age, Gross speaks with the confidence and self-awareness of a born winner. She has made it in a man's world, passing every test thrown before her. Like Harriet Tubman, she reaches out to women who are stumbling as they try to follow the same path. Her firm grasp, pulling them forward, belies the troubles of her own past.

You would never know, watching her teach a class or swing a hammer, that she has been poor, abandoned, addicted to drugs, in prison, on welfare, sexually abused, and otherwise drawn bodily through the cycles of deprivation that do-gooders fret about. Bernadette Gross, journey-level carpenter and nontraditional skills instructor, went from nowhere to somewhere, and affirmative action helped.

She was the youngest of eleven children, born to a mother who, though trained as a nurse, ended up working two jobs as a domestic. In those days in Washington, D.C., raising other people's children was what Black women did, and little else was available. "I ran wild in the streets, wore the same clothes every day to school," Gross recalls of her earliest childhood. By the time she was five, the health department was threatening to take her "away on the wagon. They did that in those days."

That threat resulted in the only day of her childhood when she was the center of her mother's attention. "She took me to the clinic, then she took me for an ice cream soda, then she sat me down and told me she couldn't raise me and was sending me to my grandmother's. My grandmother saw it as her appointed duty to break my spirit," she says. Severe physical abuse was part of this process, but, Gross says in retrospect, moving there "saved my life. She taught me basic things, like hygiene. She was always telling me, 'Being poor is no excuse for looking poor.'"

By fifteen, she couldn't take the sternness of her grandmother's home; she ran away and dropped out of school. At seventeen, she had a baby and lost her a year later when a cousin left sulfuric acid in the kitchen.

Recounting the grief, abuse, and abandonment of her early years, she says she knows now that children react in one of two ways, either by saying, "I'm going to get even with everybody," or by saying, "I'm never going to let this happen to anybody else."

She remembers making that second pledge. When her next two children were born, she promised herself they would have a better life. "I never beat my kids," she says, "and they always looked good, even when I was on welfare. Other mothers would give me a hard time when we stood there waiting for our checks; their kids were running around in dirty diapers and my kids had clean clothes from the thrift store. They said I acted like I thought I was better than them." In her characteristic style, she would respond to this social shunning with a sardonic retort: "I'm standing here waiting for the same check you are, so how could I think I'm better than you?" It was a style that would serve her well years later, on construction sites.

Gross found temporary work with the Urban League in one of the job-creation programs that existed in that brief and shining moment called the War on Poverty. She got firsthand experience doing community organizing, and when she came into contact with others who recognized her talents, she was chosen for a "first generation" college grant, designed to help bright young people break out of poverty. Her patrons didn't realize she had no high school diploma, so she took the GED on the side in order to qualify for the scholarship. She left town for Michigan State's Open University.

"They looked at me and saw things in me that said I could handle it," she says, but there was much her patrons did not see or understand. She was caring for two young children alone while their father was calling to beg her to come back to D.C., professing great love. Family and friends sent the message that college was "high and mighty and white," and the political ferment of the time drew the young Bernadette to radical politics and made her impatient with the university and her scholarship sponsors. Was college the place to be when organizers were fanning into ghetto communities to empower the poor and eradicate racial injustice? In the end it was too much, and she left college to go back to Washington.

Things were not better at home. The relationship with her children's father did not last beyond six months, and she had to move in with her sister and her sister's ten children. She left there for a succession of shared housing arrangements, marginal jobs, and personal struggles.

"There were no laws then protecting people with kids who were trying to rent; it was nearly impossible to find a decent place that would take you." She solved the problem by finding an old beat-up Victorian that had been divided into a rooming house. If you give me a two-year lease, she told the landlord, I'll fix it up. Gross took on roommates to meet the expenses and threw herself into stripping, painting, and returning the house to its original configuration — a stately old home with multiple fireplaces, porches, and a beautiful façade.

"Façade" is the metaphor she uses for this period. Much was good in her life. She was admitted to a special outreach program at Georgetown University designed to teach urban planning to residents of poor neighborhoods. She explored political activism and the self-discipline of *hatha yoga*. Her precocious daughter, raised under Gross's "kids have rights" philosophy, entered a prestigious prep school under an early affirmative action outreach program. "My kid was visiting ambassadors' kids, getting rides in chauffeur-driven cars. I wanted a nice façade for her to get dropped off in front of. One day she asked me, 'Mom, why don't we have a maid?' and I had to sit her down and explain about breaking out of the cycle of poverty." Working toward that promise of a better life, she continued her frenetic remodeling of the old Victorian.

Behind this activity, all was not well. Her son was having a hard time in the urban public schools. One day Gross overheard him suggest to a playmate that they get a paper route to earn some money. "Man, we don't need a paper route; we need a gun" was the reply. In the meantime, Gross — who had never used drugs as a teenager, when it would have been easy to do so — was succumbing to what she calls "addiction as a progression." She tried drugs and thought she could use them periodically to deal with life's stresses. "I wasn't standing out on a street corner, so I thought I wasn't an addict."

She worked three jobs to save money for a move to the West Coast, "a geographical cure," she calls it, to get her kids away from guns and to get herself away from drugs.

At a restaurant in Seattle, she had a chance encounter that changed her life. Seated near an intriguing group of women, she overheard that they were feting the Asian woman in their group who had just become a journey-level carpenter. "I'm the kind of person who will talk to a stranger in a restaurant," Gross says, "so I walked up to her and said, 'Congratulations, it's something I've always wanted to do,' and she said, 'They're giving the test for a pre-apprenticeship program tomorrow.' I ended up joining their party, and afterward she gave me a sample test. I studied it all night, took the test, and passed."

The CETA pre-apprenticeship program was designed to prepare women as well as poor and minority men for union apprenticeships. It was "an intense six weeks," Gross recalls. She survived, and was sent out for her first official job as an apprentice carpenter.

The hostility to women was open and aggressive. In those days, Gross was always the only woman on the jobs she was sent to. "People dropped things on my head, sent me to get things that didn't exist, cursed, rolled their eyes. Some guys would spit every time I walked by — spit right in front of where I was walking. Sometimes it was tobacco spit. The situations were comically the same; you could almost say the words before they did.

"'Why do you want a job like this?'

"'I can't tell whether you're a man or a woman.'

"'You must think you're a man.'

"'You'd never catch my wife doing this work; she knows who the boss is.'"

Bernadette Gross heard all of this and more, and recalls with some relish her snappy replies.

"Can't you speed it up over there?" a hostile crew called down to her at one job.

"The way to get some work done around here is to do some," she called back to the hecklers.

To the more vicious taunt "Your problem is you never had a good fuck," her retort was steely: "My problem is I was fucked too much, too early, and my tolerance for your bullshit is just not there."

Was she harassed this way by Black men as well as white? "With the Black guys it's more like 'You should find a man to take care of you.' Some will even offer to buy you — turn you into a prostitute. 'You don't have to work so hard.'"

On an early job, Gross was handed a broom and ordered to sweep. "The biggest trap they have is to give you something easy to do. How would I have made it to second-year pay if I had swept all year? I was making eleven dollars an hour, and I could have said, 'Shoot, I get paid the same. I'll just sweep.'"

Instead, she complained to the shop steward and the supervisor. Sweeping is laborer work, not carpenter work, and she wanted to do the work she was training for. In retaliation, the supervisor put her on the hardest, dirtiest job. "So, you want to be a carpenter," he said. On that hot Seattle day, she donned a heavy respirator suit and "cut seams" to remove old walls, a job that held the danger of concealed wires that someone might have neglected to "cut the juice" for. With plaster flying, she worked at breakneck speed, until they had to tell her to slow down.

"They saw I was a scrapper, and they began to teach me," she says. "Men know women can outwork them. You have to be no-nonsense: 'I'm here to do a job.' There'll always be one or two guys who respect their own mothers and sisters and who will see you as a woman who has to raise a family. They'll come up and say, 'You have a right to be here and you're working twice as hard as everyone else.'"

And so, from a few good men and by dint of her own resolve, Bernadette Gross learned the carpenter's trade.

"I always wanted to do it," she says. "I love the smell of wood. I like working outdoors. I like swinging from belts. I like moving around and not working with the same people all the time." It's a job you have to love, as a woman, because "good pay will not sustain you." She perfected the sarcastic comeback and managed to avoid bitterness. "Some women, the unfairness consumes them. They don't last," she says.

Today her goal is to send "informed workers" into the workplace. Women need to know they don't have to take dangerous work; they don't have to quit when they are harassed.

She does research and passes on history: how the circular saw was invented by a Shaker woman in the 1800s; how early unions drove women trolley drivers out of a profession they had excelled in; how the end of World War II resulted in an orchestrated move to get tools out of the hands of women — from *Father Knows Best* television propaganda to openly discriminatory hiring practices.

She shows the film *Salt of the Earth*, about the struggle of Mexican

American mineworkers in the 1950s. It's a little easier for women in D.C. to talk about the race issues, she says, when it's not black and white. She quotes her favorite line in the movie, from a scene in which a miner's wife confronts male chauvinism: "For you to have dignity, must I have none?" Gay-bashing, racism, misogyny, and union busting, she says, are all "interlocking," and women may as well understand that before they go into the trades, where they will see it all.

Today, Gross says, only 2 percent of the women who enter apprenticeship programs make it to completion. Many of the kinds of pre-apprenticeship programs she relied on are gone. Employers exploit trainees by laying them off just before they reach permanent status. "Can you imagine a woman with five kids getting laid off five times a year? She has to really want it to stick with it."

Employers also now know how to avoid affirmative action mandates in their contracts. They send letters to programs like Wider Opportunities for Women, saying that they are interested in hiring, when and if an opening becomes available, and then use their letters to say they have made an effort, in order to satisfy compliance officers. Asked what effective compliance would look like, Bernadette Gross says, "Training. You can't do it without training. If you're going to have this much construction in an area, there must be a comparable amount of training in the community." Those outreach programs, like the one that brought Bernadette Gross to her calling, have been cut out. "They opened the door and let some of us in, and then closed it. They had to leave open a crack, but they set up a maze for anyone who wants to get through the crack."

She adds that "compliance" in the trades today would mean only 6.9 percent women — ten women on a job with one hundred forty workers — and no employers are meeting that. Even so few women, she says, is seen as "taking over."

A woman can't just show up and apply for a construction job; it doesn't work that way. It's harder for women today as the resistance has stiffened. "They have refined the ways of keeping women out, even as they say, 'We're an equal opportunity employer.'" At one company Gross knows of, the supervisors were saying women didn't want to do the work because it was too complex; it involved complicated schematics. When she investigated, she found that the schematics were diagrams with numbered pictures of parts, nothing an intelligent person couldn't figure out.

She points out that a new cultural backlash makes it hard for young women to risk the stigma associated with seeking a traditionally male job. "Teenage men today are talking like cavemen; they feel very strongly about a woman's place." Her advice to young women in the trades: "Know you have a right to be there. Like what you're doing and have a good time doing it. Take responsibility to see that you learn, because some will not want to teach you."

Bernadette Gross has seen a man's world up close. "Once I watched a Polish guy get it," she remembers. "They goosed him, razzed him, told disgusting Polish jokes. He held up, and when he got to the other side, he was one of them. If a woman gets to the other side, she gets let alone, she gets to come to work every day."

From the other side she watched her male co-workers and came to see the pain behind their tough-guy stances. "They are miserable inside, putting out all this bullshit that no one is buying but them," she says, and she speaks without enmity.

These days, at the age of forty-eight, Bernadette Gross calls herself "an active participant in my recovery" and she is thinking in personal, spiritual, and political terms about what she wants to do next. "The role of advocate is intense and heart-rending," she says, describing one woman she is trying to help survive an apprenticeship. "They ride you like a bronco. She's got two kids and she's about to have a nervous breakdown." Gross scrambled to get that apprentice mental health care.

In the midst of such scrambling, she feels the need to slow down and think about the bigger questions. Speaking philosophically about the change she believes must come in order to make a better world for people who start out where she did, she says, "The great and ominous 'they' play chess like they're the only players, but the thing about chess is that other people make moves too, and good and evil are subject to one another."

Looking back on her life, she speaks of deprivation as something hard to shake. Many hands reached out to her, and she was able to take advantage only of some, just as she now extends a hand to many, knowing only some will take it. Her success is not complete. "I am a first-generation high school graduate. My daughter is a first-generation college graduate. I have one child in law school and one in prison," she says plainly, revealing the deepest pain in her heart and the complex truth of her story. It is not one of gradual ascendancy through hard work and affirmative action. Rather, it is the story of a woman who started at true bottom, and made her moves in fits and starts to a place where she has great wisdom, great pain, and much to offer the world around her.

[6]

Feminism and
Affirmative Action

W HAT IS A FEMINIST?" That's the question I write on the
board the first day of class in Feminist Legal Theory.

"I want you to imagine this person. What does she look like? What
does she believe?"

The students tell me, among other things, that she is white, middle-
aged, privileged, wears Birkenstocks, likes cats, dislikes men, believes
in abortion rights, wants the Equal Rights Amendment. Several of the
students mention myopic focus on gender issues: she ignores class
and race.

"Feminism is a white women's movement." White students as well
as students of color express this view.

"What about the Asian women in San Francisco running shelters for
Asian women?" I ask. "What about the African American women in
D.C. running shelters for African American women? Are they feminists?
What about Toni Morrison, Angela Davis, Alice Walker, June Jordan,
Audre Lorde, Patricia Williams, bell hooks, Kimberlé Crenshaw —
what about Sojourner Truth? Haven't they made feminism? Do you
call yourselves feminists?"

Some do; some are proud graduates of women's studies programs or activists with front-line experience defending abortion clinics.
Many, in spite of their interest in feminist theory and their sympathy
with feminist causes, say no, they aren't comfortable calling themselves
feminists.

As I drive home that night, I think, "Perhaps twenty-two-year-olds
simply need to reject the old, need to invent their own feminism, giving

pro–women activism their own name." At other times, I fear that the propaganda campaign against feminism has worked. Bra-burners, man-haters, libbers, unshaven, chips on their shoulders, wild-eyed, irrational feminists. In addition, elitist, privileged, out of touch.

As I argue for affirmative action from a feminist perspective, I think about my students who hesitate to say "I am a feminist." I say that line myself as often as I can in public settings, along with another: "I am a proud product of affirmative action." Both disrupt cultural stasis. How can an Asian woman wearing a suit be a feminist? How come she is proud of "needing" affirmative action?

If all women supported affirmative action, no politician would dare oppose it. The political power of women united, combined with men of color and progressive white men, would render any challenge to affirmative action futile. The current backlash against affirmative action is made possible, in part, by women's ambivalence.

This ambivalence is costly, for women have the most to lose if affirmative action ends. It is women, particularly white women, who have moved forward in opportunity and income as a direct result of affirmative action. Anyone old enough to remember the beginnings of the second wave of feminism in the early 1970s knows that the pressure to include women has made visible changes in the workplace. We see women where we never saw them before: broadcasting the news, working on road crews, sitting as judges, walking police beats, serving in the President's cabinet, orbiting in space. The idea that women are entitled to inclusion, coupled with the tool of affirmative action, has made a real difference in hiring practices and in women's lives.

Because of affirmative action, for example:[1]

- The San Francisco Fire Department went from no women in 1978 to seventy women today.
- In 1971 women received only 14.4 percent of Ph.D.s. In 1991, 36.8 percent.
- The percentage of women managers in companies subject to affirmative action requirements for federal contractors went from 18 percent to 25 percent.
- The U.S. Forest Service went from 27.8 percent women in 1981 to 43.5 percent women in 1991.

- Today half of Fortune 500 companies have at least one female board member.

None of this happened without a demand for inclusion, followed by a formal and deliberate effort on the part of employers and institutions to seek out qualified women, complete with targeted numbers and in many cases the threat of sanction for failure to include women. Corporate CEOs recognize that affirmative action is necessary, and this is why they have lobbied behind the scenes to protect their interest in continuing affirmative action. Because of their efforts, all current legislative proposals to ban affirmative action exempt private enterprise. Countless businesses have seen their profits rise when they diversified their workforces. Certain car dealerships, to take an example, have quadrupled profits by diversifying their sales forces to reach previously ignored markets.[2] Although top-level corporate officers know this, the Glass Ceiling Report identified the fears and prejudices of lower-level managers as major impediments for advancement of women and people of color.[3] A deliberate effort to change male corporate culture remains critical; as one CEO told the Glass Ceiling Commission, "The old-line companies are run by the white '46 long' guys who practice inappropriate male rituals that are dysfunctional to business. Male bonding through hunting, fishing, and sports talk is irrelevant to business."[4] Given the male bonding that controls much of workplace culture, CEOs have recognized that the incentive to change must come from the top. Instituting affirmative action goals and timetables is one way to overcome cultural resistance to inclusion of women.

While women have made significant gains as a result of such efforts, they continue to need affirmative action. Even as women are admitted into professions formerly reserved for men, they face hostility, harassment, lack of mentoring, absence of paid maternity leave, inadequate childcare, and stereotypes that limit their progress. Testimony received by the Glass Ceiling Commission revealed that women are still thought of as "not wanting to work/not being as committed as men to their careers/not being tough enough/being unwilling or unable to work long or unusual hours/being unwilling or unable to relocate/unwilling or unable to make decisions/too emotional/not sufficiently aggressive/too aggressive/too passive/and lacking in quantitative skills."[5]

As a result of these stereotypes, even women who possess credentials and experience find themselves limited in their career opportunities. Only 3 to 5 percent of senior positions in American companies are held by women, and women's salaries remain well below their male counterparts', even when education is comparable. A study of Stanford M.B.A.s confirmed that women graduates fare less well in both salary and advancement than male classmates.[6] Similarly, an American Medical Association study found that women physicians under the age of forty made 66.6 percent of their male counterparts' salaries,[7] while in the academic sphere, tenured women faculty make 88.5 percent of the salaries of tenured male faculty.[8]

The economic reality of patriarchy is that there are costs attached to being female in our culture. Affirmative action is an effort to balance out those costs. This tool for equality has benefited women across the economic spectrum. Given the feminization of poverty,[9] however, the most critical need for affirmative action is at the bottom: the woman struggling to get off welfare; the woman one paycheck away from welfare; the single working mother frantically jerrybuilding childcare from neighbors, relatives, and unlicensed sitters. Whatever her chosen profession, this woman is, more likely than not, making less than a man with comparable education and background, giving her little chance to get out of poverty. Because women remain the primary, and often the only, caretakers of young children, the poverty of women translates into the poverty of children. These children need their mothers to get out of poverty: they need affirmative action.

For many women, affirmative action is welfare reform that works. Without it, a woman with a high school education is frequently stuck in the world of low-paying women's jobs: babysitters, house cleaners, nurse's aides, clerk-typists, food service workers. A woman with that same limited education who can break into the world of blue-collar, traditionally male jobs, however, can more than double her income. Construction workers, police officers, auto workers, truck drivers, computer technicians — all of these male-dominated domains pay significantly higher wages, with more secure benefits. Often, they pay even higher wages than "women's" jobs that require more education. A preschool teacher or librarian, for example, must have a college degree for a job that pays less than the typical job in the building trades, and women represent less than 2 percent of the building trades.[10]

The women who managed to break through gender barriers to enter the building trades faced significant harassment and doubt about their abilities. Nonetheless, those few who survived found rewarding work, decent pay, and better chances for themselves and their families. These women could not have stepped up the economic ladder without affirmative action offered, though often grudgingly, by contractors.[11] It was political pressure, public embarrassment, and contracting compliance pressure from public entities that created the incentive for construction contractors and unions to provide opportunities for women. If not for affirmative action, women could not have negotiated their way through the complex system of hiring halls, apprentice programs, and good-old-boy networks. Once they were in, many employers who were at first skeptical of women's abilities came to praise the skills of affirmative action hires.[12]

The demand for job access for women parallels the demand for job access for people of color. The construction trades, the professions, and the various locations of economic power excluded both men of color and all women. Women thought to knock on the hiring hall door when they saw men of color doing the same as a logical extension of the civil rights movement.

As it was one hundred years before, the second-stage feminist demand for equal opportunity was rooted in antiracist struggle. The first feminists started as abolitionists, whose work against slavery opened their eyes to the notion of oppression. If all men deserved equal citizenship, they asked, why not all women? The white women in the abolitionist movement recognized that they had no public identity. Like the enslaved Africans, they were legal nonentities, who could not vote. Their property was held in their husbands' names; they could not prosecute crimes in their own name.

The suffragists exploded the notion of a separate sphere for women by forcing their way into public debate. Through acts of public display, from picketing to civil disobedience to sabotage, they claimed a public presence and demanded equal citizenship.

This link between antiracist struggle and feminist struggle was clear to Frederick Douglass, the first male public figure to support the women's cause. He came to understand that woman's subordination was no more "natural" than slavery. He recalled:

In a conversation with Mrs. Elizabeth Cady Stanton when she was yet a young lady and an earnest Abolitionist, she was at pains of setting before me in a very strong light the wrong and injustice of [women's] exclusion. I could not meet her arguments except with the shallow plea of "custom," "natural division of duties," "indelicacy of woman's taking part in politics," the common talk of "woman's sphere," and the like, all of which that able woman, who was then no less logical than now, brushed away by those arguments which she has so often and effectively used since, and which no man has yet successfully refuted.[13]

What Douglass and the early suffragists shared was a recognition of structural inequality. The choice to see a culture of exclusion, to name it, and to disrupt it is what made feminism in this country. The name feminists called out was "patriarchy."

Patriarchy makes the subordination of women seem natural and unremarkable. Through the years, feminists have forced us to see a hundred and one manifestations of its structure. Some are economic, such as laws limiting women's property rights and wages that keep women economically dependent on men. Some are social, such as high-heel shoes, which make running impossible, and divisions of labor that force women into the second shift of caring for home and family. Some are cultural, embedded in language and stereotype: the use of the male pronoun as a universal, the icons from "sacrificing mother" to "castrating bitch." Feminists have also dared to locate patriarchy on the pinpoint of the private: in sex. What we see as sexy (power over), who initiates sex, who is seen as "getting," and who is seen as "giving up" — all of this, too, reveals patriarchy.

The nonfeminist explanations for the disadvantages women experience are basically only two: women like it this way, or women are predestined to live this way — by God or genes or by some other natural determinant. The alternative explanation is rooted in feminism: men have a monopoly on power, and though they are reluctant to give it up, gender inequality is not inevitable. Because Frederick Douglass knew this was true of racism, he could see it was true of patriarchy.

A hundred years after Douglass championed equality for the enslaved and for women, a new civil rights movement rose up from those same country roads he had traveled. The sit-ins, the Freedom Rides, the marches that ignited freedom movements the world over, also lit a fire for women. The second wave of feminism in America decried the wasted lives of women, from the domestics who left home before dawn to clean other women's homes to the suburban "housewives" whose wasted talents and martini-soaked bitterness became a newly recognized social problem.

One of the key goals of the feminist movement of the 1970s was workplace equality. The demand for job access, at its origin, was a demand to share power, and it was much more than the simple individualist claim of any one woman for equal treatment. Moving women into formerly male occupations changes the culture by designating women as people who participate in public life. The new woman cop on the beat, represented not just her own hopes and aspirations, but the aspirations of a movement. Her access to power had meaning for the workers in the women's shelters who knew that then-current police practices meant brutalized female bodies. It changed the aspirations of the young girls who watched her walk down the street dressed in the symbols of public authority. It made a difference to young men of color, caught up in the criminal justice system, that there was now a woman present, a potential traitor in the conspiracy of silence that protected perpetrators of police brutality.

Affirmative action, because it is a structural remedy addressing a structural problem, coincides with feminist theory. While feminist theory is a rich and complex body of thought, I refer here to the idea that gender plays a significant role in the allocation of life chances, income, violence, political power, and social roles. Who cares for the children? Who initiates sex? Who fears rape in the parking garage? Who makes more money? Who calls whom to say that "Ace Construction is hiring; just ask for Joe and tell them Buddy sent you"? In a patriarchal culture, gender distributes tangible goods. Feminism says that these distributions are neither natural nor necessary. They are created by patriarchy, and their existence means that women are subordinated.

Because patriarchy is structural, feminist practice must dismantle that structure. Patriarchy disadvantages women as a group: although particular women may be more or less affected by patriarchy because of race, class, or other distinctions, all women live with the fear of rape and other forms of antiwomen violence. All women suffer economic uncertainty because of the gender gap. Women share greater responsibility for reproduction and childrearing. In short, women suffer group disadvantage, and ending this group disadvantage requires group remedy.

It follows that the solution to gender subordination must be gender based. Just as "colorblindness" is no solution to entrenched racism, ignoring gender is not the way to end gender oppression. If our culture and history place women outside the corridors of power, we must find ways to bring them in through affirmative action.

In contrast, anti–affirmative action rhetoric is grounded in a narrow, nonstructural understanding of inequality. For example, faced with irrefutable statistics demonstrating the persistent wage subordination of women, those who follow the economic model of rational free choice suggest that women may be choosing to work at jobs that pay less. Women, the argument goes, may have an aversion to risk or to working in stressful or dirty conditions. Aside from the fact that women have always done stressful, dirty work — nursing, parenting, farm work, etc. — placing the blame on some natural proclivity is a way to avoid looking at such systemic problems as institutional sexism, sexual harassment, child-rearing responsibilities and culturally entrenched stereotyping that limits women's choices.

Even if large numbers of women are "choosing" low-paying jobs, such as cosmetologist and childcare worker, a feminist with an eye out for cultural coercion might ask why the girls' aisle at Toys R Us is full of dolls, dress-up props, and housekeeping toys, while the boys' aisle is full of action toys encouraging building, driving, fighting, and heroic rescuing. Our culture sends messages about gender roles that permeate children's lives before they reach what the philosophers called the age of reason. A woman's decision to limit her economic advantage is not a free choice when she is deprived of the information and the socialization required to take advantage of a range of choices.

Affirmative action expands the choices. Programs designed to encourage women to break out of stereotyped roles recruit, train, hire, and inform so that women have an equal chance to pursue blue-collar jobs, such as auto mechanic, where the average weekly wage of $523 is significantly more than that of "women's" jobs such as cosmetologist or lab technician, with an average weekly wage of $247.[14] In fact, 90 percent of women in apprenticeships are presently working toward such low-wage jobs.[15]

We need to recognize that distinguishing choice from coercion is the wrong inquiry. From the explicit coercion of verbal and physical harassment that women encounter in nontraditional jobs, to the guidance of well-meaning counselors who believe childcare is a nice job for women, to the socialization that teaches that trucks are for boys and dolls are for girls, women's choices are affected by patriarchy. If patriarchy is acknowledged as what it is, a social phenomenon with real effects, then the structural remedy of affirmative action for women is appropriate.

When I present students with statistics indicating that women with law degrees make less than their male counterparts, I sense an unwillingness to believe that patriarchy is at work. One student asked, "I know women who have quit high-paying law firm jobs because they just didn't like the pressure and they were willing to take a pay cut to improve their quality of life. Wasn't that a free choice?" This question goes to the heart of the debate. The choice of a highly educated woman, with options in life, certainly seems close to the rational actor whom free market economists speak of: someone who expresses uncoerced preferences in the marketplace. If it is largely women who choose to forgo financial reward in order to raise families, or simply to have the leisure for maintaining friendships and reading novels, why should society have any concern with that choice? This question presumes no benefit to society as a whole from reshaping the world of work.

If, through affirmative action, barriers fall and women enter all segments of the work world, the landscape of choices may change. For example, the 1993 Family Leave Act — the first piece of legislation recognizing that people who work frequently have families to care for — came into being when large numbers of women entered the workforce. The pressure for change, the women waiting to testify about what they faced in a world where having a baby meant losing a job, came about because women were there. They were working; they were in a position to testify, lobby, speak, and be heard. In this sense, affirmative action furthered the democratic process.

What if all of the people who wanted to do a good job at work and have enough time left over to read a story to a child stayed in the market instead of "choosing" to leave? Perhaps the world of work would change in humanizing ways. Affirmative action, justified first and foremost as a guarantor of equality, becomes more than that in its full potential. It can change world views and bring new ways of being to our work lives.

Feminist affirmative action must go beyond merely adding women to the world of men. Women who have made it in a man's world are embittered by the result; more women are working double shifts because of their second jobs — maintaining home and family — and their larger earning power is offset by a rising cost of living and declining real wages. Women who went to work to seek liberation found, instead, exhaustion and the frustration of doing an incomplete job at work and at home. As they collapse at the end of yet another day of barely making it, some even fantasize about the lives of those calm, stay-at-home sitcom moms on early television.

The solution is not a return to traditional gender roles but a reconfiguring of social structures. Feminists, having long known this, demand such things as wages for housework; free public childcare; and the professionalization of women's work. That is, the people who clean homes, prepare food, and care for children, so that large numbers of women can enter the work world, should have good wages and good working conditions. Longstanding demands of the labor movement are also key to workplace equality for women: workers need more leisure, paid leave to attend to family and personal needs, and a living wage.

Even women who do not identify themselves as feminists know they need a living wage. The decline of real wages means that the average family — the single mom with kids or the traditional nuclear family — relies on women's wages. Over 80 percent of married first-time home buyers, in fact, rely on women's income to help pay the mortgage.[16] Affirmative action, as a tool that breaks down economic barriers for women, is something all women and their families need.

Listening to women, as the method of feminist consciousness-raising requires, reveals a longing for a world of decent pay for labor and time off for leisure. As nineteenth-century factory women sang, women today want bread and roses too. A feminist version of affirmative action works toward both.

If women need affirmative action, the question remains, however, why they don't demand it.

For many women, affirmative action triggers a particular form of denial, one made complex by the large number of women who see heterosexual relations as critical to their happiness. If the angry white man is painted as the victim of affirmative action, then the white woman who defines self-fulfillment as loving that man may hesitate to support affirmative action, even when she needs it for her economic well-being.

Women have fathers. Women have sons. Women are conditioned to have male lovers, boyfriends, husbands. These relations are fulfilling, primary, and joyful for many women. They are sometimes dark, painful, violent, and damaging for others. Regardless of their success or failure, many women continue to see these relations as a significant part of their lives. The personal obscures the political.

Feminism, as a theory of gender oppression, sees economically privileged white men at the top of a pyramid. Below the apex, women make their lives. Dismantling the pyramid means that men will have to give up their privilege and live in equality with those they have dominated. Quite predictably, most men do not want to move down from the summit. As Frederick Douglass said in the time of slavery, power concedes nothing without a struggle. Women are often surprised to learn this truth, to discover that a little challenge to male supremacy can unleash a flood of rage and danger.

Feminists have explored why women stay with men who abuse them physically or emotionally, why women accept unfulfilling relations and fail to require change. Change is costly. Men may react with violence, verbal aggression, denial, withdrawal of economic support, withholding of affection, and a range of resistances when women attempt to change or end abusive relationships. Because women are often socialized to make peace, to attend to the needs of others, to put others before themselves, and to see relationships as primary and all-consuming, they are easily disciplined not to seek change. Women who believe that living without a man is worse than living with an abusive man will not leave. This psychology writ large is part of the explanation for some women's acquiescence in patriarchy, part of the reason for their absence in the vanguard defending affirmative action.

Many women who live peaceably with patriarchal men do so by limiting their efforts to alter the power relationship. From the mother who hushes her children because Daddy is in a bad mood, to the secretary who sits silently through a boss's tantrum, to the girlfriend who forgoes complaint about yet another lovemaking session that left her unsatisfied, women everywhere are choosing silence in the face of male privilege. Sometimes this is a weighted and mournful silence. At other times it is a survivor's reasoned choice: I choose this compromise because it keeps a roof over my head, and there are many ways I know to make this life my own.

Some women who have sons make a deal with patriarchy. They love their boy children with the fierceness all children deserve and believe that these boys must learn active, tough, male stances to make it in a patriarchal world. They give their children over to patriarchy, with varying degrees of resistance, and never stop loving their sons.

Women who live with men see private male pain. Male privilege does not mean a life without pain. Patriarchy hurts everyone, as oppressions hurt everyone. The stark loneliness that comes from living on either end of the spectrum of dominant and subordinate is subordination's paradox. To gain the privilege of power over someone else, men under patriarchy must accept the ever-present threat of someone else trying to gain power over them. Women hold grown men in their arms, men crying like babies behind the curtain of their private lives, because somewhere out there in the public world of economic death battles and political machination, workplace hells and statehouse arbitrage, men are chewed up and spit out in the way of the patriarchal world.

Women know men's pain. So when men come home and say, "I didn't get the job because they were looking for a woman," women are the witnesses. It was a mother who told another that her white son didn't get into Harvard because of affirmative action. It was a wife who called in to the talk show to complain that her all-American husband lost out when a contract bid went to a "foreigner."

When these same women go into the workplace, either to supplement the family income or to replace it when husbands leave or lose jobs, they face the gender gap. Their wages, their job options, their chances of advancement, are all limited.

While some women recognize that affirmative action puts food on the table, others hesitate in deference to the male anger they see. Under no other form of subordination do the oppressed sleep in the same bed with the oppressor. The identity that many women feel with men makes the struggle to end gender oppression unique, and it is what led to the feminist battle cry "The personal is the political."

Complicity with patriarchy, and hence with anti–affirmative action forces, is further fueled by racism and homophobia. One of the discoveries of feminist practice is the inter-relation of all forms of subordination. The activist-theorist Suzanne Pharr has expanded on this point, showing how homophobia is used to scare women out of the feminist movement.[17] She discovered that women who speak up for women's rights are frequently lesbian-baited and called homophobic hate names. The predominant message that heterosexuality is good, right, and normal, combined with irrational and visceral fear of homosexuals, was particularly a problem in the beginning of the second wave of feminism. Organizations like NOW had to struggle in early days to confront internalized fears that "mainstream" feminist organizations could not have an active lesbian presence.

While homophobia within feminism remains a serious problem, many feminists now see that lesbians are at the core of feminism. Lesbians were there on the marches, in the shelters, at the fundraisers. Lesbians were there at the birth of feminism and its subsequent rebirths. Lesbians were there because lesbians by definition are women-centered. They are less inclined than straight women to feel the loss of male approval and companionship as a price too great to pay. As a consequence, they have less fear of feminist activism.

Like homophobia, racism also divides women, particularly on the issue of affirmative action. A key strategy of the architects of the anti–affirmative action backlash is to equate affirmative action with Black beneficiaries. The mythical undeserving, unqualified person who received something because of affirmative action is given a Black face in the media, in political speeches, and in private conversations recounting affirmative action horror stories.

This counterfactual move erases white women as what they are: the primary beneficiary of affirmative action. It plays on the culture of racism to get white women to oppose affirmative action. The coded racism in the anti–affirmative action movement tracks the coded racism in the anti-welfare movement. The right has succeeded in coding "welfare" as Black, even though the majority of people on welfare, and the majority of poor people in this country, are white.[18] The attack on the poor is made more palatable by packaging it in racism. Rather than facing the reality of taking food from blond, blue-eyed children, which is exactly what so-called welfare reform will do, the public is fed racist images of wanton Black "welfare mothers." Similarly, Jesse Helms did not run ads portraying white men losing jobs to white women. He needed white women's votes, so he could not afford to emphasize that the most impressive result of the affirmative action programs he would dismantle has been increased job access for white women.

Feminist activists have long recognized that the struggle against racism is inseparable from the struggle against patriarchy. The reliance on homophobia and racism to undermine women's support for affirmative action is yet another reason that women must fight all forms of subordination as part of feminist practice.

Complicity with patriarchy is also generated by the possibility of buying in. One of my students, in describing the reaction of some of her women classmates to the affirmative action debate, spoke of this form of complicity; of the will to believe that a person doesn't need affirmative action because the boys' club is already open to talented women. She described women classmates who believe they can go anywhere and do anything, that the barriers of patriarchy do not apply to them. For these women, choosing to identify with an oppressed group would deny their individual talents. They prefer to identify with the most privileged group in society and to assume that all the privileges of that group will accrue to them. In many cases, their fathers, their brothers occupy that world, and its manners and customs are familiar. Who wants to believe she is on the receiving end of a bad deal, particularly when her talents, drive, and class position belie any notion of structural subordination? Such a woman believes her life course will defy the facts, despite the persistent gender gap in lawyer salaries, the statistical proof that 39 percent of law firm associates are women while women account for only 13 percent of law firm partners, 9 percent of judges, 8 percent of law school deans, and 17 percent of law professors. There is one segment of the bar where women predominate: 67 percent of the nontenure-track instructors in law schools, positions that typically pay less and offer little job security, are women.[19]

Catharine MacKinnon has said gender neutrality is a theory that works for "women who have been able to construct a biography that somewhat approximates the male norm."[20] For many women, the time at which they learn they cannot approximate the male biography is when they choose to have children. The male workplace, MacKinnon points out, was structured with the assumption that the worker was not the primary caretaker of young children. The career tracks of privileged male workers — medical residents, law firm associates, executives in training, tenure-track professors at universities — require maximum expenditure of career-making time and effort precisely during the period that coincides with women's childbearing years. That large numbers of talented women have not risen up in collective rebellion against the impossibility of matching the traditional male biography is testimony to the power of the belief that equality is attainable for privileged women.

Those women law students who line up confidently for interviews with corporate firms have reason to believe their talents, not their gender, will determine their fate. After all, women are entering law school in roughly the same numbers as men. The barriers seem to be down. Any inequalities they see — that most of the partners coming to interview them are still men, for example — are easily dismissed as remnants of a system that used to discriminate but no longer does.

This rationalization ignores some hard facts.[21] First, even among the younger attorneys who entered the profession well after the formal barriers to women's admission to law school were lowered, the bulk of prestige positions — positions on law review, federal court clerkships — are going to men. Five years out of law school, men make more than women, even when grades and class rank are taken into account. Women fade away in practice. Fewer become partners; fewer take up leadership positions in the bar. Many leave law practice altogether. The confident belief that a woman can make it in a man's world gives way to a range of iconoclastic life choices: you may know her, she used to be a lawyer and now she sells antiques or works for a nonprofit or raises children or llamas.

True equality for women requires not only affirmative action but a radically expanded notion of affirmative action. It is not enough that one out of a hundred police officers on the beat is a woman. It is not enough that the women who manage to approximate the male biography, often by contracting out responsibilities for care of house and children, are the only ones who can approximate male privilege in the work world. True affirmative action calls for not only the entry of women, but a change in the culture of the places they enter.

The workplace that is inhumane for women who want to parent is ultimately inhumane. Period. Within white male culture there is a long-standing and eloquent critique of that world. The description of the fictional Willie Lomax, broken and discarded by a world that demands more than ordinary human beings, with their complex, uneven lives, can give is a description supporting the feminist notion of expanded affirmative action. Let women enter the workplace, let them live the lives they choose, alive with passions — for raising children or running marathons or organizing political campaigns. Let work accommodate this, augmenting life rather than replacing it. The gain is to all when work becomes so.

In class one day, a woman mentions being assaulted by a "groper" on the subway. She was stunned into silence, she says. Other women chime in, reporting verbal and physical assaults in public places: a man coming up and whispering obscenities in the supermarket; a man yelling homophobic epithets from a passing car; a man grabbing and then fleeing in a library basement. "It happened so fast. I just froze. Before I could think of what to do, he was gone."

A man in the class shakes his head. He was touched on the crotch on the subway, he says, and he spun around and slugged the assailant. "I didn't think. It was just a reflex."

This spontaneous consciousness-raising session was one the students remember. Our small sample was in no way scientific, but it represented, in their experience, a difference in typical male and female reactions.

Long after that class, I am sitting at the dinner table with friends, one of whom is a professional pollster.

"So what about the California anti–affirmative action initiative?" he was asked.

"Seventy-five percent of white men are for it," he says. "It's up to the women now."

Where are the women? Feminist activists are in the streets, as ever. Organizations like NOW have campaigned actively and aggressively for affirmative action. They followed Pete Wilson around the country, demonstrating at his public appearances and contributing to his withdrawal from the presidential race. They have led pro–affirmative action demonstrations in every large city, coast to coast.

Some women have learned to spin around and slug back when attacked; to do it reflexively, quickly, decisively.

Others stand frozen. It happened so fast. I didn't have time to think. Affirmative action is a complicated issue, made more confusing by the rhetorical war that pits "reverse discrimination" against "colorblind." The repeated use of the colorblind metaphor turns affirmative action into "race preference" and masks a critical fact: it is women who have the most to lose if affirmative action is outlawed, for it is women who have made the most significant gains in job access and wage increases since the advent of affirmative action and the pressure to diversify.[22]

In the early days of women's suffrage, women who had organized precinct by precinct for the right to vote found that their organizations could swing elections. More funds for education, maintenance of temperance (then seen as a women's issue because of the effect of alcoholism on the family), programs for infant and maternity care — candidates who supported those things were swept into office on a wave of women's votes.[23]

The women's voting block that suffragists imagined and began to realize never came to full fruition. Racism, among other things, split the women's vote as nativist politicians lured some white women away from a progressive social agenda. So did the decline of the grassroots local organizations that had fought the suffrage battle.

While the elusive "women's vote" is still watched by the pollsters, there is no guarantee that women will vote decisively in favor of affirmative action, even when their self-interest is at stake. "I am not comfortable calling myself a feminist. I am not sure where I stand on affirmative action. I can see both sides." The many good women — intelligent, concerned about ethics, civic-minded — who feel this way are the swing votes in this round of the affirmative action battle.

It's not the same as being grabbed on the subway. There is time to think. To think about the job you didn't get because someone thought you weren't assertive enough; to think about the job you did get because of affirmative action pressure to hire women; to think about the gender gap in wages — closing slowly since the advent of affirmative action and sure to widen once again if affirmative action ends.

Time to think, spin around, and fight back.

BARBARA BABCOCK

_____

"Before affirmative action, there was discrimination"

WHEN WORD GOT AROUND that Barbara Babcock was about to make a final argument, young D.C. lawyers would slip out of their offices to watch the show. "We all used to feel she was the one who could really argue a case to a jury. She could convey enthusiasm and belief and translate her defense into an understandable account, a story, a mosaic, that twelve people on a D.C. jury could buy," a colleague from those days recalls.

Thirty years later, students in Professor Babcock's law school classes are not surprised to learn that she was known as a girl-genius trial lawyer early in her career. The skills of trial lawyering — the ability to hold an audience enthralled, the empathetic knack for making complicated concepts accessible — are the skills of a master teacher. She is the most beloved professor at the Stanford Law School, regularly showered with awards and accolades for her teaching.

Awards have followed her all her life — the best grades, president of this, chair of that, valedictorian, Phi Beta Kappa, Order of the Coif, honorary degrees, trophies, plaques, and testimonials. When Barbara Babcock passed through the doorway of any institution, from kindergarten to chaired professorship at Stanford, she knew the awards would come. She always knew she was smart, and she consistently added to that natural edge a winner's dose of effort.

Her success seems easy. The bright laugh lines around her eyes; her wickedly humorous, molasses-paced storytelling style; and her passion for life's bounty — for students, friends, artsy clothes, good food, and good times — make it seem as though every blessing falls at her feet with neither effort nor heartache on her part.

Anyone who has been the woman who has it all knows it is never so.

Barbara Babcock's career as "first woman" and "best" is marked by valleys she refuses to let dominate her life. The first was the little secret her model family valiantly hid during her childhood. Her father, a brilliant and gregarious man, was a drinker. Their beautiful Victorian house in a Washington, D.C., suburb, decorated with her mother's artful touch, was set askew by the uncertainty of alcoholism — of never knowing when the next binge was coming.

"I never doubted for one moment that my father loved me above all else," Babcock recalls, and therein, perhaps, is the explanation for her leaving her childhood with sense of self and love of life intact. She doesn't dwell on her family's problem, preferring to recall the raucous fun of their good times, and the love of humanity that her father brought to his solo practice of law.

"Barbara, a funny thing happened today at the office . . ." he would begin, launching into yet another captivating tale, told in his Arkansas drawl, of a person in the middle of an urgent, quirky problem that only a good lawyer like Henry Babcock could set right. From earliest childhood, young Barbara began telling adults she was going to be a lawyer, drawing friendly laughter in those days when a girl child's unrealistic ambition was a good joke on a slow day.

The fact that women were widely thought incapable of certain work, the blatant exclusion and harassment they faced at every turn, was "not something we thought of as discrimination in those days. It was a handicap, like being plain or not as smart or not being rich would be. Something you lived with and overcame," Babcock explains.

School was her sanctuary, a place where the rules were fixed, and "overcoming" through achievement always resulted in recognition. "I was going to take care of myself and be well known; there would be no question about my standing in the community," she says of the pledge she made to herself as a schoolchild. A full scholarship to the University of Pennsylvania — including everything from tuition to train fare — was the ticket out of her small world. Washington, D.C., and Hope, Arkansas, her mother's hometown, were the only two places she had ever been.

"I should have gone to Radcliffe," she says, "but I didn't know about such things. I had never been *anywhere*. I went to a high school where there were no Blacks, no rich, no poor, no Jews who we knew were Jews."

At Penn, there were "*Jews* — those people I had only read about in books — and I fell in love with the first one I met." A thread in her life's story begins here: Barbara Babcock, raised by traditional Southern parents in a lily-white suburb of the nation's capital, has a habit of attraction to difference.

Her Jewish boyfriend at Penn was an experienced debater. As a team, they traveled up and down the East Coast for marathon debate tournaments, winning most of the time. She whizzed through the university, becoming valedictorian of the women's college, and thereby gaining admission to the Yale Law School, as one of a dozen women in her law school class.

When she arrived at Yale, her father was at her side. They looked up at the Gothic turrets and massive façade of the law school and saw something out of a European travelogue. Henry Babcock, the general practitioner who had taught himself law in the days when ambitious men could take the bar exam without a degree, turned to his daughter and said, "Barb, you've made it. You never have to do another damn thing as long as you live."

It was heaven. "I was indescribably happy," Babcock says. The gargoyled buildings, which some might see as cold and garish, retained a beautiful glow for her. Her love of Yale only exacerbated her hurt at being left out of one of its central privileges: only male students were allowed to live within the castle walls, in suites, with fireplaces, that wove through the inner courtyards of the law school.

Babcock bounced back from this exclusion, finding an apartment with two women classmates. One, Eleanor Holmes Norton, now a member of the U.S. Congress, became a best friend for life. Their tiny apartment in a crime-ridden part of town became known for the best parties and as a way station for traveling luminaries of the nascent civil rights movement. "Everyone who was anyone in the movement came through that apartment. We fried tons of chicken and did the dishes in the bathtub. The history of our time passed through our place," Babcock recalls.

By moving in with a Black woman, Barbara broke a social taboo that was inviolable in the culture of her Southern parents. She hesitated only for a moment, out of deference to them, before solidifying her alliance with Eleanor Holmes. Thus she pulled her parents into the reality of the twentieth century and made a friendship so precious to her that her eyes fill with tears as she describes it.

"You may have noticed," she says, with a barely perceptible touch of irony, "that most white people don't have any Black friends."

Barbara Babcock, collector of people, has Black friends — along with Asians, Latinos, gays, lesbians, Jews, and atheists — dear friends whom she worries about, cajoles in letters, feeds at her table, pries for private information, visits, sends gifts to, and otherwise becomes thoroughly involved with. She is not above expressing frank curiosity about cultures she knows nothing about, or pressing point blank for the details of the lives of others. Sharing as she does her father's gift for making people fall in love with her, she finds the targets of her amateur anthropological digging revealing more about themselves than they ever thought they would, and feeling just fine about that.

With this probing, Barbara learned about the world of Eleanor Holmes. In many ways it was a world she knew — the same landscape in the shadow of the Capitol, the same trips downtown for shopping — but the elegant department stores would not let Blacks try on clothes, and a geography of segregation determined, street by street, who could live where. Barbara became familiar with the embittered but dignified life of the thousands of middle-class Blacks who made the city run — who built it, maintained it, and served as the backbone of the workforce that kept the federal government functioning.

Barbara and Eleanor, two women who shared a hometown, a drive to excel, and a reckless exuberance, began to take on the world at Yale Law School. There had never before been a woman in the final round of the moot court competition. The entire first-year class was required to participate, and in that intense competitive environment, where every student had been the best all their lives, the competition was the first head-to-head challenge to determine who would come out on top of this new pile. The prep school boys, the Ivy League princes all were eliminated in the initial rounds of competition in 1960, leaving two women, one black and one white, in the final elimination.

With the whole school watching, Eleanor Holmes and Barbara Babcock held forth with presence beyond their years, filling the austere space of the moot courtroom. Babcock won, and everyone took quiet notice. Years later, when both names were on the front pages of the nation's papers as high-level "first woman" appointees in President Jimmy Carter's administration, those who had known them at Yale were not surprised. Whatever their private insecurities, Barbara Babcock and Eleanor Holmes carried themselves like people who were going places, ignoring the matter-of-fact exclusions they faced as women.

Babcock's top grades meant she was appointed to the Yale Law Review, but a deserved editorial position was voted down with the classic line "We tried a woman editor once, and it didn't work out." Similarly, as classmates competed for coveted federal judicial clerkships, the standard beginning for a fast-track legal career, the women were told they could forget about applying. No justice on the Supreme Court would hire a woman.

The next tier of top judges — the ones known for liberal politics, history-making legal analysis, and the wielding of inordinate political power — were clustered in the U.S. Court of Appeals in Washington. Names like David Bazelon and Skelly Wright were annexed to opinions changing the shape of American law, consistently expressing an abiding concern for the have-nots. And they never, ever hired women.

We work late, judges said privately, in our shirtsleeves. The clerks work hard and play hard — they cuss, they drink, they play high-stakes poker. Women would intrude on the sanctuary of our world. They lack the cutting-edge sharpness it takes to work as hard and as smart as we work here.

Alan Dershowitz, a Yale graduate who was already clerking in Washington, told Babcock to forget about even trying for one of those preferred clerkships, but he offered a helpful tip: Henry W. Edgerton was a senior judge who, though semiretired, still hired clerks and was willing to consider women. Thus, while Babcock was denied the Supreme Court clerkship her grades should have guaranteed, she did get into the D.C. courthouse, where she saw that she could flourish in a world considered too tough for women.

Edward Bennett Williams was the premier criminal defense lawyer of the day. The major national law firms refused even to interview women, but Williams had already taken notice of Barbara Babcock when she was a student at Yale: young, ambitious, smart, and, not incidentally, confidently attractive. He offered her a job following her clerkship, and she joined his firm. Arguing his motions, writing his briefs, carrying his bag to the courtroom, she learned trial lawyering from a master. "Your girl," other lawyers called her when speaking to Williams.

The legal culture was hostile to women. "[W]hen I started out, the things that we young women lawyers underwent as a regular part of the scene would make your hair stand on end . . . [p]eople grabbing you and threatening . . . you if you didn't go to bed with them. That's the way it was in the rough and tumble of litigation, which people said women shouldn't be in . . . You had to take it. And I really hated it."

Babcock took all this in without complaint. "It was in my preconscious days," she says. She was fulfilling an ambition she had had throughout law school: to become a criminal defense attorney, an unusual ambition for a Yale graduate. Criminal work was seen as less prestigious and less intellectually and financially rewarding than the other opportunities that fell in the laps of top law school graduates, but Babcock could not shake the romantic definition of "lawyer" she had learned at her father's table: the underdog's only chance.

A few other brilliant young lawyers were beginning to share her view. The Legal Aid Agency — the public defender for the District of Columbia — had attracted a small band of aggressive attorneys of stellar pedigree. They found that criminal defense work fulfilled a male fantasy of life-and-death struggle against the odds. Sharing this taste, and knowing she would never try her own cases at Edward Bennett Williams's firm, Babcock made the move to the Legal Aid Agency. Soon she was handling major felony jury trials.

"Above anything else, she had an overwhelming desire to win," one colleague recalls. With her love of the battle, Babcock soon rose to the top, becoming the first woman to head the Public Defenders. A front-page *Washington Post* article featured her photo, and the headline THIRTY-YEAR-OLD TRIAL LAWYER TO HEAD PUBLIC DEFENDERS. That's what I am, she thought to herself with satisfaction, a thirty-year-old trial lawyer and head of the Public Defenders. With an enlarged, reorganized staff, the newly named Public Defender Service became the leading public defender office in the country, a model for others. Babcock, as administrator of PDS, was known for her ability to find and keep talent, creating a team to which every player contributed with passion.

While she was building PDS, Babcock's prefeminist days were ending. Like every smart, educated woman of her day, she read *The Second Sex* and *The Feminine Mystique,* and she began her own analysis of how the legal system treated women. What had once seemed the natural burdens of womanhood were redefined as discrimination. After years of championing civil rights for racial minorities and indigent criminal defendants, Babcock realized that the quest for equality must include women.

Propelled by a new generation of women law students who were pushing for courses addressing women's rights, Babcock hastily put together a set of readings, and taught the first course on Women and the Law at Georgetown. Next, Yale asked her to teach the course, and she commuted from D.C. to New Haven to make history there as well. Soon, other law schools were after her, and an invitation came for a tenure-track position at Stanford.

It was too soon to leave the love of her life — the Public Defender Service — but, Babcock says, "I knew this door would open only once. The top law schools were embarrassed that they had no women faculty. They were all scrambling to get one, and only one, and then the door would close. This wasn't a job I could wait to retire to."

Teaching jobs in those days were reserved for a narrow range of candidates: Supreme Court clerks and hand-picked graduates of top law schools who were recommended by their professors for the academic life. Because women were excluded from this process, the law schools recognized that if they were going to find their "one, and only one," they would have to exercise affirmative action.

Recovering from a hurtful divorce, and recognizing that law teaching was a wonderful job available on a now-or-never basis, Babcock made the decision to move to California to become Stanford Law School's only woman professor. From there, she collaborated with Eleanor Holmes Norton and two other emerging feminist lawyers to publish a breakthrough casebook on *Sex Discrimination and the Law.* The authors of that text stated at the outset: "We believe that women suffer inequality, reinforced and at times created by laws, and that law can also be used to remedy many of these inequities. We also believe that American life would be immensely improved were women to enjoy a social, economic, and legal status truly equal to men's."

With that modestly partisan statement, the book broke ground, for it abandoned the perch of the detached and objective author. An entire generation of feminist legal scholars, emboldened by that explicit feminist stance, began to see a new way of doing scholarship.

With her name on the spine of one casebook, followed soon by a second on civil procedure, Babcock settled in for a good life in the academy, until affirmative action knocked on her door a second time, in 1977.

Responding to pressure from the women's movement, Jimmy Carter had pledged in his campaign to appoint women to significant positions. Babcock, with her academic, trial lawyering and administrative credentials, was an obvious pick to become assistant attorney general of the United States, heading the Justice Department's Civil Division. Nonetheless, detractors alleged quotas.

"How does it feel to have got your position because you were a woman?" reporters asked again and again. She developed a stock answer: "It feels a lot better than not getting it because I am a woman."

In private she says, "Look, before there was affirmative action, there was discrimination. I have a hard time sympathizing with those who worry that with affirmative action someone will think they are not really good because they are a minority, white woman, et cetera, because there is an immediate and obvious answer — just be great at the job, and then nobody has anything to say about how you got it."

The country had never before seen a woman in such a high-profile legal position. Babcock recognized the significance: "Putting women in high positions changes overnight, for women, the idea of what life can be like. It's like integrating the lunch counters — the minute one Black person sits, it changes everything forever."

After serving intrepidly as one of the highest ranking woman attorneys in the United States, Babcock returned to Stanford and stepped out of the whirlwind. She continued to collect awards and reign as a much-sought-after public speaker — both because she is a symbol of women in high places and because she is an incomparable raconteur. At present, she is consumed by her major life's work: a biography of Clara Shortbridge Foltz, the first woman lawyer in California and founder of the public defender movement.

When Bill Clinton was elected, the papers once again buzzed with her name. Would she become attorney general? She ended the speculation before her name went forward; it's nice to be on someone's list, she said, but I am not the right person. The attorney general is, among other things, America's prosecutor. Barbara Babcock will always think of herself as a public defender; her heart is with the criminally accused. "To go to prison is a horrible thing, for anyone," she says. She has never had a problem with giving her all to save someone from that fate, and she is inexorably opposed to the death penalty. A fair-minded woman prosecutor, like Janet Reno, should become attorney general, she insisted when pushed to consider the job for herself. Only half-joking, she told more than one inquiring reporter she couldn't go to Washington because she had to finish the biography she was writing.

In defending Clinton's effort to find a woman for the job, she told one reporter, "It's not as if there's just one person qualified to do the job and that person is a man, and here we've got a gender quota that makes you put in a woman instead. That's silly. There're lots and lots of people who can be attorney general. Lots. And since some of them are women and there's never been a woman and it would be such a great thing to have a woman for the equality principle, what's wrong with just looking at women?"

When students organizing against the California anti–affirmative action initiative asked Babcock to join the fray, she showed up ready to perform, gracious and adamant. She headlined a campus press conference and made passionate speeches to community groups. At one local bar meeting, she said:

> I take the side of affirmative action for the most personal of reasons. I am its direct, immediate beneficiary. I'm proud of that fact, and proud to be living in a country where a woman without the backing of old or new money, social standing, political or family connections, can become a chaired professor at Stanford Law School, and an assistant attorney general of the United States.
>
> Affirmative action is still young as a legal concept, while discrimination against minorities and white women has been with us for three hundred years. We should give affirmative action a chance before abandoning it . . . We are a long way from that nirvana — the colorblind, equal opportunity society. When people can honestly stand up and say discrimination against people of color and white women is no longer a serious problem — then we can give up one of the tools we have developed.

Other than occasional public speeches like this one, Barbara Babcock now lives largely out of the public view. Friends can picture her in her idyllic private life: traveling with her birdwatching spouse to beautiful environs, where they read great books aloud to each other. It is a life full of gifts given freely to others: hours in research so that future generations will know about early feminists like Clara Foltz, intense involvement with students, selective activism in public affairs.

Without affirmative action, Barbara Babcock, the self-described "optimist of an extreme sort," would have had a good life. The loss would have been ours. Affirmative action enlarged the universe of students, readers, friends, and colleagues who feel enveloped by her embrace, and it is not exaggeration to say the world is a better place because that happened.

[7]

Affirmative Action, Class, and Interethnic Conflict

A YOUNG AFRICAN AMERICAN student tells us that in her experience as a Stanford Law student, she felt affirmative action helped only "people like me, who had parents who were educated. It didn't help the neediest."

A young Chinese American woman says, "I support affirmative action, but my brother doesn't. He believes Asians will make it without affirmative action, because other people already think of us as smart and hard-working. We shouldn't antagonize them with demands for affirmative action. We grew up in the same housing project in the Bronx, but I just can't get him to see it the way I see it."

An older Chinese American veteran of the civil rights movement admitted, "I'm conflicted about set-asides. Some of these people — new Asian immigrants who take advantage of minority business programs and then turn around and exploit Chinese workers — frankly, I don't see why they should have anything more than Russian immigrants." When he senses resistance in the listener, he adds the killing blow: "I sit in meetings with them and they say really racist things about Blacks. You should hear them."

A historian comments on National Public Radio: "One of the reasons for results-oriented affirmative action has been that African Americans have a legacy of slavery and caste which is unique in American history. There is nothing like it. All other groups except for Native American Indians — and that's a totally different subject . . . are either immigrants now or the descendants of immigrants who came free."[1]

Even within communities of color, the debate continues. Unlike race traitors, these debaters want affirmative action to work, but they aren't sure about how it should work, given the dynamics that divide us both within and among minority communities.

In San Francisco, the Chinese American community is bitterly divided, with the Chinese American Democratic Club on one side and Chinese for Affirmative Action on the other. The Democratic Club has brought suit against the San Francisco school district, attempting to dismantle a civil rights consent decree that requires numerical racial balance in the public schools. The consent decree, which resulted from a history of *de jure* segregation in San Francisco schools, set forth a desegregation plan under which no one racial group would constitute a majority in any school. The decree thus dismantled years of entrenched segregation in San Francisco schools, segregation that Chinese American activism helped end. Why, then, were so many Chinese families opposed to the consent decree? There was one academic magnet school, Lowell High School, that was now turning away Chinese applicants in significant numbers. Under the consent decree, the school district was compelled to make sure there were not more than 40 percent Chinese at Lowell. This meant that Chinese applicants had to have higher grade point averages and higher test scores than students of all other races in order to get into Lowell. Chinese Americans were asked to step aside in order to make room for "underrepresented" groups, including whites, Blacks, Latinos, and non-Chinese Asians. Quoting Martin Luther King, the Chinese American Democratic Club called this a discriminatory quota. Chinese for Affirmative Action responded by pointing out that similar consent decrees mandating fair representation of all racial groups in the city had opened doors for Chinese in the fire department, the police department, in government contracting, and in the private sector. The principle of affirmative action and the cause of civil rights are central to Chinese-American self-interest, Chinese for Affirmative Action argued, and the fact that some Chinese might not go to their school of choice was a reasonable price to pay to meet the broader goals of the civil rights coalition.

I raised the Lowell case with students. Some echoed the position of Chinese for Affirmative Action. Wanting to push them, I asked, "What about the mother in Chinatown — a garment worker who has no pension, who wants an elite education for her children because the entire family's economic future depends on it? What are you going to tell her when she sees others with lower scores getting into Lowell while her kids are left in a neighborhood school from which few go on to college?"

"I could not look her in the eye," said one thoughtful young man, the president of the Asian Pacific American Law Students Association, "and tell her it is for the greater good."

Who should the immediate beneficiaries of affirmative action be, and at what cost, to whom? People of color have worked hard to raise consciousness about the complexity of the experience of race in the United States. Asians and Latinos are quick to point out that "black and white" does not capture the full picture. Asian Americans struggle against the model minority myth, demanding examination of class stratification and the disparate experience of various Asian subgroups: Filipino Americans are not the same as Japanese Americans, are not the same as Korean Americans, and so on. Similarly, in the Black community, Caribbean Americans, Afro-Latinos, and recent immigrants from Africa represent a diversity of culture and experience, and different — though not completely disconnected — relations to the African diaspora.

Added to this fragmentation within each group is the growing number of biracial-multicultural people who, by either descent or practice, live on the borders between ethnicities. Emphasizing the complexity of racial categorization makes the application of affirmative action complex, and that, in the eyes of certain right-wing analysts, is a reason to abandon it altogether. If race is complicated, then racial remediation is impossible, they seem to argue. If race is complicated, then racism must be over.

This is a copout at best and a deliberate reinvigoration of white supremacy at worst. The call to get smarter about race, to understand the rich texture of racialized experience in America, to acknowledge racism as a force operating in many guises, is a call for intelligent thinking about how to end racial oppression. Ignoring racism is not an intelligent response to the complexity of race.

The social construction of racial categorization, the history of cultural interaction, and the reality of class stratification within racial groups is part of the story of how racism affects our landscape. The complex and intersecting social planes of racism and class stratification call for expanded affirmative action. If all Asians are not alike, having a token Asian in any given setting does not achieve fair representation. If class stratification and racism plague particular groups, adding affirmative action for those disadvantaged by class is part — and only part — of the solution.

The myth that affirmative action helps only the privileged is often accepted, even among students of color. It assumes that the sole beneficiaries of affirmative action are "privileged" women and minorities. In fact, the opposite is true. Affirmative action has been least effective in forcing integration of high-status jobs — professors, CEOs, law firm partnerships — where subjective evaluation and white male social capital still reign supreme.

Affirmative action is the only reason that women and people of color who were historically excluded from such jobs as those in the building trades, in mining and industry, and in police and fire departments have had a chance to enter those professions in the small numbers they have. Affirmative action in the trades has brought more than a few single mothers off welfare, and it has helped move significant numbers of poor people of color into the middle class. The courageous lives of those who have used affirmative action to become the first in a range of hostile blue-collar environments show how affirmative action can put food on the table. Deleting this story from the current dialogue is part of a propaganda campaign intended to make affirmative action seem like cream-skimming for the privileged.

Similarly, many first-generation college graduates are the products of affirmative action. It is not surprising that students of color at elite universities look around and see privilege among their peers. Admittedly, the limited form of affirmative action that some universities have undertaken picks out those students of color who are most like the economically advantaged white students who predominate on campus. Nonetheless, affirmative action programs at the universities have given sons and daughters of migrant farm workers, garment industry toilers, maids, busboys, and janitors the chance to gain an education.

There is still far to go.[2] Minority enrollment in graduate schools remains way behind that of whites and is in danger of declining, a fact not unconnected to class. In 1975, during the first wave of affirmative action, 650 Black men received Ph.D.s. By 1986, that number had dropped to 320. Black graduate students come from the poorest socioeconomic backgrounds of all graduate students, and Black candidates are among those most directly affected by the shrinkage of available loans and financial aid.

Affirmative action in the academy is about ensuring access, not maintaining privilege. In our own teaching experience, we have seen a generation of students brought to the law schools by affirmative action and can testify that they were largely *not* from privileged backgrounds. They are not all "Cosby kids"; they don't have cars, trust funds, or family friends who are doctors or lawyers. Because they are the students who successfully acquired the skills — both social and educational — to move confidently in elite institutions, their humble origins are often masked. Their peers and professors don't realize that they are sending half of their financial aid check home to help their parents pay the rent. They "don't sound like" people who grew up in public housing projects or who have siblings in prison. Only those whom they trust with their stories will find out how hard they must work to act as though they belong where they are.

Even among the students of color who do come from middle-class families, we see a moderate level of privilege that rarely matches that of their white peers. The social workers, teachers, and even doctors and lawyers of color who are able to provide their children with outstanding preparation for higher education are themselves often limited in their opportunities for advancement and are seldom notably wealthy. The reality of the glass ceiling, and the history of professional barriers, have ensured that the income of white professionals is significantly higher than that of people of color with the same level of education.[3]

More than one law professor of color can attest that her educated, middle-class parents had to go down to the principal's office and make a scene when the school tried to place her on a "nonacademic track." When they become parents themselves, our professor friends often find themselves engaged in the same fight on behalf of their children. We have heard this narrative so many times that we believe it is the norm for middle-class families of color. In a racialized society, economic and educational privilege does not equate with equal opportunity.

We have worked with generations of students who came to law

school through affirmative action, and we testify that it is a lie that affirmative action "only helps the privileged."

The portraits throughout this book are our way to give a human face to the truth we know: the beneficiaries of affirmative action need and deserve the gifts they receive, and they return those gifts tenfold to the community. Thus, our first response to those who worry that affirmative action is reproducing privilege is empirical. Those who are actually helped by affirmative action are deserving and talented people who never would have had a chance without it. Our second response is to acknowledge a partial truth in the claim: yes, affirmative action does not go far enough. It does not and cannot do enough to help the neediest, but that is not a reason to roll it back.

It is important to ask who is making the criticism of privilege and to what end. When neoconservatives argue that affirmative action is a handout to upper-class Blacks, that it does nothing for the disadvantaged, we are unimpressed.[4] The depth of their concern for the poor is questionable, given their opposition to social welfare programs designed to eradicate poverty. When our students, uneasy about their own privilege, make the criticism, however, we would like to respond thoughtfully.

At one level, it is true that those who can take advantage of affirmative action at the college and graduate school level are children of privilege. Something in their lives, often intelligent and aggressive parent advocates who value education, has made it possible for them to attain the level of preparation necessary to enter the university. It is neither surprising nor unjust that students with this kind of advantage are those who come to the university under affirmative action. Open admissions and programs extending academic opportunities to students who are not as well prepared are innovations that should exist alongside traditional affirmative action programs that consider race and gender in deciding among many well-qualified applicants.

In our experience, the students of color who are able to survive under the present system of higher education are those who bring a diversity of thought and experience to the academy, regardless of their privileges. Racism crosses class lines in America. Even relatively privileged students of color have had encounters with the police, for example, that reveal the racist structure of law enforcement. Immigrant students who have benefited from their parents' work ethic and emotional support also know subtle and blatant disadvantage. They witness how bankers who don't trust a foreign accent treat their parents. They know what immigrant families are really like, and they can dissolve the myth that "those immigrants" are lazy welfare cheats. That students admitted to the university under affirmative action are not always the most financially needy in their community takes nothing away from the perspectives they bring to academic life.

The "but they are all so privileged" argument adopts a narrow and ahistoric interpretation of affirmative action, as though the program's only goal is the eradication of poverty. Furthermore, it ignores the fact that poverty is connected to race and gender bias, such that working toward race and gender equity is a means of working against poverty. The number of women in poverty is related to the fact that women are underrepresented in the jobs — both white collar and blue collar — that pay the best salaries. The number of Black children who die before their first birthday — more than twice as many as white children[5] — is related to the fact that Blacks are underrepresented in medicine, public health, and, most significantly, in the "managerial class" jobs that produce the information and public policy decisions governing distribution of resources in this country.

To say "our law school's affirmative action program isn't going to do anything for the kids in the barrio" is both true and untrue. Untrue, because some kids from poor neighborhoods do manage to take advantage of affirmative action, and because middle-class Chicano students are far more likely to know and care about the barrio and to act on that basis in their life's work. It is true, however, that most kids from the barrio will not take advantage of the law school affirmative action program because most of them won't make it to college. That brings us to the rethinking, once again, of merit.

Affirmative action admissions programs currently in place rarely make the effort to evaluate entry criteria critically. If the mission of the university is to serve the elite, then it makes sense to use entry criteria that replicate the elite. The present system, which rewards the prestige and level of a student's prior education, and which relies on tests that measure social and educational privilege, is an excellent system for identifying people most like those who already hold power. Most law schools, for example, recalculate grade point averages by a numerical factor that gives a bonus to students who went to Ivy League schools. For the large numbers of working-class students who go to state universities, this means that their grade point average is discounted: a B at Harvard is worth more than a B at State U in the graduate school admissions process.

A version of affirmative action that serves elite needs uses such standard admission practices, perhaps "lowering the threshold" slightly, in order to recruit the people of color most likely to assimilate and thrive in the business-as-usual environment of high-status education.

Seeing the mission of the university differently, however, suggests different admissions criteria. Among the many goals of the university, reproducing an elite is the least legitimate. Other goals should be to serve underrepresented communities and to promote the general increase in knowledge that comes from interaction among different cultural perspectives. These additional goals suggest different talents, measured by different criteria.

The most radical mission of the university is to expand both justice and learning, as part of a claim that neither can proceed without the other. A just university seeks to end subordination of all kinds by making higher education available to the least advantaged. This mission statement calls for a major retooling of every aspect of the university, from admissions to curriculum to staffing to research. It will require that universities commit vast resources to early childhood education, public health, high-quality public schools at all levels, and remedial education for those who fall through the cracks, so that all children have the chance to benefit from the riches of higher learning. From the many critics, liberal and conservative, who have complained that "affirmative action helps only the privileged," we have never heard an argument for such re-envisioning of the obligations of the university. While they deride affirmative action for not going far enough, the critics show no intention of actually working for a less class-bound distribution of educational resources.

If it were factually true — and our experience tells us it is not — that the overwhelming majority of the beneficiaries of affirmative action are concerned neither with justice for their communities nor with making a difference in the battle against sexism and racism in the fields they have entered, then that is reason to expand affirmative action, not to contract it. We should return to the original criteria for affirmative action, asking whether helping a particular individual will help end the subordination of the community she comes from. This would mean asking more than the question of identity. From among the pool of women, people of color, and other excluded groups, we might ask who among them has the demonstrated ability and commitment to serve as an agent for change. This question may mean one thing when it is asked to determine who is best qualified for graduate school and another when we are deciding who should get a blue-collar job. A Black woman who wants to work on a construction crew, for example, may have no interest in uplifting her race; her main concern may be uplifting herself. Her very presence, doing the work Black women are usually denied and making a decent living for her family, makes her an agent for change. For more privileged benefits, however, it may be fair to ask a greater level of commitment to work on behalf of others.

When earlier generations of students sat in, organized, and agitated to implement affirmative action at universities across the country, they insisted that the criteria for selecting beneficiaries go beyond mere identity. They wanted inclusion of those who had overcome disadvantage, and expansion of the pool of talent that could serve underrepresented communities. The first affirmative action programs inquired specifically into these things and involved students and community members in identifying those who met the criteria. This form of community-based affirmative action by definition was immune from the charge that it helped only the privileged. At school after school, however, the student members were dropped from the admissions committees, and community participation disappeared as the initial activism faded and university bureaucrats took over and redefined affirmative action.

We challenge those who are concerned about the limited reach of affirmative action to call for a return to the community-based model, and for an expansion of affirmative action to include the economically disadvantaged.

The argument that affirmative action helps the undeserving crops up with specific reference to business set-asides for minorities. Why should we set aside part of public expenditures to benefit minority-owned businesses, the argument goes, when for the most part anyone with the resources to go into business is well off to begin with? Why should we assume that racial or gender identity makes these contractors more worthy than others who may suffer various kinds of disadvantage? For grassroots activists concerned with providing jobs, housing, education, and basic needs, it is sometimes difficult to see why we should care at all whether Mr. Black Enterprise television station owner or Ms. M.B.A. Asian American stockbroker gets a government contract, particularly when he or she has shown no commitment to the principle of "lift while you climb."

The first and least radical reason for maintaining set-asides is the argument of plain old fairness. In California, before the current assault on affirmative action there, the state goal for contracting with women-owned businesses was only 5 percent. In Los Angeles, with a 66 percent minority population, minority-owned businesses received only 5 percent of public works expenditures. In short, set-aside programs have achieved nothing even approaching parity.[6]

Set-asides were originally devised to counter corrupt and discriminatory practices that reserved the benefit of government work for the buddies of those in power. Whom a person knew, bribed, or supported in an election, along with garden variety racial exclusion, determined who had access to government largesse. Processes for submitting bids for jobs, for finding out about available work, for meeting complex qualifying criteria, for meeting the requirement of "prior work," were sufficiently complex and obscure to keep outsiders — typically, women and people of color — from getting government work. Bank loans, insurance bonding, credit with equipment suppliers, access to a high-quality workforce and sufficient capitalization to survive lean times and to benefit from economies of scale — all of these were easier for established, well-connected businesses to obtain. To the extent that business connections facilitated government contracting, private club discrimination became a relevant factor. As Edwin Lee, director of the San Francisco Human Rights Commission, stated in defending set-asides, "Business relationships reflect the social relationships within our communities. Private social clubs (e.g., country clubs) spawn such business connections."[7]

Reserving construction work for insiders, given that the work represents a distribution of tax dollars collected from all citizens, results in an upward redistribution of wealth. In fact, because many capital improvement projects are supported by regressive revenue sources — user fees, lotteries, and excise taxes — women and people of color, who have lower incomes, pay more than their fair share into the funds that are passed out to government contractors. The contract set-aside is an expedient way to see some of the revenue return to those who generate it. It is the primary way that the small percentage of women and minority-owned businesses that participate in government contracting have made modest advances.

Like all expedients, set-asides are imperfect. There is no guarantee that minority contractors will hire, train, and promote more people of color or that their business practices will ultimately reflect community values. Nonetheless, many minority contractors bring new cultural values to the marketplace, respecting and promoting the needs of underrepresented communities.

Black-owned entertainment companies, for example, have provided culturally diverse programming and created an entry point for new media talent.[8] Minority building contractors have hired and trained people of color who would not otherwise get a foothold in the building trades.[9] Having a modest part of government expenditures go to individuals who are willing to put aside racist stereotypes and give a young person a job is an important gain.

Set-asides also help to dispel cultural stereotypes about who can be a contractor. Given the deep race and gender coding that tell us "network CEO" or "stockbroker" or "building contractor" means white and male, it is important to have visible examples that defy the code. Government can use part of its spending power in an affirmative way to teach an important lesson: a woman can do this; an African American can do this. Set-asides are government speech on behalf of equal opportunity. If images, ideas, and speech affect action, it makes sense for the government to use these tools in the fight against discrimination.

Contrary to the race-baiting complaints, the majority of minority contractors are not rich. Many woman- and minority-owned businesses were started by individuals who were frustrated by prejudice in the job market: immigrants who were kept out of jobs because of their accents; women who hit the glass ceiling; people of color "down-sized" under last-hired, first-fired policies. Entrepreneurship is an alternative to welfare or joblessness for those who run small food, cleaning, and service firms that rely on government contracts. Those small contractors often live on the economic margins, working long hours with none of the security or benefits of an ordinary job.

Set-asides represent only a tiny part of government spending, directed to qualified firms. None of the criteria for qualification is lowered or altered in the set-aside process. The programs typically require that, from among the qualified contractors, a small number of minority- or woman-owned businesses share in the work.

There remains, however, the legitimate complaint that not all set-aside beneficiaries are sensitive to community needs and that some programs can invite fraud and windfalls. These problems are endemic to any contracting program that hands out millions of dollars without public scrutiny or oversight. Witness the repeated scandals in military procurement. If fraud and windfalls are problems, they are best dealt with by restructuring the program to penalize fraud and redirect benefits to communities rather than individuals. As one commentator noted, those voicing recent complaints that FCC licensing set-asides have made overnight "black millionaires"[10] ignore a history of an FCC that has created overnight white millionaires.

Similarly, if labor exploitation is a growing problem as government outsources its functions to private contractors, then all contracts should require hiring union labor under decent working conditions. These problems are not created by set-asides. It is important to understand that present affirmative action plans represent a compromise, a concession. Set-asides came about because poor people in Chinatown got sick of seeing crew after crew of white construction workers building the redevelopment projects. Added to the insult of evictions and dislocations brought by these projects was the sting of showing up day after day at the worksite only to see the jobs go to whites from outside the community. Organizers developed the tactic of shutting down construction projects: "If we can't have a share of the jobs, we will sit down in front of the bulldozer until you have a change of heart." The potential for disruption by such actions in impoverished communities throughout the country was dealt with by making a concession: contract set-asides.

Under the community control model, affected families would

control every aspect of a new development project, from design to construction. They would hire and fire the contractors, considering a range of community needs, from nondiscriminatory employment practices to reasonableness of costs to health and safety to sensitivity to the particular cultures of residents. Community control also would provide an equity interest in construction companies so that the profits from development would return to benefit the community.

Community control is full-scale affirmative action directed at the most needy. Set-asides are a weak tool by comparison, but one that makes sense in the struggle between the forces of change and the status quo. Set-asides allow the large corporations that currently monopolize the building trades to continue to do so, provided they make the minor concession of hiring a few minority subcontractors. The arrangement keeps profits returning to banks and outside corporate investors, and does nothing to redistribute wealth.

One possible alternative is to rework set-aside programs to evaluate not only ownership but community connection and commitment to include those traditionally excluded. A white-owned business with a demonstrated track record in hiring, training, and promoting members of excluded groups, for example, might be more deserving of a contract than a minority-owned business with a history of worker exploitation and union busting. A community-oriented set-aside program could recognize this distinction.

Fine-tuning qualifications for set-asides is an adjunct to, not a replacement for, old-fashioned headcounting. Headcounting is simplistic and is not an end-all. Nonetheless, when we look around a room marked "tax dollars spent here" and find that all the people in the room look the same, we should ask why, and understand what institutional and historical factors keep some people out of the room.

The complaint that set-asides shoot too broadly at a narrow target, benefiting the undeserving, is like the complaint that affirmative action in college admissions helps only the "Cosby kids." The demand that the remedy work with precision, that it benefit only the neediest, disregards the persistent reality of white male privilege. The overwhelming majority of government contracts, of graduate degrees, of teaching positions at the universities go to white men, a group that represents a minority of the populace. All the talk about class, the endless citings of the "poor white male from Appalachia," cannot avoid the reality of race and gender privilege. No antipoverty program can end that privilege. Only affirmative action, targeting race and gender, can end it.

Affirmative action is imprecise only under an ideology that ignores group advantage and disadvantage. The demand that we find the one Black person who best represents the race, and who is the least advantaged, ignores the power of group disadvantage. Patriarchy doesn't pick out certain women to disadvantage the most. The virulence of patriarchy — the reason a women's movement rose up to fight it — lies in its stunning breadth.

Similarly, racism doesn't reside in pockets of the Black community. It travels up and down the class ladder, appearing in a variety of forms, from residential steering to cross burnings to media stereotyping. Indeed, Blacks frequently get blindsided by racism where they least expect it, making the constancy of wary watching one of the saddest parts of existence on the downside of the color line.

Given this group experience of racism and patriarchy, group remedies make sense. Such remedies do not focus on individuals precisely because the evil to eradicate does not focus on individuals. The demand for precision — "show me you are a bona fide victim before you sign up for this benefit" — misunderstands the problem to be corrected and the historical origins of affirmative action.

The myth of the undeserving minority is used to fuel resentment among poor and working-class whites, leading some to ask whether the breakdown of any possible coalition between working-class whites and people of color is a price worth paying for the remedy of affirmative action.

Does affirmative action pit have-not against have-not? Both within communities of color and between people of color and working-class whites, affirmative action can be used to set up a competition for a perceived limited pile of goods. Historians tell us, however, that this competition predates affirmative action. In 1949 a union-backed Democratic candidate for the mayor of Detroit lost an election to an anti-integration race baiter. Union activists were stunned. How could this happen in the heartland of the New Deal coalition, a district that was solidly working class, solidly pro-union, solidly Democratic? Union voters dropped the Democrats the minute the blockbusters appeared, paying Black women to walk their babies down the street in white neighborhoods, while anti-integration activists warned of a coming invasion.

This story, described by the historian Thomas Sugrue,[11] is one of many that show that the divisiveness attributed to affirmative action is in fact part of the history of racial division that marks any attempt at civil rights advancement in this country.

The solution is not an end to civil rights initiative, but coalition building that starts where human needs are: better schools, decent jobs, childcare, health care. These shared concerns can unite working-class whites with people of color. There is a history of interracial coalitions forged around those needs that we can learn from.[12]

There remains, though, the problem of special claims to affirmative action — or affirmative action plus. There are some groups — like African Americans in relation to slavery, Native Americans in relation to the genocide of their people, Chicanos in relation to conquest of Mexican territories in the Southwest and the abdication of the treaty of Guadalupe Hidalgo, and refugees from conflicts generated by particularly egregious U.S. foreign policy debacles — that justifiably see their claim to remediation as unique in the context of American history.

There are some claims that command recognition as peculiarly American horrors. How we choose to acknowledge and heal ourselves from those parts of our history is the test of our national integrity. Some want to use the reality of particularly horrific harms to limit affirmative action, as if to say, "All right, slavery was wrong, so let's give something to African Americans and that's it: we won't hear any other complaints." This kind of rhetoric contains both a notion of desert (only a few true victims deserve remediation) and a notion of hierarchy (make an ascending list of the aggrieved and lop off everything below the top as beyond our capacity to care for). The most progressive, active, and thoughtful members of communities with longstanding grievances recognize the limitation of this rhetoric: it is concerned with keeping narrow accounts rather than with rectifying our troubles in a forward-thinking way. The argument that people of color other than African Americans should be excluded from affirmative action is not being made by the leaders of the African American civil rights movement, for they know that it will not bring liberation to any of us.

Foes of affirmative action love to point out that among subordinated groups in our society there are disputes and tensions, such that affirmative care directed at one group can cause resentment within another. The reality of the history of interethnic conflict means that we have to work consciously to forge interethnic coalitions and to build increasing opportunities, so that no benefit to one person or one group is seen as taking away from others.

Asian Americans have lived in the buffer zone of racial relations since their arrival on this continent. Courts debated whether Asians were more like Indians or whites or Africans for purposes of the racial classifications critical for maintaining racial hierarchy. Could Asians serve on juries? Could they become naturalized citizens? Could they marry whites? Nineteenth-century judges searched through the literature of the pseudo-science of racial classification to find the answers. The answers were equivocal, with the result that Asians occupy, historically, an uneasy place in the middle of a constructed racial hierarchy.

In right-wing proclamations in the affirmative action debate, Asians are either the unfortunate victims of quotas, the undeserving beneficiaries of preferences, or the success story proving that no one needs affirmative action. Asian Americans are a rhetorical Ping-Pong ball in the debate.

"Asians are facing a real danger of being discriminated against because of the number who are getting admitted to places like Berkeley and Cal Tech." House Speaker Newt Gingrich.[13]

"Are Asians an oppressed group in the United States today? Are they worse off for lacking sizable representation on the faculties of American law schools? Are Japanese and Chinese Americans in particular, whose incomes and education compare so favorably with those of white Americans, really entitled to a leg up in law school hiring?" Judge Richard Posner, U.S. Court of Appeals for the Seventh Circuit, arguing against affirmative action for Asians.[14]

"Why should Americans of Irish descent, who are in the median-income range, be discriminated against in favor of Americans of Chinese or Japanese ancestry, who are at the top?" Patrick Buchanan.[15]

"By all major measures, the 7.5 million Asian Americans (3 percent of the population) are big winners in American life. They are more likely than white Americans to have college educations, high-status professional careers, and high incomes . . . Asian Americans have been succeeding without affirmative action. The ultimate problem is not that they may make blacks and Hispanics look bad — it is that they are making the civil rights bureaucracy look irrelevant." Columnist in *Fortune* magazine.[16]

"Quota systems hurt Asians the hardest." Dana Rohrbacher, member of U.S. Congress.[17]

In the rhetoric of anti–affirmative action, Asians are both victims and success stories. As victims, they are painted as brilliant and hardworking, the ones who get shut out of jobs and educational opportunities in order to maintain quotas for others. As a success story, questionable statistics are cited to "prove" that Asians have made it and that they don't need affirmative action.

An article in the Duke Law Journal inaccurately notes, "In 1980, Japanese-Americans had incomes more than 32% above the national average, and Chinese-Americans had incomes more than 12% above . . . Also in 1980, 17.8% of the white population aged 25 or over had completed four or more years of college, compared to 32.9% of the Asian-American population."[18] We were curious about these statistics because they contradicted both our own experiential knowledge and the statistics we were familiar with. Here is the empirical truth: Asian Americans make less than white Americans. In 1990, the average Asian American per capita income was $13,638, compared with $15,687 for whites.[19]

The author of the article, Judge Posner, relied on a chart in an old anti–affirmative action essay by Thomas Sowell for his claim.[20] It turns out that the source of the chart was Sowell's dubious compilation of three different statistical sources. Contrary to Posner's date, 1980, the data Sowell used for Japanese Americans was from 1969. Moreover, the chart was based on family income, not individual income, as Posner's footnote implied. Japanese Americans, for reasons having more to do with economic deprivation than with economic privilege, have always had a higher number of wage earners in the family than the national average. This was particularly true twenty-five years ago, when fewer white families were headed by two wage earners. The chart was further confused by the fact, revealed only in the endnotes at the back of the

Sowell book, that Sowell used different sources for his raw data on different ethnic groups, including two separate U.S. censuses and a private study. No controls for sample size, method of inquiry used in various years for various groups, size of families, or number of wage earners were suggested in Sowell's endnote, although the chart itself purported to rank ethnic groups by income. Similarly, neither Sowell nor Posner mentioned a number of facts that make comparison of average white family income and average Japanese American income misleading, such as the fact that Japanese Americans are largely concentrated in geographic locations, such as Hawaii, urban and suburban California, and New York, where both wages and cost of living are higher than the national average.

Sowell's chart also claimed that Jewish families had the highest income in the United States. The endnote, however, revealed that no census data were available for Jews and that data from a private study were used for the Jewish figures. The reader was given no information about how that study was conducted, or why data collected from a noncensus source were used in a chart that supposedly ranked according to one set of criteria. The dangerous anti-Semitic myths surrounding the belief that Jews possess economic advantages should call for the utmost care in presenting charts that purported to show Jews as being "better off" than every other ethnic group.

Why is it that Sowell's initial editor, as well as Judge Posner and the editors of the Duke Law Journal, were all willing to accept Sowell's ranking? Some cultural knowledge precedes the facts. It is a widely held belief among Americans that Jews and Asians have extraordinary economic advantage, that they have made it, that "ordinary" people are at a disadvantage in competition with them. Recent books suggesting the genetic inferiority of some racial groups have concomitantly suggested that Asians are superior in natural intelligence.[21]

All of these praises of success are connected to a dark undercurrent of anti-Semitism and Asian-bashing. "Smart" and "hard-working" so easily degenerate into cunning, inscrutable, taking over, running everything, secret cabals, and the Protocols of the Elders of Zion.

Similarly, Posner's statistics on educational attainment are questionable. He suggests that Asian Americans have won the sweepstakes of educational advantage in this country. In fact, Asians are still underrepresented in significant sectors of the academy, still have disproportionately low rates of admission to elite schools, and virtually disappear at the graduate and faculty level in most fields, including all of the humanities and social sciences. That many Asians do show up on the census as having had four or more years of college is due, in large part, to immigration policies that favor people holding technical degrees. The Glass Ceiling Report stated that "two-thirds to three-fourths of highly educated Asian and Pacific Islander American population are foreign-educated or immigrants who initially came to the U.S. as foreign students."[22] Anyone familiar with the Asian American community can talk about immigrants with Ph.D.s who drive taxis, scrub floors, or struggle to run marginal small businesses because their foreign degrees are not valued in the marketplace.[23] Raw census data cannot tell this story, nor do they account for the age differentials in the white and Asian populations. The latter is younger as a whole than the white population, factors contributing to the greater concentration of college-aged individuals.

It is thus inaccurate to use gross census data to support the claim that Asians have better access to education than the average American. Nonetheless, since the 1980s, a rash of news stories and media portrayals have further perpetuated this myth of Asian success.[24] Because of this construction of "Asian" as "success story," other stories get squeezed out of the cognitive marketplace. Within the Asian American community, the story of Asian American poverty, social dislocation, and economic uncertainty is often told, but it never makes the networks.[25]

The true story of Asian success is that it has a high price. Many Asian Americans do value education and do excel in the academic arena. Unfortunately, they receive fewer rewards for their excellence than do whites with comparable education. As the Glass Ceiling Commission reported, "Despite higher levels of formal education than other groups, Asian and Pacific Islander Americans receive a lower yield in terms of income or promotions."[26] According to U.S. Census data, whites with college degrees make almost 11 percent more than Asian Pacific Americans with college degrees, and white high school graduates make 26 percent more than Asian Pacific American high school graduates.[27]

The reality of wage differentials and glass ceilings makes academic overachievement all the more important to Asian Americans and sets the context for the affirmative action drama at Lowell High School.

The decline of public schools in most American cities signals a trend of wealthy urban parents tending to rely on private schools. Parents who are poor or working class, or members of the relatively well-off but economically insecure middle class, are left to hustle their children into the few public schools that are still considered good. The average parent looks for a school where guns and drugs are relatively absent, whose graduates go on to college, and where advanced placement classes and extracurricular activities create an atmosphere of success. Unfortunately, good public schools are rarities in urban America.

Devoted parents hire coaches for entrance exams, camp out all night on enrollment days, lie about their residency, cajole principals, and cruise the PTA meetings for scraps of information about how to work the system. They also bring lawsuits. To anyone who finds these efforts extreme, parents say fiercely, "These are my children and I must do what I can to assure their educational survival."

Few parents feel comfortable doing less in a world of rapidly shrinking opportunity. The economic forecasters tell us that the gap between rich and poor is growing at unprecedented rates, and that the demarcation between have and have-not is, more and more, drawn according to education.[28]

San Francisco's Lowell High School litigation is a story of interethnic conflict over diminishing educational resources.[29] Lowell was originally the exclusive domain of wealthy whites. The school produced Nobel laureates, a governor, and a Supreme Court justice. As a result of the desegregation consent decree, Lowell High School has added to its academic reputation an unprecedented racial diversity. The school became a model of advanced academic achievement in an integrated setting, and the students at Lowell, along with their parents, agreed that this new, integrated Lowell was a success.

The success was flawed, however, in the eyes of those outside the gates. The problem with using a magnet school to save public education is that many students are excluded from the showcase schools that exist amid otherwise decaying systems. Lowell would be a nearly all-Chinese school if test scores alone determined admission. Because of the consent decree, however, racial balance was maintained by drawing from the top scorers in each of the city's racial groups. Asian Americans remained 70 percent of the enrollment at Lowell, with the Chinese subgroup capped at 40 percent.

To maintain this cap, many talented Chinese students were turned away, which is particularly troublesome because the high scores of students of Chinese descent are often as much a product of their subordination as of their privilege. Immigrant parents who fear racism teach their children that academic achievement is the key to survival. The children, knowing the economic uncertainty of their parents' lives, hear the message that it is up to them — that their admission to Lowell is the insurance policy for the entire family during hard times. Excelling in academics is a matter of survival. First-generation Chinese Americans regularly outscore fifth-generation Chinese Americans on the Lowell entrance exam, and they react with understandable rage when their efforts are rewarded with a hike in the entry requirements for them alone.

With real individuals standing outside the school gates, it is indeed difficult, as our student said in class, to speak blithely about the greater good. We have to speak plainly about the cost and dilemma of redistributing educational opportunity and the goal of racial justice. We have to ask, "On what ground, through what pain, do we make our multiracial coalitions?"

Chinese for Affirmative Action argues that integration, equal access to education, and multiculturalism are the foundation of the consent decree and are essential to the Chinese American community. When privilege was the order of the day in San Francisco, they point out, Chinese exclusion was absolute: no admission to Lowell, no political office, no public employment. The civil rights movement is what opened doors for Chinese in the city, and the principles of that movement are what Chinese must support. Integrated schools are successful schools. Racial balance is what keeps the majority of the public behind the public schools and provides the ethnic interaction that defines high-quality education in a changing world. An all-Chinese or predominantly Chinese Lowell High School could not provide this and would sacrifice the excellence — based in significant part on its diversity — that makes Lowell so desirable in the eyes of the students who want to go there and the college recruiters who seek out those students. And there is a practical reality: an all-Chinese magnet school would not survive the budget-cutting reflexes of the broader community. All taxpayers pay for Lowell, so its benefits must be available to a wide range of San Franciscans. Integration is morally right, politically astute, and educationally sound.

Those parents who feel their children are excluded argue that these are not goals they care to achieve at the expense of their own children's immediate needs. At one level, this is an irresolvable conflict. It is dishonest to claim that we can rectify racial injustice without immediate cost; affirmative action is not cost-free. Not every child can go to Lowell High School, and the just world in which every child can is beyond the schooldays of any child now living. This is the hard truth from which we start.

It is also not enough to point to past injustice to explain present remedy. In San Francisco no group can beat the Chinese in a contest comparing the historical wrongs inflicted by racism.[30] The history of racism in the Bay Area is, in large part, the history of Chinese exclusion, of Chinese interned on Angel Island, of violence against the Chinese, of sweatshops filled with Chinese workers, of Chinese deployed in the most dangerous jobs in the mines, in the fields, and on the railroads, creating much of the wealth that made the city.

The reality of the Lowell consent decree is racial remediation in a school system that lacks the resources justice requires. Even as progressive people of color support the consent decree at Lowell, they decry, loudly, any school system in which desperate parents know that only a few schools can offer their children a decent education. A good education for all was the original plan for public education in this country. It is supported by the majority of citizens, and it is attainable. That we have fallen so far from our goal is tied to the history of racism. In many communities, public schools are associated with children of color, and the political will to make those schools places of excellence is gone.

The consent decree was the product of a multiracial civil rights initiative. Although it was not, as legal remedies often are not, the ideal or most elegant way to tackle the longstanding racial exclusion at Lowell, it did transform a monocultural school into a place where young people of all races sit down in the same classrooms, interact, and obtain a first-class education. That is a success story. Not one without cost, but also not one we should abandon at this point in history.

On the timeline toward justice, the consent decree is not a permanent solution but a roughly hewn one that requires continual reassessment. As group dynamics change, as relations of relative privilege change, those sensitive to racial justice will note that the remedies must change. It may be that the large numbers of working-class immigrants of Chinese descent who are entering the public school system can show that their needs, their present disadvantage, justify modification of the consent decree. The high test scores of the group may mask pockets of exclusion within the Asian American community. Immigrants with particular histories — those from home countries where education is less available; those from ethnic subgroups for whom access to higher education is still an impossible dream; those who must overcome language barriers; or those who get those high test scores at the sacrifice of their carefree childhood — might offer a story that calls for a different interpretation of their scores as compared with those of a privileged child for whom high scores are an unthinking result of living in a home where parents leave the *New Yorker* magazine on top of the toilet tank and listen to NPR while driving to the grocery store.

A variety of alternatives to the present system exists. Some suggest a lottery from among the many students qualified for an advanced program like Lowell's. That is, set a minimum standard of excellence, and select students at random in proportions that will meet the 40 percent rule.[31] This will avoid the perceived unfairness of a system that sets different score requirements for each racial group. Under a lottery system, a few high-scoring members of each group will lose out to others with slightly lower scores, but this will be the product of chance rather than of a command to put higher scorers of one race below lower scorers of another race. It is critical to remember that scores and GPAs are not magic numbers. Any individual will score differently on different attempts at the same test, and the difference between the low end and the high end of the students admitted to a school like Lowell is insignificant in relation to their difference from the mean. That is, they are all excellent students. Given the relative meaninglessness of test-score differentials at this level, some reformers have suggested de-emphasizing test scores and adding criteria that reward overcoming disadvantage, such as attendance at one of the elementary schools known for providing substandard education — the schools in poor neighborhoods, the schools plagued by urban disarray.

While some alternatives may suggest a way out of the bitterness created by the test-score focus, racial balance remains a legitimate end. Places where people of different races can work together and learn about one another must exist. As residential segregation becomes more entrenched in this country, and as voluntary social interactions among races remain exceedingly rare, schools remain an important place to practice that which is essential to our survival as a multicultural country. We must learn enough about one another to live and work and govern together for the common good.

In this we differ from our student. We do believe we have to look each other in the eye and speak about the common good. Whether to the mother in Chinatown or the unemployed white construction worker who will vote for a race-baiting Republican candidate for the presidency, we need the courage to say, "The uncertainty facing all of us will end only when we pick up the least of us and rebuild this economy from the bottom up. Your anger and uncertainty are the beginning from which we can unite."

In our nation's capital, there are schools with fire code violations, schools with lead in the water fountains, schools with plaster falling from the ceiling. We could rebuild those schools, putting thousands to work. We could hire more teachers, at better salaries, and demand excellence from them. We could make every school — as was once this nation's dream — an excellent school, and every child a well-educated child. A magnet school may help a child get on the track for the managerial class, but it will not end the economic uncertainty that child faces, as recent downsizing, outsourcing, freelancing trends make clear; nor will it begin to deal with the general decline of public education that diminishes the human resources of this nation, worsening our stagnation and decay.

Through DNA studies, anthropologists now know that all of the human race once dwindled down to about four thousand to five thousand people many eons ago in the great cataclysmic periods that wiped out most other species. We almost didn't make it, and it is a miracle that we billions who descended from that small band even exist. In a magazine interview, one researcher was asked, "Why — why did we make it against the odds, when all those other species could not?"[32] The answer is haunting: we had large brains, and we were social, the anthropologist said. We lived in groups; we cared for one another; we figured out ways to change, to move, to adapt to great shifts in geography, climate, and available food.

Ours is a grieving species; we care for our young with desperate concern and remain forever inconsolable if we lose a loved one. Ours is a dynamic species; we invent and reason and struggle and strive in our efforts to adapt to changed circumstance.

To all the questions of interethnic, intraethnic, and class-based division that mark the affirmative action debate, we offer a lesson from our common ancestors: we are smart and we are social. We can figure out a way to bring up the bottom first, showing care for those persistently excluded from the processes and institutions of our society. We can reward the bridge-builders as we do this. In choosing from among the high scorers for admission to Lowell, in deciding who goes to graduate school, in awarding government contracts, we can add to the qualifying criteria questions designed to find those who can best deepen the understanding within our divided family and who will work to pull up those in danger of being left behind.

Finally, we can acknowledge complexity. None of the categories or criteria we use is the final word on how to deal with our problems. Knowing as much as we can about our own social conditions, becoming empirical, debating the hard questions, we can reshape the criteria and categories when we need to. We cannot, however, avoid the politics of power in any of this. Thus as we complexify, we also struggle, holding fast to the original purpose of affirmative action: to bring to the place of power those formerly excluded. In the spirit of the five thousand who chose change over death, may we, too, transcend the limits of past thinking and move forward as one social, inevitably connected tribe.

LAWRENCE LEVINE

"The unpredictable past"

THE STUDENTS IN Lawrence Levine's seminar at Berkeley are discussing a reading about the European immigrant experience in the early twentieth century. A Latina student explains her reaction to the article: "I've been having a lot of problems with my parents lately. I thought it was only because of a generation gap. Now I understand how much of it is because I was born here and they are immigrants." As she speaks, her voice breaks, and she begins to weep quietly.

It is no accident that this student finds herself confronting deep emotional responses to the immigrant experience. The watchword for Levine in his study of history is "empathy." The past is not a list of events to memorize; not a cast of characters to adulate. Whether we like them or not, people make up the past, and our job is to understand them.

In Professor Levine's history class, the students are called on to do just that. To know, understand, and empathize with the different inhabitants of the past. His own genealogy, from *shtetl* to working-class Manhattan to esteemed university chair, is always present in his conversations with students and colleagues. Asked how he negotiates so easily as a senior white man in a multicultural university that others find balkanized and filled with tension, he says, "I come at people with my immigrant experience. It disarms tensions and reduces barriers."

It was jazz, played in small Manhattan clubs, that planted the seed of an idea for Levine, one he claims to share with Benny Goodman and a generation of working class immigrants who fell in love with Black music: there is a way to live that is both on the margin and in the middle of what it means to be American. There is an excitement in that life far greater than that of simple assimilation. In jazz, Levine heard this message: you don't have to leave behind who you are.

We write of Lawrence Levine — white, Jewish, male — as a product of affirmative action in this sense: he is one who embraces newcomers to his world, who says with open enthusiasm that affirmative action has made his professional life rich beyond the limits of what earlier historians believed possible.

History, as this noted historian first learned it, looked nothing like the history he teaches today. "We had thick, dry books of narrative history, listing one event after the other, telling the same story of gradual progress centered on Northern Europe. I didn't know how to study then. I would make long lists of kings and queens and dates, and bring them home and memorize them. My mother would watch me, and she was so proud, so impressed. Who knows what she would have thought if I brought home a reading about the *shtetl*?"

When he went on to graduate school at Columbia, "clutching that City College degree," Levine says, "I knew nothing about the history of the lives of workers, children, women, slaves. Nothing about Africa other than ancient Egypt, nothing about Asia, nothing about South America after the age of exploration, nothing about Native Americans, about Canada, about Australia, nothing about most of the world and most of its cultures, past or present."

The curriculum today is thicker and deeply challenging, Levine says. Students are expected to know more and to think in more complex ways. This is the university after affirmative action — after women demanded attention to gender; after students of color demanded attention to ethnic history; after unquestioned assumptions about the centricity of European-derived culture were exploded by newcomers who insisted on the acknowledgment of difference. There is a paradox in Levine's assertion that historians got smarter when the newcomers challenged existing presumptions, for he himself is a staunch defender of the ability of scholarly outsiders to understand a culture, study it, and describe it. If he is right, why, then, do we need diversity in the academy? Why not let the dominant elite study diverse cultures without actually bringing to the university those who are culturally different?

In answering this question, Levine turns to his experience as a teacher and scholar. What women bring, he says, is an immediacy of commitment to and an insistence on asking the gender question. "It is in the front of their minds." Similarly, Black students think about slavery and the role of race when the classroom discussion focuses on topics like the Founding Fathers. "They ask the questions I used to have to ask for the class when I started teaching," bringing an urgency to the discussion that was missing before. "Sometimes it is cantish, but even then it is useful," he says. Sometimes there is tension and conflict, "but you don't change from a homogeneous to a heterogeneous university without that. The simplest time in the university was that time in the nineteenth century when young men of the same class and culture dominated. Things were easier because homogeneity ensured that there was more unanimity about what constituted acceptable ideas and behavior; because there was *more*, not less, of what today is called political correctness."

Levine himself was part of a post–World War II vanguard that made a return to the "simplest time" impossible. As a Jew and a child of an immigrant father, he was part of a generation that some historians feared could never understand the American past. In 1962, as Levine was revising his doctoral dissertation on William Jennings Bryan for publication, the head of the American Historical Association delivered a prestigious presidential address lamenting the changing demographics of the professorate:

> Many of the younger practitioners of our craft, and those who are still apprentices, are products of lower middle-class or foreign origins, and their emotions not infrequently get in the way of historical reconstructions. They find themselves in a very real sense outsiders to our past and feel themselves shut out. This is certainly not their fault, but it is true. They have no experience to assist them, and the chasm between them and the Remote Past widens every hour . . . What I fear is that the changes observant in the background and training of the present generation will make it impossible for them to communicate to and reconstruct the past for future generations.[1]

Levine and others like him were warned by a placement officer at Columbia that Jews would not be welcome on the faculties of many elite universities, and that they should apply to the City Colleges of New

York, where Jews could be hired and given tenure. In a sense, the fear that newcomers like Levine would change everything was well founded. Levine went on to become a prize-winning American historian and a recipient of a MacArthur "genius" grant, known for his gifted analysis of the history of American culture. His work — which includes studies of the culture of enslaved Africans, of nineteenth-century theatergoers, of twentieth-century American film — is marked by a deep appreciation of ordinary people and the dynamic interplay of their cultures. This son of a grocer who worked "fourteen hours a day, six and a half days a week," who grew up in a world populated by Jews on one side of the trolley tracks and immigrant Catholics on the other, became a skilled interpreter of cultural interactions, an intuitive reader of the social conditions that give rise to such phenomena as the popularity of Shakespeare on the Western frontier. His familiarity with cultural diversity, his empathy for the common person, his love of human beings, are revealed in his books and articles, part of the wave of social history that has changed his profession.

Affirmative action is threatening to some who come from a similar background: working-class ethnics who have succeeded in the intellectual world and who enjoy concomitant privileges. As a white who has written extensively about the lives of Black people, Levine is open to the charge of colonial scholarship, yet he speaks without a trace of defensiveness when asked about this possibility. "Anyone can write without understanding. A Black person can write colonial history. Outsiders always write history, because by definition the historian writes from outside the past. I have never felt personally under attack," he says.

He notes that he has been occasionally condescended to but never told he should not write about what he writes about. In fact, leading Black historians appreciate the "blackness" of his work. Larry Levine, the historian whose pledge is empathy, writes about Black people with the feel of the insider.

"Our obligation to the dead," he says, "is to understand." In his classes he sometimes passes around a picture of a white woman holding a small child, watching a lynching. We can all empathize, he tells his students solemnly, with the terror felt by the victim of that lynching. But what in the world was going on in *her* head, he asks, referring to the mother. He hesitates in recounting this bit of pedagogy: "Maybe you'd better not write about that." Maybe the reader — not knowing who he is and how his classes are conducted with such deep affection and respect for all students that taking risks is possible — will not understand what he is trying to do. He turns the story on himself, in a technique reflecting his skill at negotiating through difference. "I would be a lousy historian of the Nazis. I don't want to understand them. That is my disability. To understand," he continues, "is not to forgive. We need to get rid of that platitude. Understanding is not the same as liking, promoting."

When talking to Larry Levine about the changes he has seen in the academy, one gets a sense of boosterism. "Whites are a minority at Berkeley," he says; "it is what the whole country is going to look like by the year 2050." He speaks of the American nativist tradition as something we have seen before, a last gasp of empire sinking before an inexorable reality: this is a nation of many cultures, all rich, all bringing things worth knowing about. Rather than run from those differences or deprecate them, Levine, in his life and work, exudes a joyous, intelligent, appreciative, and critical view of America's cultures.

He has supported affirmative action in his profession and at the distinguished universities where he has taught. He says affirmative action has made everything better: the students, the curriculum, the scholarship. How do we understand him, his refusal to feel he is a target of others' nationalist anger; his open embrace of newcomers who might challenge his established position; his deep appreciation of cultures as foreign to his own as his once was to the intellectuals who ran the academy? In the end, what distinguishes him is intelligence, comfort with his immigrant roots, and genuine fascination with the complexity of human experience. As he talks about new research, the words tumble out in authoritative and excited pronouncements: what the primary sources reveal, how this connects to the insights of another historian, what this tells us about a misunderstood pocket of the American experience — all spoken of with an overarching sense of fun. Isn't it great, this life, this world, these amazing human beings who make up, as he has called it, "the unpredictable past"?

In his latest work, *The Opening of the American Mind*, Levine explores the history of the attack on multiculturalism in the university. Once again, he sounds his theme: ours is a country of cultures interacting in complex ways, against a background of ever-changing economics and demographics. The debate in the academy reflects this, Levine argues, and in this sense is inevitable: "We can no more escape history than the Americans of Lincoln's time could, and we are no less in need of his advice to 'disenthrall ourselves' from 'the dogmas of the quiet past.'"

In the men's room at an academic conference, a young untenured professor from a small Western college approaches a large, exuberant man whose long graying hair flows in slightly disheveled locks. The young professor says, shyly, "You're Larry Levine, aren't you? I just want to thank you for your presidential address. I made copies for everyone in my department. We've been debating some of those issues, and you put them in a way that people could understand."

Levine's address was a spirited defense of multiculturalism and social history, with pointed criticism of some of the big names in the profession who were lamenting the loss of "real" history. Although he thinks of himself as an outsider, his position in the academy gives him a voice of established authority. In spite of his characteristic self-deprecation, his encounter with the young professor reminds him of his responsibility to use that authority. There are many universities where social history is still considered aberrant, where young scholars face career uncertainty because their seniors do not know what to make of the culture wars. With his large intellect and confident presence, Levine urges his colleagues to keep their own minds open. In the closing words of his latest book:

> We need not a new history but a more profound and indeed more complex understanding of our old history. The need presses down upon us relentlessly, and we will ultimately be judged by how well we meet it, by how able we are to keep our understanding of the American past — and present — open, dynamic, and responsive, free of the weight of fixed symbols and rigid canons.

[8]

It's All the Same Thing:
Multiculturalism, PC, Hate Speech,
and the Critique of Identity Politics

"I can't even tell a joke anymore without someone calling me a sexist."

"Those immigrants move here and they won't even bother to learn English."

"People are teaching multicultural literature when kids don't even know Shakespeare."

"I couldn't even get an interview because they were looking for a minority."

"All of this focus on racial identity is leading to Balkanization."

"When you walk into a New York City subway car or a Los Angeles public school, it feels like you're in a third world country. Citizens should not be made to feel like strangers in their own land."[1]

WHEN WE LISTEN CAREFULLY — and even when we try not to hear — we encounter some version of complaints like these every day. We hear them from people whom we recognize as enemies. We also hear more subtle versions from friends and allies who share our vision of a just world. At first glance the grievances seem unrelated, but they have a ring of familiarity that tells us we've been here before. The debates over hate speech and sexual harassment, multiculturalism in the curriculum, "political correctness," English only, and identity politics raise substantive issues that we all need to talk about, but when we hear those sentiments expressed today they are too often in defense of the status quo. The troubling subtext of these comments is "Go back where you came from." They reflect a tremendous social anxiety brought about by the important but still small civil rights gains of the past three decades. In other words, they are both created by and directed against affirmative action.

We can trace such notions back to the eighteenth-century idealism of our forefathers. J. Hector St. John de Crèvecoeur emigrated from France to the American colonies in 1759 and settled in rural New York. In his *Letters from an American Farmer*, published during the American Revolution, he marveled at the diversity among other settlers, commenting on "a strange mixture of blood" that one could find in no other country. "From this promiscuous breed," he wrote, "that race now called Americans has arisen." Crèvecoeur reflected on this new American, "who, leaving behind him all his ancient prejudices and manners, receives new ones from the new mode of life he has embraced, the new government he obeys, and the new rank he holds . . . [and] who acts upon new principles." America was a place where "individuals of all nations are melted into a new race of men."[2]

As the historian Arthur Schlesinger, Jr., reminded us, in a similar vein, the motto *E pluribus unum* ("One out of many") holds the genius of the United States. "The goals of those who came to America were escape, deliverance, assimilation. They saw America as a transforming nation, banishing dismal memories and developing a unique national character based not on common ethnic origins, but on common political ideals and experiences. The point of America," Schlesinger wrote, "was not to preserve old cultures, but to establish a new American culture."[3]

But if a new race called Americans had indeed arisen, it was white. If America's European immigrants found unity in the shared political principles of self-government, individual freedom, and equality before the law, they were also made one by a shared belief in the racial superiority of whites and the preordained subordination of women.

Job Lawrence, my great-grandfather, shared Crèvecoeur's longing to embrace a new life, to leave behind the ancient prejudices, to disregard the badges and incidents of slavery, race, and to class, and to become a new man in a nation where the many would be one. My father first told me about my great-grandfather in a letter I have kept to remind me of my own American heritage.

Job Lawrence, as you know, was born in slavery and knew the ignominy of having his own father and title-holder sell him and my great-grandmother to his father's brother. It is not clear whether it was being sold or the silver dollar which my great-grandfather gave him that earned his everlasting enmity; but my grandfather later changed his name to Lawrence. (Lawrence is, thus, not our "slave name," but the name of a Pittsburgh paint manufacturer who befriended young Job after emancipation and encouraged him to get an education.)

Great-grandpa Job went to Maryville College in Tennessee and to divinity school at Howard. Like Crèvecoeur, he reached out to the new nation, serving as chaplain at a freedmen's hospital and establishing and pastoring colored churches along the foothills and valleys of the Great Smoky Mountains. He had a long and fruitful pastorate in Knoxville, Maryville, and Columbia, Tennessee. My father, always the sociologist, described him as "a prime example of Max Weber's 'ideal, typical this-worldly aesthetic' and a dyed-in-the-wool Calvinist." But America did not embrace Job Lawrence as it had embraced Crèvecoeur. As W.E.B. Du Bois wrote so eloquently of my great-grandfather's generation, "The Nation has not yet found peace from its sins; the freedman has not yet found in freedom his promised land. Whatever of good may have come in these years of change, the shadow of deep disappointment rests upon the Negro people."[4] Job knew well the horrors of the Civil War and the terrors of the Ku Klux Klan.

In 1888, when he was elected to the Knoxville school board to represent the town's colored population in matters concerning the segregated colored schools, there was an immediate outcry from the town's white populace, and the white board members refused to allow him to attend their meetings. The *Knoxville Daily Tribune,* in an editorial with the headline SOCIAL EQUALITY, called his appointment one that raised "serious questions," including the fact that Lawrence was a graduate of Maryville College, a school that advocated "the coeducation of the races" and trained its students to believe in the "idea of the social equality of the races as the thing to be desired, and that ought to be secured." The *Tribune* editorial noted with alarm that one of the professors at Maryville had even said that "the state statute forbidding the intermarriage of the races was a shame and disgrace to the state." The editorial closed with a call to action: "Let parents arise in their might and nip the coming of mixed schools and mixed everything in the bud. The parents of Knoxville seeing the evil can crush it."[5] Job sued the school board for denying him his seat, but the thinly veiled threat in the *Tribune's* editorial was not mere rhetoric in the days of lynch law. He left town in fear for his safety and that of his family.

The contradiction between the unifying American dream of inclusion and the reality of America's racism is what the Swedish sociologist Gunnar Myrdal called the "American dilemma."[6] Myrdal's comprehensive and influential mid-twentieth-century study of American race relations saw opportunity in the tension between ideal and reality. He believed the "American creed" was a beacon of hope for those excluded by the nation's racism and a spur to the white majority to live up to their proclaimed principles. Yet my great-grandfather Job knew that he must fight more than hope to make the American creed a reality, that he and his children's children must themselves become the spur to remind white America that its darker brothers and sisters are among the *pluribus* and that there can be no *unum* without us.

He also knew that neither he nor his children would survive the struggle for inclusion without the protection and nurturance of the communities that did embrace them, that he must teach his children pride in their race and culture so that they would know the full measure of their humanity in this land that valued them so little. If the ideal of one people was to become reality, the differences among the many must be treasured.

What we learn from studying backlash in social relations is that changes in conditions of domination are almost always initiated by the oppressed, not the oppressor. While the oppressed person has often internalized the ideology that rationalizes her subjugation, and both people in an unequal relationship have some investment in maintaining the status quo, the dominant person is likely to resist change with more predictability and greater tenacity.

This resistance is reflected in the backlash against affirmative action and multiculturalism in our universities. In the 1960s outsiders demanded access to education. In the 1970s they demanded access to *relevant* education, and after a series of student strikes and demonstrations at places like Harvard, Cornell, and San Francisco State, new disciplines joined the academy: Afro-American studies, Asian-American studies, Chicano studies. The sister discipline, women's studies, followed closely behind. Thus, those seeking inclusion first demanded the right to sit in classrooms and, second, the freedom to develop an identity, a history, a theory.

In the 1980s universities moved further toward full inclusion of those groups, histories, and cultures previously excluded. It wasn't enough, for instance, for feminism to exist only in women's studies, or for race-culture analysis to remain in the backwaters of ethnic studies. This is the natural progression of affirmative action: in every discipline — history, science, literature, law — the upstarts began to ask "How would the entire universe of truth, as presently constructed, change if the world view of subordinated groups was taken seriously?" The question posed, and continues to pose, a serious challenge to the legitimacy of established canons, and it generated tremendous backlash. As Catharine MacKinnon put it, "The anxiety about engaged theory is particularly marked among those whose particularities defined the prior universal."[7]

A bumper crop of books lamented the loss of real scholarship, real literacy, real (Western) culture, and revealed the uneasiness with which many regarded the transformation of the canon. Allan Bloom's *The Closing of the American Mind*, a runaway best seller in 1987, and E. D. Hirsch's *The Dictionary of Cultural Literacy* in 1988 were followed by Dinesh D'Souza's *Illiberal Education* in 1991.[8] It was but a short step from their work to the revival of biological determinism and social Darwinism in Murray and Herrnstein's *The Bell Curve* and D'Souza's thinly disguised hate tract, *The End of Racism*. First came the assault on multiculturalism, then the assault on the multicultural themselves.

An unprecedented outpouring of magazine articles, editorials, opinion pieces, letters to the editor, and talk show appearances proclaimed the impending doom of education as we know it, presaging the decline and fall of the very foundations of liberalism on which our democracy rests. The politicization of intellectual life, the end of rational discourse, the abandonment of academic standards, and the end of academic freedom — all of these ills were laid at the feet of the newcomers to the academy. Simultaneously, economic and social dislocation, poverty, and crime were the fault of racially or culturally inferior others — the same others who were assaulting Western culture in the academy.

When *The Atlantic* previewed D'Souza's *Illiberal Education* in a cover

214] EACH OTHER'S HARVEST

story, the cover design featured an old white man in academic robes being drawn and quartered by faceless persons. Only the hands of his tormenters are visible, one black, one brown, one yellow, and one white, pulling the aged body in four different directions. Immediately behind the soon-to-be dismembered victim a pile of books has been set afire, and in the far background is a crumbling columned building. The word *Veritas* is inscribed on its toppling façade. The old academician's fractured body is depicted as a book on which appear the words "Behind the campus controversies over quotas and curriculum lies a larger battle over the very meaning of 'knowledge,' 'diversity,' 'standards,' and 'education' — and an assault on the foundations of Western culture."[9] This graphic portrayal of newcomers to the academy as a faceless, violent, book-burning mob appeals to our deepest fears of difference and change. The images of invasion and destruction of an old cherished order are not accidental. They tell us we must defend what is ours against outsiders. What is perhaps most revealing is that D'Souza directly links the controversies over "quotas," "curriculum," and "the very meaning of knowledge."[10] His opposition to affirmative action, conveniently caricatured by the hot-button word "quotas," is part of a larger war over who will define what is true and good — over who will own culture.

The critics of multiculturalism recognized the importance of the power to shape ideas, and thus it was not surprising that they chose to focus their attacks on the nation's elite universities. For example, when the faculty of Stanford, after two years of discussion and deliberation, voted in 1988 to expand their core humanities curriculum to include important works by women and people of color and to confront issues of race, gender, and class, Secretary of Education William Bennett admonished the university for being "brought low by the very forces which modern universities came into being to oppose — ignorance, irrationality and intimidation."[11] Bennett's doomsday rhetoric and demonic imagery notwithstanding, the Stanford faculty had voted for the changes in the freshman humanities requirement not as a capitulation to the "intimidation" of "ignorant" minority students, but after what many faculty members, including some who were opposed to the changes, described as "the most spirited educational discussion on campus in two decades." It was the kind of intense and honest intellectual conversation that required people on both sides to move beyond their fear of change and each other and search for common ground, where all would be made richer. A member of the English department, who had initially resisted change, described the new requirements as a recognition on the part of those teaching the course that race, gender, and class "deeply affect the world in which we live and in which our forebears have lived."[12] Stanford's then-president, Donald Kennedy, called the changes "practical." "I want Stanford students ready for the world as it will be, not as some would like it to remain," he said.[13]

Renato Rosaldo, the chair of Stanford's anthropology department, called the debate and the new curriculum that emerged from it part of the process of creating an "educational democracy." He said that such a process involved asking "questions of cultural citizenship," such as "How can diverse groups retain their diversity and participate in a democratic community? Can they be full and equal citizens who enjoy the privilege of shaping their destiny? Can they do so without having to surrender their heritages?"[14] At Stanford, where over 40 percent of the entering class were Asian Americans, African Americans, Native Americans, and Chicanos, these questions were critical. Students had rightly asked, "Who is the 'we' [in this course about] our heritage?" Certainly Stanford had not answered these questions in the debate, but in beginning to ask them they had taken an important step toward the inclusive vision of America that is the goal of true affirmative action.

For those of us who know firsthand the history of the struggle to build a more inclusive educational community at places like Stanford, D'Souza's and Bennett's attacks on affirmative action and multiculturalism seem at best silly hyperbole and at worst a sophisticated, pseudo-intellectual assault on the status, reputation, and psyches of women and people of color in the academy. But it is difficult to dismiss the invective lightly when it is part of a backlash that includes more direct assaults against outsiders in the form of hate speech and violence. When a feminist studies center at a West Coast college is vandalized with sexually explicit graffiti by residents of a neighboring fraternity house, when, at a prominent Midwest university, African American students arrive at class to find written on the blackboard "A mind is a terrible thing to waste — especially on a nigger,"[15] when a Stanford law student yells a homophobic death wish at a gay classmate as he passes him in the dorm, we are witnessing a time-honored American cultural practice of using verbal slurs to put people in their place and remind them that they don't belong. These incidents of gutter hate speech, and thousands of others like them, coincided with the high-brow verbal assaults of D'Souza and Bennett, underscoring the resistance to change and showing that much work remains to be done in creating an educational democracy.

Conservatives have turned the harm of hate speech on its head, citing efforts by universities to protect students from such verbal assaults as further evidence that feminists and people of color have seized control of our campuses and imposed a "new McCarthyism" in domains where scholars once were free to search for truth and justice. Conservatives' attacks on "political correctness" coincided with their attacks on multiculturalism and affirmative action, and the right became conveniently enamored of free speech when the issue was freedom to hurl racial epithets rather than the right to protest racial exclusion.

"Sticks and stones will break my bones, but words will never hurt me." This retort to verbal taunts teaches us that words are harmless, but the victims of assaultive speech learn that words do wound and that they are important weapons in the arsenal that maintains race and gender hierarchies. As a small boy, I was assaulted by a word so filled with cultural meaning and power that it shouted of my subordination and divided me from my white playmates. My parents taught me to ignore such words. "You must not allow those who speak them to make you feel small or ugly," they said. "You must know they only speak these words because they do not feel good about themselves." My parents' answer to the words was to "represent the race," to be smarter, cleaner, and more morally upright than the white folk to prove that we were not what they called us, that we were fully human. But I watched my father's jaw go tight when some white adolescent called him "boy," and knew that even he had not escaped the wounds.

Today the words still hold their power. Only a few years ago, I arrived at my law school office to find, shoved under my door, a hate tract depicting a Black man as a gorilla with the caption "jungle voodoo apes" and calling for "death to devil niggar [sic] beasts," and a "White Students Union" newspaper, along with an application form that warned away "all Jews, queers, race traitors and other filth who are considering the infiltration of the WSU." I filed these in a folder marked HATE SPEECH and sat down to finish preparing my lecture, but it was several minutes before I could think clearly about my subject. The heat at the back of my neck and the pulse I felt at my temples subsided by the time I got to class, but the images on the hateful flyer stayed with me for the rest of the day. None of my white colleagues had received the tracts, and I knew I had been targeted.

The racist messages shoved under my door derive their meaning and power from the historical and cultural context, from the background of minstrel shows, of racist theories about brain size and gene pools and biblical ancestors that has shaped our conscious and unconscious beliefs. The students at Dartmouth who called an African American professor a "welfare queen" drew on a cultural capital well known to themselves and their target.[16] Their message was "Our degrading image of you, and not your intellectual or academic standing, is how this society sees you, and we will use that image to annihilate you." The words were not intended to initiate discussion. They were attacks on their target's standing to engage in intellectual exchange. Their purpose was to draw a circle that keeps people of color out.

The last two decades have brought an alarming rise in the use of assaultive speech to threaten, terrorize, wound, humiliate, and degrade people of color, women, and gays and lesbians. The increase in acts of violence against these same groups is not unrelated to the rise in the incidence of hate speech. The National Institute Against Prejudice and Violence, in its 1990 report on campus ethnoviolence, found that 65 to 70 percent of the nation's minority students had experienced some form of violent racial harassment.[17] Of course the epidemic of hate speech and violence is not restricted to college campuses. According to the June 1994 report of the FBI Criminal Justice Information Services Division, there were over 7,969 incidents of hate crime reported to the FBI during 1993. Of these incidents, 6,746 were crimes against persons that claimed over 8,293 individual victims.[18] Sixty-two percent of the incidents were motivated by racial bias; 18 percent by religious bias; 12 percent by sexual-orientation bias; and the remainder by ethnicity and national origin bias.

Sadly, none of this is surprising. History teaches us that in each period where outsiders have made advances in the struggle for inclusion there has been a corresponding rise in hate speech and violence from those who feel threatened by their presence. The Ku Klux Klan has had three periods of strength in American history: the later nineteenth century, in response to Emancipation and Reconstruction, the 1920s, when it exploited the nation's xenophobia and expanded its list of enemies to include Catholics, Jews, Asians, and other immigrants, and the 1960s, when the civil rights movement was at its height. The Klan also had a resurgence in the 1970s, with the advent of affirmative action, and although it has not reached its past level of influence, the Klan is now just one of many organizations involved in a broad variety of white supremacist activity. From 1987 to 1990, the country experienced a nationwide surge of violence against minorities and gays and with it a new generation of racist terrorism from neo-Nazi youths who called themselves Skinheads. The year 1994 saw an alarming revival in the Aryan Nations and the racist, anti-Semitic militia movement. The Southern Poverty Law Center's Klanwatch listed over 250 active hate groups, including Klan, neo-Nazi, and Skinhead organizations, operating in forty-four different states in 1995.[19]

This overt form of backlash signals the most conspicuous connection between affirmative action and hate speech. Gutter hate speech is always the first line of defense against integration. When nine young Black students walked the gauntlet of an angry white mob to integrate Little Rock's Central High School in 1957, they were spat upon, called "nigger," and threatened with lynching. Those of us who must do our work while being verbally assaulted, threatened, and demeaned know that the words are weapons used with intent to frighten, anger, and wound us; to make us question our worth, to diminish us and devalue our work in the eyes of others, to send us back where we came from. The message of assaultive hate speech is anti–affirmative action, and it is the modest gains of affirmative action in integrating schools and workplaces that generate the assault. No crosses burn when white supremacists are secure in their position.

Few of us would use gutter hate speech, and most agree that it is condemnable. Nevertheless, racist, sexist, and homophobic speech is defended in the name of free speech and academic freedom. The syndicated columnists George Will and Nat Hentoff have called cautious attempts by universities like Stanford to draft hate speech regulations the work of "thought police" and the "new McCarthyism," even when the regulations would limit only intentional face-to-face epithets.[20]

The debate over the regulation of hate speech, furthermore, has deeply divided the liberal civil rights and civil liberties community. Many honestly believe that the regulations pose a grave danger to First Amendment liberties, and others have argued that we must protect hate speech to reinforce our commitment to tolerance as a value. We do not lightly set aside these arguments. Our nation's history of intolerance to minority views, and the lessons of parents and grandparents who knew political oppression and fought mightily against it, have made us jealous guardians of the right to free speech. But our people have also experienced the injury of historical, ubiquitous, and continuous defamation. The tension between our Constitution's commitment to speech and its commitment to equality cannot be resolved by protecting speech whose purpose and effect is to exclude, demean, and maintain structures of subordination. We do not believe that pornographic, racist, or homophobic speech directed at women, people of color, and gays and lesbians in schools and workplaces should be tolerated. The racial epithet written on the blackboard, the sexually demeaning slur hurled across a campus lawn, do more to shut down speech than to expand it.

The most strident cries against "censorship," "orthodoxy," and "political correctness" have come not from those in the civil liberties community but from the *National Review, Commentary,* the American Enterprise Institute, and a growing network of externally funded right-wing student newspapers, such as the *Dartmouth Review* and *Stanford Review,* a farm system where young Dinesh D'Souzas hone their race-baiting skills. These born-again champions of free speech are also the leading voices in the assault on multiculturalism and affirmative action and the chief revivalists of discredited theories of genetic and cultural inferiority.

Ideological and psychological attacks on newcomers to the academy are accompanied by material barriers to change. Tuition is up, loans and grants are down, and financial support for oppositional scholarship is disappearing. Academic funding is increasingly governed by commitment to conservative agendas — from private foundations that require allegiance to *laissez-faire* economic theory to a Congress that threatens to cut funds to the National Endowments for the Arts and the Humanities and the Corporation for Public Broadcasting.

This heightened backlash was not an accident. The moment when conservatives took control of the federal government coincided with the flowering of the most powerful second-generation criticisms of heterosexist, white, male, upper-class subjectivity. This created a contradiction, a tension, that has propelled us into the 1990s on a wave of rising hatred and anxiety, coupled with an emerging, genuinely multicultural movement for full inclusion.

To dismiss the backlash against new faces and voices in the academy as the work of right-wing ideologues, however, is to underestimate the anxiety about change among liberals and the seductive power of "change back" tactics as a response to the discomfort of having to abandon an old and familiar world.

Those who share a vision of a world that belongs to us all are sometimes among those who are fearful of the risks of new relationships with new ground rules. We hear colleagues say they are reluctant to take on issues like rape, abortion, homosexuality, or affirmative action for fear that they will say something that will offend their students. Even as these professors express their honest dilemma, they sometimes reveal a longing for a time when they did not have to watch their words, when they could engage in the pursuit of knowledge and truth uncensored by "political correctness."

The story of Professor Stephan Thernstrom is a favorite example cited by critics of multiculturalism as proof that the left has imposed unprecedented academic censorship on American campuses. One morning in 1988, Thernstrom, one of Harvard's leading history professors, opened his campus newspaper to discover an article accusing him of "racial insensitivity."[21] The article reported the complaints of several Black students in his class and cited two incidents to support the charges. Thernstrom had read aloud from the journals of plantation owners in his course The Peopling of America, which was designed in part to "consider the origins, history, and legacy of racism in America." The Black students criticized his failure to include the voices of slaves among the narratives he used to depict the master-slave relationship as well as his use of a text, which he had edited, that described affirmative action as "government enforcement of preferential treatment in hiring, promotion, and college admissions."[22]

"I was absolutely stunned when I read this," said Thernstrom. "None of the students had come to me with their complaints. And the comments they attributed to me were a ridiculous distortion of what I had said in class."[23] Thernstrom's colleagues rose to defend his academic freedom, but he felt he had been unfairly attacked. "Some of these questions are simply not teachable anymore, at least not in an honest, critical way,"[24] he said, explaining his decision not to offer the course in the future.

This story about the "silencing" of an eminent professor by powerful know-nothing multiculturalists became part of the culture wars. In an article in the Heritage Foundation Reports entitled "Radicalism in Power: The Kafkaesque World of American Higher Education," Thernstrom's story is told under the subheading "Running Afoul of Orthodoxy."[25] This telling inverts the real power relations. Young people, newly arrived outsiders to a world of prestige and power, become powerful oppressors; the Harvard professor with an endowed chair is powerless and oppressed. The slave narrative becomes the imposed canon, the master narrative the excluded text. The same critics who protested that the regulation of assaultive racist and sexist speech was censorship, and argued that more speech is always the best answer to speech with which we disagree, have turned the speech of a student criticizing a professor in a newspaper article into an infringement on the professor's academic freedom.

What is going on here? Our point in telling Thernstrom's story is not simply to turn the story right side up. Maybe there is no right side in the relations between the professor and his students until they can all confront the master-slave narrative, until they can talk to one another with candor and empathy about how both slaves and masters were dehumanized by the institution of slavery, about how the legacy of that dehumanization lives with us still and inhabits twentieth-century classrooms. Of course, the faces of the students in Professor Thernstrom's classroom look quite different from those he knew when he was a student. The difference, though, goes beyond physical appearance. During the past thirty years women and people of color have come to our classrooms in greater numbers, *and* they have demanded to be seen and heard. Today's minority and women students may seem less radical than the student generation of the late 1960s and early 1970s, but this may prove only that they take as given the changes that earlier generations fought for. When a white male colleague complains that he can no longer talk honestly about rape or race in his class, we hear him saying he can no longer talk the way he used to, with the confidence, comfort, and predictability that accompany a conversation with like-minded peers.

A woman of color who is on the faculty of a prestigious law school says that when she visits her colleagues in their offices or has lunch with them at the faculty club, their way of speaking and body language, their casual talk about sports and politics, the way they sit in their chairs and put their feet up on the desk, convey an ease and comfort in their workplace that she has never experienced. "It's as if they're sitting in their own living room," she says, "while I feel as though I'm a visitor on my best behavior."

A generation ago, when there were few minorities and women in graduate and professional schools, professors told jokes and stories they had heard from a previous generation of professors. They knew that they and their students shared a world of experience, expectation, and sensibility, and were confident that the young men in their classes would laugh at the jokes and nod with understanding and appreciation when the moral of a story was revealed. Harvard, Yale, and Princeton men had a sense of belonging to and propriety over the institutions where they studied and taught. Today, when minority, women, or gay and lesbian students object to a story, joke, or opinion related in good faith and humor, these men may experience a sense of loss. They lose the good feeling of being at home. With the arrival of new and different people, what was once a private space has become public. Harvard does not yet look like a New York City subway car, but sometimes it may feel "like a third world country" to those who knew it when it was all male and almost all white.

"Why won't they just come talk to me?" "Why do they assume I'm a racist?" When white colleagues ask these questions, they are saying they want to be treated as individuals. The reactions may be natural, but they assume a world free of the fallout from a long history of racial insult and exclusion. The faculty member who wants the benefit of the doubt doesn't understand that his students hear his plea in the context of a world still racist, sexist, and homophobic, where they are daily confronted with multiple messages that demean and exclude them. If they have misinterpreted his meaning and misjudged him, he must speak directly to their responses, searching with them for the source of their misjudgment. If he cares about teaching them to think honestly and critically about ideas, he cannot take his course and go home. If he does so, neither he nor they can learn or change.

An African American friend who is a filmmaker was invited to Harvard Law School several years ago to show his extraordinary documentary on the life of Malcolm X. During the question-and-answer period that followed, a white student asked a question that suggested Malcolm's rhetorical attacks on Harlem merchants may have been anti-Semitic. Before the white student could complete his question, he was shouted down by some of the Black students in the room. "Unfortunately, the question was framed so that the Black students heard it as an attack on me, or Malcolm, which it may have been," our friend recalled. "But the question also identified an important and complicated issue that needed talking about." The Black students' angry response to the white student's question made it impossible for the filmmaker to respond to the question. As he tells the story, his frustration and sadness are still palpable. This was a lost opportunity for both white and black students, and for the gifted artist to do what he does best: communicate.

It is easy to hear this story as further proof of the excesses of political correctness and the mistake of affirmative action, but, as was true of the Thernstrom story, we cannot understand the incident without knowing more about its larger setting. Years of sit-ins, boycotts, and demonstrations have produced little change at Harvard. The law school is notorious for its failure to hire feminists and critical race theorists and for having no professor who is a woman of color, despite decades of student protests in support of diversifying the faculty. Black students do not shout down the student whose question offends them because they feel powerful and validated. Rather, they need to silence him because they feel isolated, vulnerable, and excluded from the daily discourse of the school. They have no forum for discussing the issues that concern them most.

This is so because, among other things, our universities have not been serious about affirmative action. Most of our students have not had the benefit of professors of color, of feminists, and out gay and lesbian faculty who understand their isolation and vulnerability, who care enough, and are trusted enough, to talk with them in honest and challenging ways about race, gender, and sexuality. The students have not had the experiences that would let them know they can talk about these issues without being assaulted. They have not had professors who can teach by example the difficult work of bridge building and resistance, of succeeding in a world not of their making and making it theirs, of fighting subordination and fighting the slave within. When there is no progressive presence or agenda to provide a place and way to talk about injury and anger and self-doubt, students of color, for lack of an alternative, turn to shouting down what threatens them, to pseudo–Mau Mau nationalism, to militant public figures spouting anti-Semitism and theories of Black supremacy. When minority students engage in reactionary, nonprogressive politics of this kind, it is a desperate response, a symptom of their alienation in a world where, despite right-wing tales of universities overrun by multiculturalism, they seldom see themselves at the front of a classroom or hear their voices in the books that are assigned.

When students of color sit together at a lunch table or choose to live in a theme dorm or pledge a Black fraternity or sorority or speak Spanish to each other, they face reproachful cries of "self-segregation" and "balkanization." This, too, is an inversion of reality, as if the African American or Latino or Asian students huddling in the corner were excluding the roomful of Anglos, and not vice versa.

Newcomers to formerly segregated schools and workplaces frequently seek the company of classmates with similar backgrounds and interests for the same reasons that the students from Andover and Exeter or Southerners or the children of left-wing intellectuals do. They want to feel comfortable and at home in a new place. When white students sit together or join the same clubs and fraternal organizations, it seems racially neutral and goes unnoticed. Only students of color face charges of self-segregation and balkanization.

When more than two minority faculty members meet by chance in the hall and stop to chat, one will often joke that our white colleagues may think a conspiracy is being hatched. The observation is made only half in jest. The meager numbers of minority professors on predominantly white faculties make our gatherings conspicuous events. Even among well-meaning colleagues, an anxiety about whether we will "fit in" with the larger group is often translated into apprehension about our spending too much time with each other.

That it is not students of color who are primarily responsible for the segregation of our campuses is demonstrated by the findings of a national study of student interactions across racial lines. The 1994 survey of more than six thousand students at campuses across the country found that minority students frequently studied or dined with students of other races, especially whites, and that they engaged in these interracial activities much more regularly than did white students.[26]

There is a political agenda that lurks behind the charge of balkanization. If claiming ethnic identity is the cause of ethnic strife, the solution becomes "Stop asserting your ethnic identity and be just like me." The result is to disguise the effects of systems of domination. It assumes that racial identity is the cause of racial subordination, rather than the product of it.

The identities of people of color are constructed by America's racism even as we embrace, or more accurately reconstruct, those identities to fight racial subordination. Our culture, our identity is not entirely of our own making. We participate in and act upon what we are handed by history. One author of this book is the granddaughter of immigrants; the other is the great-grandson of slaves. We choose to remember this and to celebrate the survival, resilience, and culture of our people as part of our political identity, informing our struggle against all forms of domination. There is agency involved in this use of our identity, but it is not completely autonomous from what history has handed us. How the world treats us, and how it treated our ancestors, is significantly tied to race.

Often, when colleagues express antagonism toward multiculturalism, we sense that they are experiencing an unacknowledged feeling of loss of their own identities, as if our choice to make our racial, cultural, or gender identity part of our work reminds them that they have been forced to abandon significant parts of themselves to fit in where they live and work.

My sister Paula Lawrence Wehmiller, a brilliant teacher and teacher of teachers who is studying to become a priest, wrote about leaving home in 1963 to attend Swarthmore College. She carefully packed a large suitcase with all her favorite clothes. Along with the clothes, she said, "I packed my music and art, and dance, my love of sports, my imagination, my stories, my humor, my dreams . . . my optimism, my toughness and stubbornness, my strictness and high expectations of myself, my visions of all it was possible to be. I packed, too, the re-sounding notes of my parents' frequent refrain to all their children: 'You know who you are and you can be yourself.'" She arrived at the cam-pus, looked up the broad walkway at the forbidding gray buildings, and thought, "I'd better leave this suitcase right here. I will never be able to dance and dream, and sing and laugh at this scary place. This is no place to tell my stories." So there the bag sat while she plowed through four years of lectures, labs, papers, and exams. "Now and again," she wrote, "I would peek out of the dormitory window to see my big old suitcase covered with snow or leaves or soaked by the rain, patiently waiting for me to be done fitting in the best I could."

I read my sister's story to a group of colleagues from law schools across the nation who were attending a workshop to talk about affirma-tive action and the resistance to change as new voices came to their campuses. We were sitting in a large circle, and at the beginning of the session I asked each participant to introduce his or her maternal grand-mother. It was a mostly white group. They were, on the whole, more liberal and more hip than most law professors, but they were to all appearances a fairly typical group of academics. When they introduced their grandmothers, I was struck by how wonderfully different those women were. They came from a wealth of cultures and traditions: suffragettes, vaudevillians, ranchers, union organizers, and keepers of kosher kitchens. Many did not speak English; every one of them was an outrageous character; and every law professor revealed a strong sense of admiration for and identification with the grandmother.

Suddenly we seemed much less homogeneous, more interesting, more human — no longer generic, objective, dispassionate, perspec-tiveless law professors without kith or kin, without history or commu-nity or culture. Many of us who had known each other professionally for years were, for the first time, seeing a part of our colleagues that could find no place on their résumés. We had revealed a significant piece of ourselves that our hiring committees would have deemed ir-relevant to the question of our qualifications. It was apparent that many of my colleagues, like my sister arriving at Swarthmore College, had left large parts of themselves outside the university's gates.

Paula's story and the story of the grandmothers are related to the backlash against multiculturalism and affirmative action, as well as to our vision of what multiculturalism and affirmative action ought to be. The resistance to new faces and new voices in the academy is not just a fear of people with dark skins or women or gays and lesbians, although that is part of it. Nor is it only about the fear that, with limited space in the classroom and the canon, new faces and voices mean less space for the old. There is something else going on.

That something is the fear of facing our own identities. We are afraid of going back and opening that bag of gifts, of passions, talents, and history that we left at the railroad station each time we were forced to redefine ourselves to fit some neutral, identity-less mold that really was someone else's identity. Multiculturalism has become a lightning rod for backlash in part because, when an Asian American, Latina, African American, lesbian, or feminist student comes to the academy and insists on bringing along her bag of gifts, those of us who have left our identities outside are forced to reckon with our loss.

Consider the gay white man who has made his way in the world and achieved professional success by hiding his sexual identity. When a new colleague who is gay and "out" arrives and insists that his identity as a gay man is one of the gifts he brings to his work, the closeted gay man could respond by joining those who say identity is "irrelevant," or "your identity has no value here," or "claiming your identity divides us from one another," as if the prevailing culture claimed no identity as straight. When the closeted gay man joins this homophobic chorus, he denies a part of himself.

Another possible response is to "come out." Coming out is risky. The man who has made his career in the closet will pay a significant price for leaving it. But coming out is liberating.[27] It is liberating not just for the individual but for all of us who, in some way, remain closeted. It is liberating for the enterprise, for the canon, the classroom, and the workplace, because who we are is redefined. There is a new, different, honest, inclusive *unum*.

Crèvecoeur's "new race of men" was defined by white supremacy and patriarchy. We outsiders cannot become one by assimilation into that which defines some of us as less. Multiculturalism has never been about balkanization, but it must be about transformation. We must redefine the one so that it can truly embrace the many. Transformation is frightening. It requires us to face our individual and collective identities. It requires us to confront the sometimes horrific history that has shaped those identities. It requires a faith that, when we make space for others' gifts, the pie will expand; that when the culture, the *unum*, really includes us all, ownership will be beside the point.

The attack on affirmative action is about closing doors. The attack on multiculturalism is about closing minds. The attack on PC Thought Police is an effort to make door-closing look heroic and libertarian. It is neither. The backlash represents fear and aversion to liberty, sentiments that cannot win the day in a nation born with a promise of freedom, born of many cultures, moving forward with more richness in cultural variety now than ever before.

[III]

THE WELCOME TABLE

*Expanding
Affirmative Action*

[9]

The Telltale Heart:
Apology, Reparation, and Redress

I tremble for my country, when I reflect that God
is just. — *Thomas Jefferson*[1]

They shall build up the ancient ruins,
they shall raise up the former devastations;
they shall repair the ruined cities,
the devastations of many generations.
— *Isaiah 61:4*

ONE SUNNY DAY, on the island of Yap, in part of the Pacific
island group of Micronesia, I was running a course designed to
teach the common law of torts to Micronesian judges. I posed a hypo-
thetical designed to illustrate the master rule of fault-based liability in
tort. "What if," I asked, "a little boy runs out from behind the high
brush, into the road, and is hit by a car? The driver was driving carefully
and could not have stopped in time to avoid the accident. The child is
killed instantly."

This was the easy case, the first of a series of hypotheticals designed
to show that once fault is unclear, liability becomes unclear. To the
judges, however, it was not an easy case. It was a false case. No one
could respond to it justly without more facts.

One of the judges, enjoying the Socratic method and intending to
teach me a thing or two, asked for more facts. How many sons, he
asked, in the family of the driver? How many sons in the family of the
injured child? How did the family of the injured child learn of the
injury? How soon, and from whom?

"Okay," I said, "I give up. You tell me how you would decide the
case."

What the judges learned that day was the peculiar habit, in Western law, of limiting the relevant facts. All an American jurist would want to know is whether the driver was at fault in the accident; there would be no liability if the driver was exercising ordinary care.

What I learned from the judges that day is that there is a universe of relevant questions to ask after an accident if one lives on a tiny, isolated island, and if it is an absolute imperative to live in peace.

Fault is irrelevant, the judges explained. If your driving hurts someone, you should make sure you go immediately to the family to tell of the tragedy and of your grief. They should not hear the news first from someone else. Your remorse must meet the test of sincerity. Your kin should come quickly with food and gifts to show their intent to make amends. If you are lucky, you will have a son to work the taro fields of the family who lost a son. Your son will work for them all of his days, as part of your apology, and the apology, sanctified by elders and sacred ritual, must find a gracious welcome in the wounded family. If they allow their loss to overcome them, such that your sincere apology is received insincerely, they will lose status in the community.

This system of repairing great loss is not about account keeping. It is part of the sacred, in a culture that does not separate the sacred from the secular. The longstanding customs that govern reactions to the tragedy of an automobile accident guarantee the spiritual wholeness of all citizens. When either side — what we would call in Western law the plaintiff or the defendant — fails to comport itself according to custom, the well-being of the entire community is in jeopardy.

If the judges' system works in the idealized way they described, it achieves something the American legal system does not: both the plaintiff and the defendant walk away at peace.

In another part of the Pacific, Native Hawaiians speak matter-of-factly about the payback for human failings. Traditional Hawaiians place value in the concept of *pono,* the state of being that is peace, repose, goodness. Upsetting *pono,* disrupting the rhythms of the land and its people, is a wrong — not only to fellow human beings, but to the cosmology. The price is illness, misfortune, cataclysm. When the volcano erupts, taking out roads and villages, the Hawaiians look around for someone who acted against *pono* — perhaps the developer who bulldozed old burial grounds, or the politician who acted out of greed, or a family whose feud was left to fester.

In the Judeo-Christian tradition, the Lord says, "Vengeance is mine."[2] There is a wisdom beyond human comprehension that determines what pain to exact for human transgression. Few cultures exist that do not have some notion of judgment. Actions have consequences. This is a law of physics we transmute to a law of our lives.

Those cultures which make active use of apology rituals are often the ones that acknowledge the importance of community cohesion. Apology rituals, within societies that depend on the clan or village to provide a social safety net, are essential for survival. A dispute resolution mechanism that results in one party's walking home happy and the other's walking away from the village forever is an utter failure. To make the community whole, to erase the bad feelings of the past, to come jointly once again to the table, is imperative. In the Jalé villages of New Guinea, for instance, elders require feuding clan members to come together to feast on pig, each tearing the best morsel from the bone to place in the mouth of the former foe. This is what makes the elders smile.[3] An apology in such communities leads to a gain, not a loss, in status.

This approach contrasts with the modern Western view that an apology diminishes status. Typically, in American society, when someone confesses an error or wrongdoing, he is seen as weak and vanquished, disempowered and vulnerable. Ask an American lawyer what to do at the scene of an accident, whether a car crash or a nuclear meltdown, and the first rule is "Don't apologize."

In America we have no comparable clan, no network of kin and near kin with whom we must maintain peace, with whom we must ceremoniously share our food even when we don't want to. The failure to know that the globe is our village, that every act of disregard for the planet and its inhabitants sets in motion disruptions of the good, is the curse of modernism. It is what makes us unable to see affirmative action as bringing balance to all our lives — not just the material balance of integration, but the emotional and spiritual balance of healthy souls.

The case for affirmative action includes notions of reparation, rectification, and redress: the deliberate effort to identify and make amends for past wrong. Reparation is not all there is to affirmative action. It is

234] THE WELCOME TABLE

neither the most compelling nor the most persuasive reason for it, but it is a reason worth considering, for there are costs in the refusal, ever, to apologize.

As the fiftieth anniversary of the end of the Second World War approached, refusal to apologize became a leitmotif. The Smithsonian canceled the Enola Gay exhibit because some felt it focused too much on the horror and not enough on the military rationale for dropping the atomic bomb. Meanwhile, the Japanese government was persistently embarrassed by the claims of its victims: brave women in Korea and the Philippines who came forward to tell how they were raped, imprisoned, tortured, and forced into prostitution, as well as POW survivors of death marches and horrific abuse. No one in a position of power in either country could say he was sorry for the lives lost and damaged in the horror of war, or suggest publicly that some of the loss was unnecessary, wrong, or evil.

Whatever the record of history will bear, and I believe it will show that the bombing of Hiroshima was racist, as were the many atrocities committed by the Japanese army, there is a social code that stands in the way of even asking the factual questions that might lead to the need for an apology. We don't need to look back at American military action, this code tells us. The war is over, the cause was just, we will only hurt ourselves, our prestige, and the honor of those who sacrificed all by asking, Was there anything we could have done differently, more justly, with more care?

What does it do, to a nation and the world, to refuse to look back? When someone else, someday, is making the decision about dropping the bomb on me, I want him to face a record of history that judges the United States wrong for what happened to civilians in 1945. When someone, someday, is preparing new internment camps for citizens rounded up without habeas corpus, I want him to know the judgment of both courts and Congress: the World War II internment of Japanese Americans was unconstitutional. This historical memory, the careful judgment made on the record of history, is the only inoculation we have against future harm. This is not endless, useless guilt; it is judgment with utility. It takes past harm as the teaching that will shelter future citizens.

The way to imprint that teaching is through reparation. To the extent that at least part of the justification for affirmative action is reparation, affirmative action rests on a notion that is alien to modern jurisprudence. Oliver Wendell Holmes — seen by some as the architect of modern American legal thought — saw as his life's greatest work his distillation of the common law into its basic principles. At the core of his conceptualized system of justice was the notion of objectively determined, fault-based liability: if a person does something that is unreasonable under society's objective rules of behavior, that person is at fault and must pay compensation to the victim.

Reparation, affirmative action, and the remediation of past injustice look like nothing Holmes envisioned. Rather than defying societal norms, the perpetrators of racial and gender injustice acted precisely in accordance with those norms. They had no particular victim in mind, nor a comprehensive plan, for example, to perpetrate the genocide of Native Americans. It was just something that happened on their way to achieving a destiny made manifest by their casual belief in superiority and entitlement.

The standard liberal legal ideology, which focuses on individual fault, clashes with the ideology supporting reparation. A standard legal claim pits an individual victim against a perpetrator of recent wrongdoing, whereas a claim in reparation pits victim group members against perpetrator descendants and current beneficiaries of past injustice.

A reparations claim lacks the logic and efficiency paramount in the Holmesean world view. It is out of control. In reparations, the lines delineating liability are fuzzy, the exact identities of parties in action are unknowable, and the costs are potentially bankrupting. Under a regime of reparations, no individual actor could calculate in advance the parameters of potential liability.

The logic of reparation lies beyond the logic of the law, raising predictable objections. First, critics claim that reparations are politically untenable: divisive, obsessive, distracting from real issues. Second, they argue that the historical basis of the claim is invalid: either the past harm did not occur, or it was somehow justifiable. Third, the imprecise outlines of both the victim and the perpetrator class render reparation claims fatally imprecise. Fourth, the passage of time renders connection between the original wrong and present effects of that wrong vague and unprovable. Fifth, damages for past wrong are impossible to calculate and to distribute fairly. Finally, to the extent that reparation is aimed toward a group rather than an individual, it raises the ethical objection of disregard of the individual.

We reject these arguments. Correcting past wrongs, such as discrimination, through programs like affirmative action is divisive because it just might work. It may open the doors of opportunity and break down barriers to power sharing. It is, indeed, less divisive to let power and privilege stay where they are. The uneasy peace gained from silence in the face of oppression is a known quantity, one that even the disenfranchised sometimes choose over the unknown.

Every movement for progressive social change is called "too divisive," which often translates as "Keep the status quo." The objection that reparations set up a hierarchy of suffering, however, merits a thoughtful response. We are leery of proclamations that some wrongs are worse than others or that some people are particularly privileged in their pain. Experienced seekers of justice usually conclude that ranking oppressions is a useless exercise. At the same time, asserting the pure equality of pain deprecates human experience. In our own lives we know that some losses are greater than others, some pain easily surmounted, other pain a lifetime's burden. In an account of justice that takes history seriously, we do need to say, with caution, that there are losses of such magnitude that we, as Americans, need to recognize them as our particular obligation to address.

In the United States, a key question is whether a certain historical wrong bears any relation to our ongoing culture of subordination. The enslavement of African Americans and the genocide of Native Americans are parts of American history that gave rise to particular forms of current American racism. This is not the same as saying that only members of these two groups are the victims of racism, nor is it the same as making the moral evaluation that what happened in these cases was the worst thing ever experienced by any group of human beings. Rather, these events loom large in the origin of our constitutional order, our economic development, and our shared culture. The slave ships brought to the United States an institution that indelibly shaped our understanding of race. Similarly, the massacres of Native Americans required a rationalization and a psychology of denial that mark American colonialism. White supremacy, sometimes expressed explicitly, and just as often denied vehemently, is the legacy of these events.

The record of broken bodies is on the ground we tread; the narrative traditions of native people and of African Americans tell us that something extraordinary happened on this land, in a time close to ours. Some 90 percent of the estimated hundred million American Indians who lived at the time of European contact were decimated, in what one author called "a demographic disaster [that] has no equal in history."[4] That number is significant enough to call extraordinary, and to suggest an extraordinary care as we consider our responsibilities to American Indians today.

Edgar Allan Poe, an American who lived in the time of slavery, understood the dark side. He wrote of a man who murdered his tormentor and hid the victim's heart under the floorboards. The investigators arrived, and the murderer proceeded with his calm rendition of a coverup. Somewhere in the background he heard a noise and realized the heart was beating. Surely the constables heard it, he thought as he escalated his professions of innocence. Unable to bear the noise, he ripped open the floorboards and revealed his guilt to the astonished onlookers.

Like the telltale heart beating beneath the floorboards in Poe's story, the weeping at the 1890 Wounded Knee massacre and the moans of the Middle Passage make a persistent pounding when we speak of liberty and equality and the greatness of our America. The casual superiority of a rich and free nation is something we maintain only by speaking loudly, drowning out the sounds that grow ever larger as our frantic efforts to deny and explain escalate. What Myrdal called the American dilemma, what Du Bois called the color line, and what present commentators call the race relations problem are all part of our national culture. Until we speak the truth about it, we cannot know the truth about our own condition.

Keeping the telltale heart under the floorboards is a preoccupation of the postrevisionist historians who argue that dredging up past wrongs is false history. When Pete Wilson announced his soon-to-fail bid for the presidency of the United States, he chose as a central theme the evil of negative history. We've got to stop talking about slavery and

Native Americans and emphasize what is good about America, he said.[5] This echoes the view of professional historians, like Lynne Cheney and Arthur Schlesinger. Why all this talk about victims? Why not admit the greatness of the United States? Why this compulsion to look for the bad?

Other detractors of reparation try to deny or justify past harm. The argument that no harm occurred presents factual claims that are refuted elsewhere. We note, however, that a denial of the harm is often not a factual claim at all, but a form of assault designed to perpetuate the harm itself.

Unlike the claim that no wrong occurred, various attempts at justification try to explain or deflect the wrong. A common explanation for slavery, for example, is that within the culture of that era, the inferiority of Africans was taken for granted. To condemn acts from the vantage point of the present is "ahistoric" or "anachronistic." It is precisely because there were many people in the time of slavery who knew it was wrong that we are able to judge it as wrong today. The truth about slavery was made plain by the enslaved Africans themselves, who in narratives and song left a contemporaneous text of condemnation. This truth was not held exclusively by the enslaved; the international anti-slavery movement brought together many, educated and uneducated, rich and poor, black and white, who studied the evils of slavery and condemned the institution in its time. It is not only from our present vantage point, but also in wise eyes of the past, including Thomas Jefferson's, that slavery is unmitigated evil.

Similarly, when feminists condemn the sexism of past political leaders and social institutions, we are warned that we are using the distorting lens of the present. This argument ignores the many noted women and some men who have condemned patriarchy for over a hundred years, as well as the anonymous women of generations earlier who sang their versions of the blues, telling us that "hard is the fortune of all womankind."[6]

In the end, however, the argument over whether what happened in American history was justified or explainable, given past realities, does not answer the call for reparation. Whether the wrong was somehow "understandable in context" does not mean it was just, and justice requires attention to harm regardless of the parameters of blame.

Regardless of past transgressions, some argue, present remedies are impossible because of imprecision. If the *res*, the thing, is stolen and the thief caught, the law returns it to the rightful owner. This is the paradigm of what the law does, and among the oldest writs are those for the return of the *res*. What if the thing that is stolen, however, is not a *res*, but rather freedom, sovereignty, dignity? What if there is no clearly identifiable thief and no single owner, but multitudes who benefit and multitudes who suffer because of some historic wrong? Lack of precision in the law weakens a claim. Those who come before the law are expected to make a coherent case against a fixed defendant: Who did this to you? How were you harmed? What was the price of your loss? If the answer to any of these is "I cannot say with certainty," then the claimant is not worthy in the eyes of the law.

In today's world, in the interests of justice, we make some exceptions to this demand for precision. When poisonous pollution enters the river from sources unknown, for instance, affecting millions of downstream users and planting in some communities the seeds of cancer that will become evident only years in the future, a so-called Superfund problem arises. The solution may be to tax all producers of the poison and create a fund for possible future harms. Though the details about perpetrator and victim are not known, there is often a sense that the law should respond in some way to the disaster, typically through legislation.

Similarly, in the world of antitrust and commercial law, it sometimes happens that a great way to make money is to bilk a million people out of a dollar apiece. The victims may never know of their loss, and identifying all who were cheated and proving their loss is a logistical impossibility. Class action suits or class remedies are possible solutions. If everyone who used a teller machine at Cheatum Savings was illegally deprived of a dollar in one year, for example, a court might require a dollar discount on fees to everyone who banks there the next year. Not everyone who benefits from the discount is someone who lost out during the period of cheating, but the fit is close enough, and the inability to identify the victims with precision is not a reason to let Cheatum off the hook. We allow this imprecision in order to uphold standards of the marketplace that are seen as critical to consumer confidence. Obsession with precision puts the demands of arithmetic before the demands of justice, ignoring the more central goals of stability and fairness.

Along with imprecision, there is the problem of time. According to

American jurisprudence, as time passes, regardless of right or wrong, claims are put to rest. For an ordinary negligence claim, states typically set the limit at two to six years. After that, it is too late for a plaintiff to bring a claim. The time bar, or statute of limitations, is said to promote settled expectations and business planning; we need to know the outer limits of our liability so that we can go on with the business of commerce.

If seven years is too long ago for a civil law suit, what are we to make of a hundred years? In most nations a hundred years is not so long ago. A theory of reparation focuses on the magnitude of harm done and its continuing effects, weighed against the passage of time. When the evidence of continuing effect is strong, the passage of time is not a reason to waive the wrong. While dwelling on the past is not always a good thing, in some cases forgiving and forgetting are impossible, particularly if the old wrongs continue to give rise to new harms.

Reflective adults ponder and regret the mistakes of their lives and recall the traumas done to them. Victims of childhood abuse or neglect may well spend hours trying to understand how their past shapes their present attitudes, relations, and personality. A common survival strategy for the most egregious abuse is to forget or diminish what happened. There is no real forgetting, however. The anxiety, flashback, depression, and other symptoms of repressed trauma remain. The body remembers, calling out with a range of illnesses and behaviors the words we cannot say: something terrible happened to me, and I am in pain. A person stuck in the past, reciting a list of grievances over and over without resolution, is not whole; but neither is the person who cannot see the past, who does not know she is sad today because she was raised yesterday by someone who saw no joy in life.

"Forgive and forget" is too simple a solution for the complex harms human beings inflict on one another. The abused child must remember, confront, and express anger before any forgiveness is mentally healthy. On a larger scale, national healing, something politicians seek in platitudinous addresses, will not come cheap. The forgiveness that is close to godliness is a deep forgiveness, the one that comes when the work is done, the past confronted, the pain acknowledged and expressed. This task is not about feeling guilty, pointing fingers, extracting vengeance. It is about liberation.[7]

* * *

No one wants to confront that which hurts the most; no one wants to open up the carefully cabined places of forgetting; but some wise souls learn that hiding from what is hard gives no shelter. The past, whether personal or geopolitical, is ours, and acknowledging our origins is what enables us to make our lives better than what the past alone might have predicted.

What is the price of peace? The story of the Native Hawaiians is illustrative. Native Hawaiians have long protested the loss of their sovereign nation, their lands, and much of their culture as a result of the U.S.-backed takeover of Hawaii in 1893. One of the specific claims relates to native lands, ceded to the State of Hawaii by the United States government, and held in trust for Native Hawaiians. The state, the Native Hawaiians claim, is in breach of the terms of that trust. They would like to sue the state to force it to use the ceded lands, as required by law, for the benefit of Native Hawaiians. There is one problem, however. State law does not give Hawaiians the right of legal action. They cannot sue in state court.

For years, the Hawaiians have lobbied the state legislature for a "right to sue" bill, which would allow their claims to come to court. In opposing the bill, the state has argued that if it is sued, it will go bankrupt. If the Hawaiians could sue, they could very well win, and the actual damages, for years of misdirection of benefits that were intended for Hawaiians, could surpass the revenues and assets of the state.

Making up for past wrong, in short, should not happen, according to the state, because it would cost too much. This argument against reparation trumps all the others. Instead of saying it didn't happen or it was too long ago, it says if the harm caused is too large, there is no remedy. The argument is somewhat disingenuous. The practical reality is that no litigant will ever collect full damages if they will bankrupt the state. At some point, the political process will have to allow for compromise. When Japanese Americans sought redress for their internment during World War II, for example, most recognized that no monetary amount could compensate them for what they lost: careers, education, land, businesses, hand-built farm houses, loved ones lost to poor medical care, a lifetime's possessions left behind for the junkman, the comfort of familiar streets and faces gone — so much, tangible and intangible, that was irreplaceable. Most significant of all, though, was the loss of rights and the shattering of expectations about freedom and citizenship. A million dollars would not have made whole what each person lost. No one asked for a million dollars. What they asked for, and got, was an amount large enough to constitute a genuine apology but small enough to pass through the legislative process. Reparations exact not a pound of flesh, but, rather, sixteen ounces of mutual sorrow over loss.

Reparation, to the extent that it recognizes group harm and group responsibility, rings of collectivism, something feared by Red baiters and derogated by those classical philosophers who ground their ethics in the individual. Although the criticism of dehumanizing individualism is implicit throughout this book, we do not reject the belief that each human being is sacred, unique, and entitled to individual recognition before the law. A simple choice that puts either individuals or groups first is not enough to resolve the reparations debate, for groups are made up of individuals. Any philosophy giving primacy either to individual rights or to the group must confront that fact of human life. The relations of individuals to groups and groups to other groups are something we cannot avoid in defining what is just.

Reparation, like affirmative action, is for everyone. The direct beneficiaries, as deserving as they may be, are not the center of reparation. All of the objections to reparation come down to one thing: the failure to see individual interest as tied inextricably to community interest. Making peace with the past, so that we can live and work together in a peaceful future, is what will ultimately save all individuals. The person free to invent himself or herself and walk unfettered, the person whose individual choices are paramount in the political philosophies of the modern age, that individual is revealed only when the legacy of past oppressions is wiped away.

Reparation is only one part of affirmative action. As we argue throughout this book, affirmative action is required in order to institute equality today. Nonetheless, part of the justification for affirmative action is and should be the correction of past injustice.

When affirmative action is defined strictly as a remedy for past injustice, it is easy to attack. Some argue that a focus on the past detracts from the issues or problems of the present; people become mired in past grievances and are sapped of the will to struggle around current injustice. Some, like the majority of the present Supreme Court, are skeptical of claims that past wrongs, such as the enslavement of African Americans, are connected to present disadvantage. The unstated message is "Get over it; it was a long time ago." Others feel that if past wrongdoing is the basis for affirmative action, then only African Americans, and not other minorities, should benefit from affirmative action.[8] This leads to a no-win game of comparing oppressions — whose suffering was the most egregious, whose claim for compensation the most compelling — and it oversimplifies the goals of affirmative action into a settling of accounts: "Let's find the true historical wrong, the clear victim, the price of their pain, and then fix it up with a direct payment."

This notion of affirmative action as simple payback for past wrong misunderstands the social function of history in our lives. We are made by our past; we can't live, breathe, act, or invent apart from it. Confronting and knowing our collective history is important because it is what shapes present circumstances; we are racist today because we were racist yesterday. The forms and the dynamics of that racism will change over time, but the root is connected to the branch in a way that is present in the here and now.

Of course, the fight for affirmative action of the 1960s and beyond was not a fight merely for acknowledgment of past wrong; it was a passionate struggle to improve present conditions, to gain jobs, education, and political participation today.

Acknowledging this doesn't remove the element of reparation from affirmative action, however. There is a past-based part of the original demand: this country must know and acknowledge past wrong if it is to progress on the road to justice. We cannot end racism without knowing where it came from and how it works in our culture. In this sense, the inability to say "We were wrong, we are sorry, we will right this wrong" means that we are stuck in time. If we refuse to confront the past, we become bound to it and cannot move forward.

What this means for affirmative action, and for progressive politics in general, is that we have to do two things at once. We should, as argued in this book, live in the present, focusing on present need and expanding affirmative action programs to reach all people who, for whatever reason, are excluded from education, jobs, and participation in the democratic process. At the same time, we can recognize our particular responsibility for correcting the past wrongs in our history. It was right for this nation to issue a formal apology to the thousands of Japanese Americans who were incarcerated in America's concentration camps. The healing of the Japanese Americans required this, as did our self-perception as a good and free country. There are apologies we have not made; atrocities carried out in our name that continue to debase our most sacred symbols of democracy. We must confront our horrors and pledge that they will not happen again.

As this book was written, the Truth Commission, charged with finding out what happened to the thousands of South Africans who were victims of atrocities during the struggle to end apartheid, began its work in South Africa, that nation determined to remember and move forward from a bloody past. One by one the witnesses came before the commissioners. The tortured whispered their survivors' stories; the parents wept describing their murdered children; some of the murderers wept, too, holding out their killing hands as an entire nation watched.

There is no more powerful process a nation can undertake. The commissioners had to halt the proceedings at times when neither they nor the witnesses could bear to continue. Counselors were called on to help the commissioners confront their own traumas at hearing one story after another of human suffering.

Nothing that happens before the Truth Commission can restore a peaceful heart to grieving parents, nor absolve the eternal guilt of the torturer. Nothing will happen except confrontation with truth, and out of that beginning the new South Africa will start its healing.

The living struggle to give meaning to the loss of the dead; the grieving heart seeks reasons. The freedom fighters of South Africa knew they risked all for their people's liberation. They did not know, when they joined their cause, that they were bringing an additional gift to the larger world. In its search to uncover the past and thereby move forward to healing, South Africa is setting an example while the world watches. No nation, great or small, past or present, has undertaken this level of collective confrontation with its own evil as part of a peaceful transition to a free and equal society.

May they find their peace, and, someday, may we find ours.

DIANE HO

"Equal application of strength"

KEOLA (the real name is not used here) was accused of killing an eight-year-old boy. The coroner reported massive injuries, over a sustained period of time. "So what's your theory, Dani? She didn't do it or she didn't mean to do it?" I asked in the jaded voice of someone who has been around the law too long.

"Mari, she didn't do it," Dani answered. Not in the law voice, but in the real voice of a human being convinced of innocence. Suddenly, the conversation shifted ground. If Dani, a woman of the toughest common sense, believed her client was innocent, she was. This was serious business.

Keola, I learned, was a troubled young woman. When she was two years old, she watched her father shoot and kill her mother. When she was five, her father killed himself. Keola found the body. She was taken in by relatives and abused by them, sexually and physically. She reported the abuse and was labeled the family snitch when she was removed by authorities. After entering the foster care system, she was abused again. Keola was a woman, in short, for whom terrible treatment and having nowhere to go were normal.

At eighteen, she found herself alone and pregnant. It was a difficult pregnancy, and her doctor warned her that she had to stay near the hospital in case her preterm labor became a medical emergency. There was only one place she knew of to go: back to the relatives who had abused her as a child. She moved into their home, then in chaos. Several of the adults living there had long criminal records of violence, often directed at each other. Neighbors reported regularly seeing abuse of the children. Two days after Keola — then nine months pregnant — moved in, the eight-year-old in the family was killed. The adults in the house fingered Keola, the one they had labeled a snitch years ago.

"How could the police believe the relatives?" I asked. "She had no motive. It wasn't her kid; she'd just moved into the house."

"Maybe they didn't believe," Dani explained. "They have a dead kid; they don't know whom to charge. They bring her in, figuring she'll break and tell them what happened." In the meantime, the rest of the family scoured the house, destroying all physical evidence, and agreed on the details in their statements pointing to Keola's guilt.

A friend of Keola's called Dani to take the case, knowing that a young Hawaiian woman wrongly accused was enough to bring Dani's full wisdom and wrath to battle against the Maui prosecutors. Dani fought the case through trial, where she held forth with a dignified Hawaiian presence. Those who knew her enjoyed watching the courtroom transformation. Her playful social persona disappeared in trial, where she was all business.

There is no happy ending to Keola's case. She was found guilty, and the good fight was not enough to pull her up from the bottom. Her lawyer is still on her side, working through appeals and strategies for making the best of her prison time.

This lawyer, to whom bottomed-out young women turn in need, this lawyer, who is educating crews of impoverished Native Hawaiian children in her spare time, who paddles Hawaiian outrigger canoes in the open ocean, who is the gray-haired quarterback of her alumni football team, was never supposed to become a lawyer. She went to law school as a single mom, part of the time with nowhere to live other than a used van.

Diane Ho is a Hawaiian. The Native Hawaiians have suffered desperate degradation in their own homeland, the result of the illegal overthrow of the Hawaiian government and the ravages of disease, land dispossession, and cultural chaos outsiders brought to the islands. At the time Dani entered law school, there were only a handful of Native Hawaiian lawyers in the state. As a result of affirmative action at the University of Hawaii Richardson School of Law, however, there are now over a hundred.

Dani's Hawaiian ethic of generosity means that her office frequently serves people like Keola, the forgotten cases that other lawyers find unprofitable. More than her law practice, however, Dani sees her life work as salvaging young people under the auspices of her canoe club. Pick any day, and you will find teenagers zipping through the comfortable wooden house that is the law offices of Ho and Hamili. There is weight-training equipment in the basement, which the young paddlers use between rounds of helping their "aunties" — the secretaries and lawyers — with office chores. The paddlers learn to use computers and to draft correspondence. Some type out their college applications there in the office, calling out over their shoulders for advice.

What is wrong with this picture? These are not the ones that are supposed to go to college. They are street kids, not on the academic track.

You would never guess, Dani brags, if you watch these kids running a meeting, that some of them live on the beach and others in the homeless shelter. She has taught them to plan their educational programs and apply for government grants. She made them write a manual of procedures, strategies, and names and addresses of resource people so that their work would benefit a new generation of youngsters. She says, "I discovered you can't help these kids one on one. You have to create a group and make it uncool not to participate. Once the word gets out, they keep coming."

At Dani's office, the kids the public schools have given up on have learned it is uncool not to learn. With the lure of Hawaiian canoe paddling as the centerpiece, Dani created a home for learning Hawaiian culture as well as academic and political skills. In Hawaiian culture, she tells them, you give to the group. What you can give is what defines you, and you must bring your best self. That means getting in shape before the paddling season starts, and improving yourself through learning and helping others. When you paddle, she says, you can't be stronger or weaker than the others. One strong paddler exerting extra effort will stop the canoe. "Equal application of strength" is required, Diane Ho explains.

The ethic of equal application of strength has meaning for these young Hawaiians, for whom individualism — acting higher than others — is a cultural sin. It means group striving for excellence. At Dani's office, they sit around the table conducting their meetings. They make calls to the mayor's office, they get results, and they learn of their own worth.

Dani is one who happily uses people who are happy to be used by her. She calls wealthy lawyer friends and urges them to open their hearts and their checkbooks to her protégés. She signs on a beauty queen to plan a fashion show fundraiser, featuring models who work painfully to overcome teenage awkwardness and unfamiliarity with the kinds of people and kinds of clothes that a fashion show entails. She calls on local designers to donate the outfits.

"You should have seen them," she says, her voice low and soft in admiration. "Some of these kids never get to wear new clothes. They don't like to walk in front of people, so we had them dance instead. They had so much pride, they came so far. The audience could see it, and some of them started to cry."

The fashion show raised enough money to send eighty kids to the sacred island of Kaho'olawe. Only a few living human beings have had the privilege of stepping on the island, which was recently returned to the Hawaiian people after years of desecration by U.S. military bombing practice. "Do you know how they got there?" Dani asked.

"No," I said, knowing she wanted to tell me.

"They paddled," she said, happily pausing to let the magnitude of the feat sink in. Open ocean channel crossing, navigating between islands, is treacherous. The ocean swells rise so high that the paddlers in their low koa wood canoes sometimes lose sight of the horizon.

"We put eighty kids on that island, and we didn't have one incident." It is unclear whether she means teen criminality or physical danger — the island is covered with unexploded ordnance and treacherous terrain — or failure to show the attitude of reverential respect Hawaiian religion demands of visitors to the island. Whatever tests were placed before them, the young paddlers passed, and Dani's pride is clear.

"They are so smart," she says, "and no one knows it." All they need is a chance and adults who believe in them. At Ho and Hamili, Dani Ho and her partner, Ruby Hamili, another Hawaiian graduate of the Richardson School of Law, send out the message again and again. Be proud you are Hawaiian, descendants of the great ocean voyagers. Paddle with equal application of strength, stand tall in the courtroom, know you belong in college, walk gracefully on the land that is yours. At Ho and Hamili, a law firm that affirmative action helped to make, the young paddlers watch and learn from two Hawaiian women who live this creed.

[10]

And Also with You: Extending the Reach of Affirmative Action

A COLLEAGUE OF OURS, who is sympathetic to the goals of affirmative action, tells us that he believes we and other progressives should drop affirmative action as a political goal. "This issue is killing us," he says. The overwhelming mood of the country, he argues, is opposed to affirmative action. A principled stand in favor of it is political suicide. We will lose not only on affirmative action, but on a range of civil rights and human rights initiatives if we demand something that the majority is unprepared to give. This is not the time, he believes, to defend affirmative action.

We disagree. Where the resistance is great is the exact location of the struggles we choose. The current backlash against affirmative action, the confusion and the anger aroused by feminist and antiracist struggles, are markers alerting us to important work.

In friendship, in love, in families, this is so. There are the things we are not supposed to talk about, subjects we draw lines around, marking where we should not venture. Carefully crossing those lines is often what cements relationships and makes love true.

The social and cultural lines that delimit race and gender privilege are much the same. The private clubs that require women to enter through a side door are more than remnants of an old era. They mark the locations of patriarchal power and privilege — places where deals are made and assumptions formed. The women in cities across the country who walked through front doors, either in open defiance or after successful campaigns to drop gender bars, were changing a culture and demanding a share of power.[1] Joining an exclusive club, of course, is not the goal of feminism. The point is that the resistance these trailblazers encountered signaled tangible consequences.

The animosity affirmative action spawns is not a reason for retreat. Rather, it is a reason to expand demands for affirmative action. Affirmative action has not gone far enough. We must reinvigorate and enlarge existing programs.

When we say affirmative action has not gone far enough, we use as our measure the goal of equal participation in economic, political, and social life. In every institution of power, there is continued exclusion of women and people of color, and disparities in power are marked by gender and race lines. The following widely reported statistics[2] portray this inequality. Only about 30 percent of all scientists are women, and in certain specialties the numbers are even more drastic — only 16 percent of physicists, for example, are women. There are fewer women doctors than men, and in every medical specialty women earn less. Between 30 and 40 percent of associate attorneys in law firms are women, but only 11 percent of partners are women. Women make up 50 percent of entry-level accountants, but less than 20 percent of accounting firm partners. They represent 48 percent of journalists, but hold only 6 percent of the top editorial jobs. Forty percent of college professors are women, but they make up only 11 percent of tenured staff. Seventy-two percent of elementary school teachers are women, but they represent only 29 percent of school principals.

Similar statistics reveal the exclusion of people of color. For example, African Americans, 12 percent of the population, hold only 2.5 percent of the managerial jobs "above the glass ceiling." In fact, a white woman with a high school degree has as good a chance as a Black person with a college degree to obtain a managerial position.[3]

Overall, the number of women and minorities in executive or management positions is paltry. Over the past decade there were two women CEOs in fifteen hundred top companies. Ninety-five to 97 percent of the senior managers (corporate vice presidents and up) were men, and of those men, 97 percent were white. The little progress that women made in upper corporate echelons was virtually reserved for white women: 95 percent of women senior managers are white. Among the women who have made it to the senior management level, 95 percent report that a glass ceiling exists to this day for all women.[4]

Most employed women are clustered in occupations that are 75 percent or more women. It's not news that female-dominated occupations pay far less, have fewer benefits, and frequently offer tenuous job security. Moreover, sex discrimination exists even within female-dominated occupations: male nurses earn an average of 10 percent more than female nurses, and male bookkeepers earn an average of 16 percent more than female bookkeepers.[5]

At the slow pace of existing reform, the landscape of privilege — where economically well-off white men run Congress, major corporations, unions, the newspapers and television stations, publishing firms, law, accounting, investment firms, and banks — will remain the prevailing picture well into the next generation. Unless we initiate radical changes now, the gender gap in wealth and earnings will not close, and the feminization of poverty will continue. Affirmative action has made small gains in the direction of equality, but small is not enough. Every corporate board, every university, every union, every branch of the media, should make full integration its goal and should accelerate affirmative action initiatives to achieve that goal today. There is no reason, given the wealth of talent available, to continue exclusion in these institutions.

We oppose subordination on all axes. In this book, we have focused on race and gender in particular both because of our own experiences and because those were the first categories in the affirmative action plans generated by the civil rights movement of the 1960s and 1970s, the plans currently under attack.

Race and gender, however, are only part of the story of how some human beings are made lesser. Failure to see the whole story is one of the reasons the civil rights movement has not brought about widespread equality. A just vision of affirmative action would include our lesbian and gay citizens, who are afraid that whom they love will define what jobs and opportunities they will have; our citizens with disabilities, who are asking not for pity but for liberation in the tradition of civil rights struggles; and the growing ranks of the poor and the working poor, to whom the basic security of adequate food, shelter, and medical care is denied and to whom decent education is largely unavailable. As advocates of expanded affirmative action, we embrace them all.

In committing to expand affirmative action, we face the complaint that now "everyone is a minority," and only straight white men are left out. This familiar inversion of the truth is contradicted by the statistical reality of extraordinary white male advantage. Others complain that affirmative action seeks "special rights" for minorities when equal rights are enough. *We demand whatever rights are necessary to achieve equality.*

To our colleague, and many like him, who counsel scaling down demands for affirmative action as the "special rights" rhetoric generates, for example, antigay legislation in states like Colorado, we answer that retreat rarely ensures safety. Backlash is exactly what we should expect when we attempt to move a culture forward. People don't always cooperate, even when their souls are at stake, in making positive social change. Even as they complain, however, they eventually do change and adjust to new demands. The requested change that seems outlandish today seems probable tomorrow and inevitable the day after that. Thus, we choose a politics of vision over one that asks, "What can we realistically hope to obtain?"

One of the most frequent attacks on affirmative action is that it fails to take into account the poor. As a prominent former mayor once exclaimed at a congressional hearing:

> How galling it is for white males to know that the children of Bill Cosby and Cosby himself are entitled to preferential treatment in a whole host of programs simply because they and he are black. It is unacceptable to fair-minded people that a poor white male from Appalachia, or other parts of the United States, or some Asians, are placed at an enormous disadvantage because of the concept of group rights. Affirmative action laws, executive orders, and regulations have created group rights in the name of equality, a contradiction in terms.[6]

While critics of affirmative action often use the "what about poverty" question as a diversion tactic, the issue of affirmative action based on economic need is an important one. Affirmative action should include the economically disadvantaged, and many of the best programs already do. The University of California, long before Governor Pete Wilson's attack on affirmative action, included in its plan the category of economic disadvantage. Many other universities, including all of the Ivy League schools, consider overcoming economic disadvantage a plus in the admissions process. A student who attains high grades and test scores in spite of growing up poor and going to low-quality public schools is considered a particularly good candidate for admission. This moderately expanded form of affirmative action, however, does not go to the heart of what is needed to overcome economic obstacles to education and opportunity, for it is exceedingly rare for students to come through circumstances of abject poverty with the ability to meet traditional admission criteria.

Real affirmative action for the "poor white male from Appalachia" and for others growing up in poverty must begin with the redistribution of educational resources. We know that intervention in the early years works to open up educational opportunity. A joint study by the University of North Carolina at Chapel Hill and the University of Alabama in Birmingham reveals that poor children who went through supportive preschool programs had higher intelligence test scores, better achievement in math and reading, fewer cases of having to repeat grades, and less special education placement than a comparable group without the benefit of such programs.[7] The academic differences between the two groups of children widened as the children got older: the preschool education had visible, lasting benefits at the ages of eight, twelve, and fifteen. Study after study shows that poor children who are exposed to programs like Headstart obtain educational benefits that last into adulthood. Headstart children are more likely than poor children who do not go to Headstart, for instance, to graduate from high school, stay out of the criminal justice system, go on to college, get a job, and stay off welfare.[8]

The proven success of early intervention programs is well known. Given this success rate, one wonders where all the affirmative action foes who lament the fate of the "poor white male from Appalachia" go when, year after year, Congress refuses full funding for social programs like Headstart, turning away thousands of families of all races who are seeking a better education for their children.

The Children's Defense Fund has reported that a child who has lived in poverty for one year or more is 3.2 times more likely to drop out of high school than a child who was never poor.[9] Poor children live around more crime but have less access to high-quality recreation, which develops positive social skills and puts children in regular contact with supportive adults.[10] Recreation programs and teen job training are labeled "pork" by the Republican Congress, which reduced or eliminated such programs as part of its crime bill revisions.[11]

In every state in the nation, there are children who go hungry when we cut school breakfast programs, who are turned away from overcrowded Headstart classrooms, whose public libraries are closed half the week because of funding cuts. For these children, the affirmative action debate is largely academic. Saying, "We will set aside 1 percent of government contracts for you if you manage to start your own business," or "We will hold a place for you at the university if you can score in the 85 percent range of the SATs" is a cruel jest. If one is denied a fighting chance to obtain the skills necessary to enter the door, no set-aside can help.

Affirmative action for the economically disadvantaged must take two forms. First, we should expand existing programs to include economic disadvantage as a category. This would provide a point of entry for the exceptions, the rare individuals who — often because of significant nonmaterial resources, such as a loving and supportive family — are able to overcome poverty and obtain the minimal qualifications for employment and higher education opportunities. We must make special efforts to include such individuals in all of our public and private institutions.

Second, we must make antipoverty, literacy, and remedial education programs a significant part of our affirmative action efforts. Some colleges, such as the prestigious City College in New York, have made this commitment, saying to students, "If you will work hard, we will meet you halfway. If you had a lousy preparatory education through no fault of your own, we will set up the courses and tutorials that can bring you up to speed so that you can compete in a rigorous university environment."

This type of program recognizes the effects of poverty and exclusion from opportunity and does something about it. Talented, hard-working individuals who grow up poor are not always able to show their talents and sometimes lack skills that they could attain with help. Giving them this help is a fair way to open doors.

Why don't we do it more often? First, it costs. Remedial education and early intervention, unlike set-asides and quotas, require upfront expenditures. Second, these expenditures are seen as redistributions — taking from the haves to give to the have-nots — which go against America's tenets of individualism, private property, and capitalism. Finally, a successful propaganda campaign has convinced even those concerned about poverty that no government antipoverty program will work. Stories of inept bureaucracies and intransigent, congenitally lazy poor people have permeated the culture, to the point where many who would give a dollar to a homeless person on a cold night would not vote to spend a government dollar on a poverty program.

To these reasons for avoiding affirmative action for the economically disadvantaged, we charge prevarication. From our mothers, who made lifelong vocations of teaching and healing young children, we learned this truth: what you give to a child is returned tenfold. The teachers who know how to do this already exist, they are good at what they do, and they could train others to do it. But they are underpaid and unsupported in their efforts.

In these days of budget-cutting madness, Congress has made a cowardly surrender in the War on Poverty. To save tax dollars today, they have committed us to untold billions of future expenditures to pay for multiplying ravages: more child abuse, more crime, more imprisonment, more untrained and unemployable workers, more citizens who believe, and quite dangerously so, that there is nothing to be gained by entering into the social compact. To live among fellow citizens who care nothing for their own lives, or ours, is a scary thing. This is the world we are creating by cutting prenatal care, cutting Aid to Families with Dependent Children (AFDC), and refusing full funding for Headstart.

Certainly, there is a cost to fighting poverty, but it is far exceeded by the cost of expanding poverty. The punishment exacted on poor children is borne by society time and again. A high school dropout, for example, will secure a low-paying job at best, will pay fewer taxes, is more likely to commit a crime, and more likely to get sick.[12] One estimate shows that each dollar cut from AFDC reduces future economic output by up to $1.51, making the cost to society $177 billion for each year that our nation's 14.6 million poor children spend in poverty.[13] Ironically, the Census Bureau estimates that it would cost only about $39.4 billion to end child poverty today.[14]

Are antipoverty programs contrary to American virtues of individualism, private property, and capitalism? The premise of taxation is that any government must collect revenues from individuals and distribute them for the benefit of the collective. We understand this when our tax money is invested in roads and highways or police and fire departments. Education is no less essential to the life of the Republic.

Two of our nation's great philosophers of education, John Dewey and Alexander Meiklejohn, stressed the importance of educational opportunity for all in a democracy. It is not just the ideal of fairness that requires this equality, but the maintenance of democracy itself. Dewey wrote that "a government resting upon popular suffrage cannot be successful unless those who elect and who obey their governors are educated. Since a democratic society repudiates the principle of external authority, it must find a substitute in voluntary disposition and interest; these can be created only by education."[15]

Alexander Meiklejohn, the educational experimentalist and constitutional theorist, understood that participation in democracy's objective, which is self-governance, presupposes education. "All human beings should have the same essential education,"[16] he argued.

Democracy works when all citizens are educated and able to participate actively in self-governance. Under this rationale, our public schools were once the world's finest, but today a devastating effect of America's racism has been the abandonment of public schools. Communities that in days past would have voted inevitably for school bonds, and in support of expanded funding to schools, now reject such proposals. In many parts of the country those with resources send their children to private schools, while public schools — other than enclaves of prestige public schools in wealthy neighborhoods — have become the domain of less privileged "others."

The notion that funding education and antipoverty programs takes from haves to give to have-nots is a perversion of individualism. It does not require confiscatory takings to right the wrongs of which we speak, but it does require that each person see self-interest as tied to the collective. We are born with great gifts of empathy for others, and we can use these gifts to see that each individual has the potential to flourish.

In 1995, on a trip to South Africa we drove through beautiful suburbs made ugly by huge rolls of razor wire coiled along the walls
surrounding gleaming mansions. The mansions had barred windows;
the residents drove cautiously out in the morning to go downtown to
work. Once at work they drove into their guarded buildings and never
ventured out onto the street for fear of robbery. On beautiful sunny
days, the office workers stayed at their desks, never leaving for lunch at
a street café or even to take a walk to the bank for errands.

Next we visited Soweto, where thousands still live in shacks with no
running water. We marveled at the patience and faith of the poor Black
populace, waiting for promised reform, living in shacks while others
lived in castles on the hill.

Go to any country where the gap between rich and poor is wide and
you will see the coils of razor wire protecting the mansions — the same
wire that surrounds prisons in our United States. Everyone is imprisoned, behind bars and alarms and barbed wire, in these worlds of
inequality. We don't want to live with such fear, and we worry that the
United States is becoming just such a nation. As individuals who wish
to walk down the street without fear, as individuals raised to care for
others, we reject mutual imprisonment as a solution for social inequality, and we call for expanded affirmative action to bring the poor back
into the community.

In addition to devoting resources to the long-term goal of ending
poverty, we need to include the economically disadvantaged in existing
affirmative action programs. These are two means to the same end.

In supporting an expansion of affirmative action to include the category of class disadvantage, we do not suggest this as a substitute for
race- and gender-based affirmative action. It is an addition. Racial remediation and gender equity are required because of racism and sexism.
The middle-class African American who is stopped by the police for no
reason, or is turned away from a rental office that has a secret policy of
not showing apartments to Blacks, needs to see an end to the culture of
racism. Poverty is often linked to racism and sexism, but it is not coex-
tensive with it. Eradicating poverty, as much as that dream is dear to our
hearts, will not eradicate racism and patriarchy. Thus, we call for expanding the categories included in affirmative action, not for the substi-
tution of one category for another.

Among those who agree that we must widen affirmative action to benefit the economically disadvantaged, there are some who will still disagree with our call to include all subordinated peoples.

It is not our intent in this book to lay out the full case for equality for gays and lesbians. We simply make the claim, consistent with the civil rights tradition we come from, that all human beings are entitled to equal dignity. We therefore oppose heterosexism — the system that says only heterosexual relationships are acceptable — and homophobia, the fear and hatred of lesbians and gay men. People are entitled to love and make love in conditions of freedom.

In addition to supporting this basic freedom for gay and lesbian individuals, we hold that it is in the interests of all of us to end oppression based on sexuality. Adrienne Rich's famous essay "On Compulsory Heterosexuality"[17] never fails to startle first-time readers. She describes, in a way that resonates with many women readers, the deeply loving women-to-women feelings that reside in families, in friendships, in social life. She suggests that the presence of homophobia and the coercion to choose heterosexual relationships are so entrenched in our society that none of us knows what our sexuality would be in a world without that coercion.

The vibrant political activism and the new academic studies coming from the gay community challenge us to expand our thinking about subordination. How is homophobia, if it is a central part of our culture, a cradle for other forms of subordination? What about poverty, and the persistent habit of making poor people, immigrants, and unwed mothers "the other"? Is this process something we learn in a state of preunderstanding the first time someone explains that girls love boys, boys love girls and deviation therefrom is evil?

We don't know the complete answer, but we do see significant evidence that the admonition not to show weakness, and the push to gain power over others, come in a package of homophobia that most young boys receive in this culture: "Don't be a sissy." Out gay and lesbian schoolteachers, firefighters, business people, and laborers, are a remedy for this coercion. Seeing gay people in these iconic positions, knowing that they are both gay and citizen, gay and worker, gay and teacher, will change us all, working against the tyranny of homophobia.

The call for affirmative action for gays and lesbians is threatening exactly because it would subvert the culture of patriarchy. The gay community itself has not demanded affirmative action, making a political judgment that the world is not ready for such a sea change. Hate-filled antigay campaigns, often couched in religious language, have created a political realm in which asking for a fair share of power and access seems like asking too much.

We defer to the judgments that come from the gay community about whether, when, and where to push for affirmative action, and emphasize that, to our knowledge, inclusion in affirmative action is not a present demand of any gay organization. Given the real threats posed by organized antigay political movements, we can hardly second-guess decisions made within gay and lesbian organizations about strategy and allocation of effort. The purpose of our call is to consider the benefit that gay affirmative action would bring to all of us. Whether or not now is the time, the time will come to put sexuality at the center of the civil rights movement, not to give anyone special rights, but simply to create full equality. The purpose of this book is to defend affirmative action as part of a dream of freedom for all. We choose to consider the full promise of what affirmative action can be, and to say to our gay brothers and sisters that when and if you choose to make this demand, we will be there with you.

Why should we care about homophobia, we are asked in communities of color, when racism is what is destroying the community we care about? There is a crisis — the children with guns, the young men in prison, the hate crimes against us on the rise. This should be our priority.

We respond by saying that homophobia undergirds systems like racism and patriarchy in ways that hurt all of us. This seems like a ridiculous idea at first encounter and like a simple truth when the examples play out.

Consider the children with guns. So many young people are shot down in the streets of Washington, D.C., that the U.S. military sends its doctors there to learn the latest techniques for patching up young bullet-torn bodies. Who is killing these children? The simple answer is the person with the finger on the trigger, most often another young person, born in poverty. The solution is to throw the shooter in prison. Unfortunately, this response has done nothing to end the violence.

Certainly racism is at work. If some disease or natural disaster struck down a number of white children equal to the number of Black children killed by gunfire this year, the President would declare a national emergency. Our willingness to let the killing continue is tied to a culture that devalues young Black lives. Poverty is also a critical explanation. Poverty made fertile ground for the guns and drug trade that have decimated poor Black neighborhoods. Without jobs, without decent education, there is nothing in the universe of these children that tells them there is another way. No sports programs, no computers, no marching bands, no playgrounds, no recreation centers, no supermarkets, no malls where a teenager could get an afterschool job. The massive abandonment of the city has taken away normal life, leaving these children to grow up where criminal activity becomes both livelihood and place of belonging.

Racism and poverty are obvious causes. Sexism and homophobia are less obvious but still significant. There is a critical fact buried in the statistics about young lives lost to gang wars on the streets of our cities: the killers and the killed are overwhelmingly male. The lesson that guns are power, that backing down is weakness, that weakness is horrible, is a lesson taught by patriarchy and homophobia. Consider how young boys are socialized in this culture. The first time they show weakness to peers in a physical confrontation, they learn its cost. Failure to participate in activities of bravado draws forth taunts of "punk," "sissy," and, as children grow older, more explicit gay-bashing. The coercive mechanism that socializes a child to grow up to hold a gun and shoot down another child in the street begins with this taunting and with a strictly enforced and gendered code of behavior.

A student who grew up in South-Central Los Angeles, a part of town notorious for having the toughest and most violent gangs, once told a story about a gang member she knew who confessed that he sometimes encountered members of rival gangs and deliberately pretended not to see them, hoping they would do the same. Two young men, dressed in street-tough colors, might pass each other in the aisles of a convenience store, avoiding eye contact, each silently praying that the other will remain in unspoken agreement not to create an incident so that each could go home quietly to his mother. If there are witnesses, other crew members, girlfriends, neighbors, to comment, the silent wish to stay safe is overcome by a lifelong message: back down in public, and you may as well be dead. The culture of male posturing takes over, often ending in tragedy. The saddest and hardest thing is that no one really wants this, neither the killer nor the killed.

Opening up gender roles and depleting the power of homophobic coercion is thus one critical step in fighting teen violence. If boys can say, "I'd rather be a sissy than a fighter," or "There's nothing wrong with boys loving boys, and I'm not scared if you think I do," then a critical mechanism of socialization to violence is robbed of power. Resistance seems unimaginable in present culture, and that is why present culture must change.

Affirmative action, as a closet-ending mechanism, can make it impossible to pretend that homosexuals are evil, other, distant, not our family, not our friends, not our neighbors, not our teachers, not members of our churches, not vital to the polity. A large, welcomed gay presence in our lives means young people are less subject to homophobic coercion.

Similarly, the visible presence of people with disabilities in a range of roles and settings reduces our fear of being ostracized because of physical difference. What we have learned from the disability rights movement is the universality of subordination. All human beings are vulnerable to disability, and all will experience at least part of their lives with physical challenges, including the vulnerability of infancy, illness, and aging. Given the universality of this experience, it is remarkable that we continue to see "normal" as able-bodied, implying that disability is somehow less than normal. Many people with physical or mental illnesses keep them hidden because of shame.

A focus of the disability rights movement is the decentering of able-bodiedness. This insight challenges us to create a physical environment that welcomes a range of physical abilities, and to modify work and educational practices to accommodate the same. More profound, however, is the cultural and attitudinal change that comes when disability becomes normal. We can normalize the use of a wheelchair or sign language, for example, so that we feel comfortable with it and lose the sense of fear that disability holds. This takes some of the terror out of the reality of our dependence on our bodies and converts a culture of distant pity into one of community; converts fear of aging into acceptance of life's natural progression. Reasonable accommodation of people with disabilities, now mandated by law, requires that we disrupt business as usual in order for all to participate. Going beyond this mandate, we should actively recruit and set aside places for people with disabilities because of what they can add to our schools and workplaces.

Back in the days when children in wheelchairs were warehoused in schools where "normal" children never met them, all children learned a dangerous message: don't be sick or weak or different, and shun those who are. At the macro level, this was an ideological base of tyranny and oppression. At the personal level, it created internal tyrannies for scores of children who lived in terror that their own difference — whether a stutter or an alcoholic parent or a chronic illness — would mark them forever as outsiders. To this day, such thinking keeps many from seeking help for mental illness or addiction.

Just as affirmative action for gays and lesbians can bring them out of the closet and end the coercion the closet imposes, at varying levels, on all of us, so can affirmative action for citizens with disabilities end another form of the closet. A large, open presence of the disabled in all our institutions says it is okay if you are in a wheelchair; it is okay if you are dyslexic; it is okay if you need an antidepressant. We are not all the same, and we can stop fearing that someone will discover and punish us for our difference.

Immigrant status and multilingualism are also potential additions to affirmative action categories that are never discussed. Present antidiscrimination laws prevent discrimination on the basis of national origin. In spite of these laws, however, it is common practice to exclude immigrants and those with linguistic differences from the workplace. Some citizens feel it is legitimate to reserve jobs and other benefits for the native born, and to demand linguistic and cultural conformity. Studies show that applicants with "foreign" accents are turned away from employment, regardless of their qualifications.[18] In some workplaces, employees are forbidden to speak any language other than English, even during breaks, on the theory that a foreign language makes English-speaking co-workers uncomfortable.

Ours is a nation made strong by the contributions of immigrants, and we can rise above the xenophobia that corrupts our national culture. In studying the history of our commitment to democratic values, we find the greatest threats to civil liberties have invariably co-existed with xenophobia. The Alien and Sedition Acts,[19] the Palmer raids,[20] the HUAC hearings,[21] the curse of McCarthyism,[22] the World War II internment of Japanese Americans[23] — these landmarks on the road of constitutional sacrilege are all painted with xenophobia. The fear of some alien outsider, intent on destruction of the United States, has led us time and again to destroy our own constitutional values in ways that shame us in hindsight.

Fighting xenophobia is an imperative for constitutionalists and civil libertarians. Paranoid belief systems about foreigners must give way to a culture of tolerance and the celebration of difference.

Affirmative action is a way to make this happen. People who think they cannot understand someone with a different accent may find they can when they are given the chance to work and learn alongside the person different from themselves. Sociolinguists tell us that the ability to comprehend across linguistic difference is more a function of attitude than phonology. People who are motivated, unprejudiced, and exposed to difference will comprehend a range of accents. People who are fearful and convinced they can't understand, won't. What would affirmative action for linguistic difference look like? We could make a special effort in hiring, in education, in granting business opportunities to seek out individuals who are immigrants or are multilingual. Including these individuals, particularly in high-profile positions, such as teaching or broadcasting, would expose others to the reality that linguistic difference is functional and beneficial. Children who grow up hearing many accents are less likely to say, as adults, that they can't understand, or that hearing another language offends them.

Of course, affirmative action sometimes brings cultural disruption. The easy assumption that we all share basic attitudes and social codes marks life without affirmative action. Without even realizing it, players in monocultural institutions live and work with this cozy ease. New languages, new etiquettes, abound in the multicultural world. While much of the new is exciting and enriching, the end of old comfort levels is experienced as a loss by many.

We can't go back to that easy world of one language, one way, because it is a fantasy. This already is a nation of multiple cultures. Gays and lesbians are already our relatives, our classmates, our co-workers.

The immigrants who pick the produce we buy every week are an integral part of our nation and economy. Languages like Chinese and Spanish have echoed in our cities' corridors for longer than any of us have been living.

The person in the wheelchair may be you, if not today, then someday in the future if you are fortunate to live so long as to know a gradual decline. None of this will fit back in the closet once we let it out, and it is already out. What we need now is affirmative action to proclaim the process of inclusion, to let our large family know its own.

In writing this book, we encountered great fears of expanding affirmative action to embrace all layers of diversity: race, gender, language, culture, sexuality, physical ability. When will it end? If affirmative action is intended to challenge norms, it seems destructive. It is like taking out the heart, taking out the greatness of a *United* States. Furthermore, it seems to remove the people at the center — economically well-off, able-bodied, heterosexual white men — and place them outside. Words evoking ritual sacrifice are used in making this claim.

Children play games like "dogpile,"[24] "cooties," and "slambook" to work through the terror of human existence, of both needing others and fearing, always, harm from them. Living in a world deeply divided into have and have-not, where the youngest children learn quickly that it is embarrassing to have friends visit when there is an alcoholic in your home, humiliating to say you can't go to the movies because your parents don't have six dollars to spare, dangerous to say you don't want to dogpile on anybody, we cannot imagine a world without such terror. This failure of imagination makes it impossible to believe that affirmative action is anything other than a reverse dogpile.

In a world marked by domination, people survive by negotiating hierarchy and struggling to stay above the bottom of the pile. It is hard to believe that those making a claim for inclusion don't intend to get theirs by taking yours. We understand this impulse even as we condemn it. There is a way, there must be, to say you can speak Spanish without annihilating English. There is a way to hear the claims of gays and lesbians without heaving the weary exclamation "You too? Now you want affirmative action too?" There is no room left on this lifeboat; it's sinking already.

Our sense that the boat is sinking and that there is no grace left to hand out, no heart left for another story of pain or exclusion, is the current crisis of the American soul. It is a metaphor that reflects a material reality. There is a true economic crisis facing us, and end-of-the-month bills remind many citizens of it. The sense that there is not enough to go around is not paranoid. Neither is it enough to guide us out of this mess.

Affirmative action is part of the way out. Using the strength of each of us, promoting multiple talents and virtues, bringing into the center those previously left out, is a recipe for economic revitalization as well as public mental health. Bringing new people into the circle of the human is not dehumanizing to those already there. It is the opposite. Enrichment, not displacement, is how we must learn to think.

Two related questions arise when we suggest the need to expand affirmative action. First, people want to know exactly what it will look like. What mechanisms, processes, and adjustments would affirmative action for the poor or gays or immigrants, for example, entail? Second, we face a specific concern that redistribution inevitably leads to tyranny. As one friend asked us, "Who makes the distributional decisions, on what principles, and how do we ensure that the discretionary power necessary for substantive justice doesn't reintroduce unfairness and abuse?"

Our goal is to set forth a way of looking at the world that makes affirmative action not only plausible but necessary. We defend race-conscious remedy in the context of a history of racism; we seek to dismantle patriarchy because patriarchy hurts all human beings in the ways it constructs gender. We deliberately avoid providing a blueprint for implementing specific affirmative action programs, because implementation must pay close attention to location and context and requires the complex work of responding to the particularities of affected constituencies. The world of simplistic answers and all-encompassing rules is what reactionaries use to attack affirmative action and other social programs. Taking race into account is racist. End of analysis. Providing jobs for the unemployed is socialist. End of analysis.

The actual world is more complex than that, and the better course is to abandon the demagogue's easy answers in exchange for what one poet called diving into the wreck. Complexity always, and, as another poet said, "Wrap your contradictions 'round you like a shawl."

In the days when the community-control model of affirmative action reigned, the specifics of local programs were hammered out in often-contentious all-night meetings. At the University of San Francisco Law School, Asian students argued among themselves about whether the social position of a third-generation Japanese American from Hawaii was sufficiently different from that of a second-generation Chinese American from rural California to merit different treatment in the school's affirmative action program. Those same students left their Asian caucus to make the case to other students of color why Asians should receive any affirmative action consideration at all, which required educating colleagues about institutionalized racism and violence against Asians. At the University of California, Los Angeles, Asian students made this case to African American students, and twenty-five years later their voices crack with emotion as they describe how their Black colleagues were moved to give up places set aside for Blacks in order to include Asian Americans in affirmative action at UCLA. This process — the lifelong alliances formed and the understanding gained — was more important than the outcome.

Figuring out whom to include, in what numbers, according to what criteria, at what cost, are institutional decisions that must take into account many factors, including the history of discrimination at that institution, in that local community, and in the country at large; the present role of the institution in perpetuating inequality; and the unmet needs of communities traditionally excluded from that institution. The principle we choose to guide this process is antisubordination. Should we make a place for a third-generation Japanese American woman from Hawaii? What are the facts about subordination of people like her? Racist violence targeting her is on the rise, though certain opportunities in professions are more open to her than they were twenty-five years ago. Her position in structures of domination and subordination is in flux. Whether she is an appropriate candidate for affirmative action will depend on the circumstances.

Saying there is no all-purpose test is not the same as saying that it is always difficult to come up with an affirmative action plan. For the many institutions that have never made room for anyone different, the need to start and the choice of how to do it are obvious. If there has never been a woman partner at the Smith firm, if there has never been a nonwhite firefighter at the local fire department, someone needs to ask why and figure out how to change the picture. The second-generation affirmative action questions similarly have some easy answers as well as hard ones. If there are no out gays or lesbians in the workplace, that is a loss to many and a gain for homophobia. It may be more important to hire any gay person than it is to figure out which gay people can most effectively reduce homophobia in that workplace. At some point, however, the antisubordination goal, which in our view is the bottomline justification for affirmative action, deserves specific attention. How can we hire and facilitate the institutional success of those gays and lesbians who will contribute actively to the eradication of homophobia? "Identity plus" as a criterion for affirmative action — that is, considering not only how people identify, but what they have chosen to do in their life with that identity — will best serve the antisubordination goal in many contexts.

A complexified approach leads to the kinds of apprehensions our friend raises. It seems amorphous, unpredictable, arbitrary and risky. The imagery of darkness and descent into chaos, the prediction of unbridled discretion, often accompany the concerns we hear about antisubordination approaches to justice.

A world that is unpredictable, unstable, and degrading to the individual is the present world for many of the people we care about. That world must enter the calculation when we worry about whether our efforts at rectification will only make things worse.

Social change movements can bring harm along with change. We call for vigilance against arbitrary power of any kind, and we challenge the bipolar thinking that puts fair process and substantive equality in inevitable opposition. This bipolarity is the legacy of the cold war and red-baiting rhetoric. Ending poverty is socialism is totalitarianism. When critical theorists critique due process as an illusion masking vast substantive unfairness, this is heard as a critique of due process itself. The thought that we could have both procedural fairness and redistribution of wealth is incomprehensible, in this view.

When we talked to jurists in South Africa, we were impressed with their deep commitment to the rule of law and procedural fairness. "You must understand," one distinguished judge told us, "for many years all we had was the rules. All we had to save a life of a comrade was the argument that the technical steps in a legal procedure were not followed. It is hard for us to give that up now."

The new South African Constitution is revolutionary. It promises substantive justice in ways that put it centuries ahead of our own. Food, water, and shelter are its core promises to citizens. It is also a constitution filled to overflowing with due process.[25]

No one who has lived without fair procedure would write a constitution that provides for less. In taking the first steps toward substantive justice, and affirmative action is one such step, fair, orderly, and humane process is a necessary adjunct.

Rethinking university admissions to include poor people; changing hiring procedures to welcome those with disabilities; including out gays and lesbians in positions of public authority — expansions like these need not take place outside a legally ordered world. These expansions are based on principle; they are not arbitrary. A careful process of fact-gathering must accompany the effort to expand affirmative action. Who is in fact excluded from the room when major decisions of public policy are presently made? Who is subjected disproportionately to violence and economic disadvantage? What cultural images and stereotypes degrade members of this group? How pervasive is the bias against them?

There are answers to these questions available from credible sources, including economic and social science evidence subject to evaluation in the same way we evaluate other forms of information we consult when making public policy. It is a fantasy of projection that says, "If we expand affirmative action, someone else will just pick people like themselves to get everything."

President Clinton, in his response to critics of affirmative action, said, "Mend it, don't end it." That is the state of present liberal defenses of affirmative action. It concedes to criticism — there must be something wrong, something to mend — and it retreats from any notion of expanding affirmative action to reach more people than the modest numbers included in existing programs.

We stake out a different position. Affirmative action works, but it does not go far enough as presently constructed. No woman, no person of color, no out gay or lesbian, has ever had the chance to stand where the President does.

His speech defending affirmative action was a good one, which we admire. Our work is not over, he said. "We had slavery for centuries before the passage of the Thirteenth, Fourteenth, and Fifteenth Amendments. We waited another hundred years for the civil rights legislation. Women have had the vote for less than a hundred years. We have always had difficulty with these things, as most societies do. But we are making more progress than many other nations. Since, based on the evidence, the job is not done, here is what I think we should do. We should reaffirm the principle of affirmative action and fix the practices."

To that we add "and expand it." Reach out and pull up the many who wish to stand beside you — not above you, not below you — to bring their hands, too, to the task of rebuilding our land.

[11]

A New Heart
and a New Spirit

A new heart I will give you,
and a new spirit I will put within you;
and I will remove from your body the heart of stone
and give you a heart of flesh.

— Ezekiel 36:26

I am not guilty of anything. My ancestors never owned any slaves. I should not be made to pay the price of their transgressions. Their guilt does not pass on to me. I did not create Plessy. I regret that Reconstruction ended in 1877. I was not even born until 1970. Racism is not my problem because I did not create it. To be sure, I do not like that the system is the way it is. If I could be all-powerful, the system would be even-steven. It is not a creation of my intent. So I am not guilty. When you point the finger and look for someone to blame, someone who must give up something in the name of equality, don't look at me, because it is not my fault.

A student in one of our classes wrote this in response to reading a draft excerpt from this book. In the same reflective piece, he also wrote:

Funny. Last week my basement flooded. So I got out the wet-dry vacuum that my landlord provides for just this situation and started to clean it up. The ironic thing is that I did not create the flood. I did not start the rain. It was not me who improperly sealed the wall. Yet, it would be folly for me to just sit there and say, "It's not my fault. I am not guilty of creating this flood. Therefore, I will not clean it up."

I view racism as my problem that I share with the rest of the country . . . Guilt or no guilt, it is something that I must deal with whether I desire to or not. But to say that I am responsible for only that damage that I caused gets us nowhere. Indeed, the moment I fail to take responsibility for the damage caused beyond my own actions is the moment that I do become guilty. It is a lesson I learned a long time ago in elementary school. It is the sins of omission that are far worse than the sins of commission.[1]

The double-voicedness of these statements was so striking, we spoke with the student to make sure we understood his intent: "Who is speaking in the opening of your paper?"

He smiled. "It's me; it's both me," he responded.

Our young student, who doesn't want to shoulder the blame for the failure of Reconstruction, who mops up the flood in his budget-priced basement apartment, is part of the audience we had in mind as we wrote this book. We thought of him, and the many students over the years who have asked hard questions about affirmative action.

Many — perhaps most — of the students we encounter in recent years oppose affirmative action or express serious doubts about it. We wanted to offer them a vision that goes beyond "somebody has to pay for 1877"; a rhetoric more forthright than "diversity is good for everybody." Affirmative action is about cleaning up the basement because it is where you live. It is necessary, just, and soul-enriching.

Once upon a time people would say, "Don't talk about race, religion, or politics in polite company." Affirmative action is one of those topics: raise it and duck, unless you are prepared for anger, resentment, miscommunication, and a good dose of personal invective.

To get students to begin a discussion of the taboo topic of our day, we used an artificial exercise in a class we co-teach. We divided the class into four groups, and assigned each a role: Group 1 was the critical race theorist/feminist activist. Picture someone like Professor Matsuda, we told the class, or someone like Professor Patricia Williams, whose book we had just read.

Group 2 was the law school dean who, while not a radical, was prepared to defend her school's affirmative action program to alumni and students.

Group 3 was the student who says, "I see good arguments on both sides, but in the end I come out against affirmative action." Perhaps this

272] THE WELCOME TABLE

person is reluctant to take a public position, but will share serious misgivings about affirmative action in private conversations. From past experience, we know this describes many law students.

Group 4 was the conservative activist who is an aggressive opponent of affirmative action and proud of it, someone, perhaps, from the Federalist Society, a conservative law student group.

We asked the students to talk about what these characters might say about affirmative action, and what background beliefs they might hold. We asked that they try to use empathic skills in taking on the assigned role. Rather than caricature, we sought a real sense of how this person sees the world.

They had no problem imagining the rhetoric on all sides, and they listed several arguments in four columns on the chalkboard.

In looking at what the students had written, we pointed out that the deepest ideological conflict is in two arguments at either end of pro– and anti–affirmative action debate. We circled them: "redistribution" on the left, and "bell curve" on the right. Both of these start from a unified factual premise: present distributions of wealth, power, education, and material benefits are uneven, with certain groups — women and people of color — less well-represented at the top. Two alternative explanations exist for this: nature or subordination. If nature is the cause, if certain classes of the human species are less intelligent, less aggressive, less able, the wisdom of nature — both the nature of Darwin and that of Adam Smith — is best left alone. If subordination is the cause, then antisubordination practices, including redistribution, are fair.

This, we suggested in class that day, is the reason the arguments in the middle of the board seem to go nowhere. Both the reluctant supporters ("diversity") and the reluctant opponents ("not at my expense") of affirmative action prefer to limit the terms of the debate, in order to avoid talking about either natural inferiority or redistribution.

In saying that people who presently have preferred tickets of admission to the marketplace have a right to keep their seats, the liberal opponents of affirmative action use a language of individualism and merit. While it was easy to see why a Jim Crow seat in the "whites only" section was an unfair advantage, it is less easy to see why the recipient of a job or a letter of admission to a prestigious university has an unfair advantage once the Jim Crow signs have been taken down. If all are given an equal opportunity to compete, let the best person win. The logical extension of this argument is that those who can't compete under existing measures are undeserving. If those who lose out in fair competition are disproportionately women and members of minority groups, that is something beyond the scope of antidiscrimination law. It belongs outside of law altogether, in the realm of what we call natural or private.

Calling exclusion natural is what theories of race-gender inferiority do explicitly. Most people, living in a century marked by unspeakable horrors done in the name of natural inferiority, reject such theories completely both as a matter of fact and as a matter of ethics. No human being is naturally inferior to another; none is inevitably limited in potential at birth by nature of race or gender.

Herein lies the rhetorical "do not enter" sign for opponents of affirmative action. Those who don't want to cross over into arguing present distributions are just — because of natural inferiority, or natural choice ("women are risk-averse and therefore take less lucrative jobs") — are left saying yes, existing distributions are not always fair, but it is also unfair to penalize someone who didn't cause those distributions as the cost of achieving equality in fact. "In the end, I just can't support affirmative action."

Similarly, the liberal supporter of affirmative action who prefers to emphasize the value of diversity sidesteps the question of redistribution. Arguments that we all benefit when new people and new ideas are welcomed to the workplace offer little solace to the individual who feels that his job was given to someone else in the interest of this vague thing called diversity. The sincere institutional supporter of affirmative action who focuses on the life of the institution over the rights claims of individuals never answers the key claim of reluctant opponents: it just isn't fair.

Without talking about structural inequality, unconscious racism, institutionalized patriarchy, and antisubordination theory, it is impossible to defend affirmative action. Redistribution is the scary word everyone wants to avoid on this side of the debate. Corporate boosters and law school deans who support affirmative action must cabin their rhetoric in the realm of maximizing institutional goals: profit making in one case, the enrichment that follows diversity in the other. Radical supporters of affirmative action are the only ones, then, who will take on the redistribution question.

We once heard a joke about a group of monks who had a policy of practicing the teaching of their religion that Christ appears in the form of the least advantaged. They always offered food and shelter to the needy who came to their door. One night as they sat down to dinner, they saw yet another hungry-looking stranger approaching the monastery. One of them looked up and said wearily, "Jesus Christ, is it you again?"

The idea that we should take in every stranger must be a joke. It must be funny, odd, laughable. Right? Of all the arguments we hear in support of affirmative action, there is only one, in the end, that counters the claim that "it just isn't fair." It is the one no politician, no law school dean, no corporate CEO, no editor of a major daily newspaper will make. It is the argument closeted in mainstream defenses of affirmative action and this is it: Yes, you should open your door to strangers because they are you, they are your God if you have one, they are your soul.

The United States Constitution forbids redistribution in several specific clauses, including the Contracts Clause and the Fifth Amendment. Our founding document reflects the fears elites expressed at the time: those without property — the debtors and the wage laborers — might, in this new experiment called democracy, rise up and take from those who have. Thus the founders commanded that the government could not erase debts, nor take private property without just compensation. Even as they created an unprecedented system of government by the people, even as they outlawed nobility, they conceded to the pressure to maintain slavery and to protect existing accumulations of wealth.

There is another kind of property the framers may well have protected if they had possessed the conceptual tools to do it. They feared the rising up of have-nots, the anger at privilege, the questioning of entitlement to economic and political power that this book represents. They didn't write into the Constitution an anti–affirmative action clause, but they might have if they had thought about it.

In spite of this history we write this book as Constitutionalists, as two who believe that the founding document is good for the long haul. The Fourteenth Amendment, added to the Constitution after Abraham

Lincoln's "Great Civil War," was consecrated, along with the ground at Gettysburg, by "brave men, living and dead, who struggled here." The Fourteenth Amendment added a new dream to the great American experiment. It mandated equality, making ours the first nation in human history to make equality the law.

Like Frederick Douglass, we choose to participate in the ongoing process of constitutional interpretation that makes democracy a living thing. Douglass knew the Constitution was born in slavery, with slavery written right into its text. Nonetheless, he chose to embrace the Constitution and claim that the promise of liberty, including the aspirational language of the Preamble, included the enslaved. His abolitionist fight, alongside Lincoln's "brave men, living and dead, who struggled here," wrote slavery out of the Constitution. Out of the most bloody war of our history, we were given the gift of a new Constitution, one that embraced equality.

After that great war, the substantive meaning of equality was clear. We could not pass from a nation of slavery to a nation of universally free and equal citizens without reconstruction. Newly freed slaves needed affirmative efforts to enforce their rights and to give them the means to exercise liberty: The Freedman's Bureau's forty acres, a mule, and the vote were promises never realized, a reconstruction ended by political expediency, nightriders, and Jim Crow signs.

The affirmative action debate today is, as our student recognized, the legacy of 1877 and the failure of reconstruction. Our nation was not able to make equality the law of the land, even on paper, until the civil rights acts passed in what some call the Second Reconstruction. In 1964 we outlawed discrimination in public accommodations, education, housing, and employment. It took us until 1972 to outlaw gender discrimination in education.

The civil rights acts, however, were not enough to unwrite a four-hundred-year history of racism and patriarchy. The reasons are many: antidiscrimination law is notoriously difficult to enforce, and race and gender subordination are deeply embedded in places the law is slow to reach: in psyches, cultural practices, unconscious exclusion. The only way to make equality real is to attack and dismantle inequality.

Affirmative action in education and hiring alone, however, is not enough to bring about the last reconstruction. To make every citizen part of the polity — valued, voting, informed, active, participating — will require substantive equality. Not just the right to go to school, but the right to go to schools that are safe and well-equipped for learning. Not just the right of nondiscrimination in the workplace, but the right to have a job, and the right to safety, fairness and dignity in that job. Not just the right to buy a house as long as you have money, but the right to basic shelter regardless of wealth. The right to health care; the right to childcare and paid parental leave; the right to prenatal care and to food.

Affirmative action is just one part of a larger claim to substantive equality. The Constitution mandates this at its core, because none of it works without the people. None of the rights guaranteed by the Bill of Rights — free speech, freedom of religion, freedom of contract — makes sense to children living in shelters or old women eating out of trash dumpsters. The great promise of mass political participation is a sham as illiteracy grows and access to information is increasingly the exclusive domain of those few with thousands of dollars worth of computer equipment at their disposal.

We could defend a utopian vision at the bottom line: The costs of refusing to provide prenatal care, preventive public health care, quality childcare, decent public schools are far greater than the costs of providing those things. Consider what we pay, for example, to fight a raging tuberculosis epidemic, caused by poverty and absence of basic public health care in this country. Consider the costs of an imprisonment rate higher than that of any other industrialized nation. Consider the costs of crime, aggression, and violence that we pay when we create a growing class of citizens who feel no reward will come to them from conforming to the laws, social expectations, or norms of the larger society. Those who are in the business of calculating these costs come inevitably to the same conclusion: pay now or pay tenfold later. Moving to the suburbs will not save us from the new resistant strains of tuberculosis, nor from the crime and anomie that city borders cannot contain.

While the cost-benefit analysis could end the argument against substantive justice, we choose to defend a constitutional vision of substantive equality on broader grounds than self-interest. The ultimate reason we should all care if anyone, anywhere, goes without is that we are all part of the human family. When human beings watch something sad or horrible happen to other human beings, they are themselves wounded.

This is the nature of the animal we are. Empathy is bred in our bones and housed in our souls.

The psychologists who study what they call "posttraumatic stress disorder" are aware of this phenomenon. The trauma of watching others in pain is deeply damaging to the psyche, even when you are in no immediate danger yourself. The rescuer arriving after the fact at a scene of disaster; the Vietnam nurse who heard the screams of the dying; the witness who watches a crime of violence from the safety of a window across the street. People react to witnessing with the same nightmares, trembling, anxiety, depression, and physical revulsion that follow from personal endangerment.

The unsafety of others is disruptive of our own quiet sleep. The woman driving home to her own warm bed spots an older woman who pushes her life's possessions in a shopping cart, wandering down the street in disorientation. The driver wonders, "Could it happen to me?" The man whose friend is laid off after twenty years with the company soberly calculates how long he could go without a paycheck; maybe six months before he'd have to sell the family home. A child coming home from the funeral of a child thinks about the randomness of gunfire in his neighborhood. He thinks, "It could have been me."

The language of individual responsibility, of free will, and of choice may create an illusion of safety by day. We believe, most of the time, that we can protect ourselves through hard work and caution. "It will never be me." In the shadow moments, however, we know we are not safe. We are desperately alone in a world in which no one is responsible for the pain of any other person.

There is only one way out of that sad place: to care for others and to know thereby that someone will care for you. The mindset that rejects everything from school lunches for poor children to affirmative action in employment is the one that believes life is a competition for a meager pile of goods: get a little and keep it away from others who want to steal it from you. In this lonely crusade no stranger, ever, will render aid or comfort. Many people have lived lives that make them believe this negative state is true and inevitable: it is the human condition.

Our ultimate message in this book is of the greater possibilities for human existence. We have known all our lives that others will care for us; that generosity, love, and deep joy are not only possible but inevitable in this life. We were blessed to come into the world surrounded by multiple communities of people who said, in repeated word and deed, "You are ours, you belong, you are special, we will care for you."

It does not seem crazy to us that people would prefer to live under that ethic, and that it is attainable not just in families, but also in broadly, encompassing multitudes.

It won't happen, we presume, in our lifetimes. The struggle for affirmative action and other forms of collective action to repair community is "no easy walk," as one anthem says. This book was written in a period of retrenchment, with courts, legislatures, governors, boards of regents, all making new proclamations of the death of affirmative action. Many of our students and colleagues in struggle are despairing, wondering what point there is to yet another protest, another book, another rally in the face of massive social resistance to a civil rights and human rights agenda.

We have two answers. First, the struggle itself is the point. To stand for a brighter vision of human possibility gives life meaning; it is a refusal to participate in the murder of one's own spirit. Second, the attack on affirmative action, coming as it does out of tremendous anxiety in a changing world, is an opening for a more progressive vision. Present social structures, from the material structure of massive inequality of wealth, to the rhetorical structure justifying that inequality, are unstable. The attack on affirmative action is an attempt to shore up a tottering tower of privilege, and in responding with an aggressive defense of affirmative action, we hope to reveal privilege and dethrone it.

As we wrote this book, we wondered if it was a contradiction to speak ecumenically (affirmative action is for everybody) and redistributively (affirmative action is about ending privilege). We decided it was not. Certainly implementing expanded affirmative action will mean an end to business as usual, with concomitant feelings of displacement and discomfort for those who were advantaged by the old order. In some cases, the displacement is real. If more women are let into the workplace, there will be fewer jobs for men, at least in the short run. If more students of color are let into the universities, there will be fewer places for whites. While this result is defensible, there are few altruistic enough to voluntarily give up what they see as an entitlement in order to make room for a stranger.

Indeed, if altruism of this kind were commonplace, we would not need affirmative action. We are faced with the tension that has plagued this nation since the beginning. We want equality, but we are mindful of its full costs. We oppose aristocracy, but we are complicit with it. We know change is necessary, but none will volunteer to make the change in their own backyard. Jefferson could not give up his slaves, even as he wrote eloquently of slavery destroying his nation's soul, even as his brilliant mind foresaw the cataclysm that occurred after his death.

When cities go up in smoke — Watts 1965, Newark 1967, Miami 1980 and 1989, Los Angeles 1992 — we stop and say we have to do something about it. When we stand amidst the rubble and carry the smell of burning cities on our clothes and home to our closets, we cannot deny the costs of present-day exclusions; we agree we must act. Affirmative action is the collective decision to resolve a historical contradiction in favor of equality and against maintenance of privilege, to pay the price that resolution entails in order to end the runaway costs of continued social stratification. Cities will burn until we decide, once and for all, to root out the cause of such self-immolation.

Affirmative action really is for everyone. We don't mean this in a shallow way — although it is, indeed, more fun to go multicultural. The definition of what it is to be human is at stake. We don't want our children to come to the end of their lives and say, "I lived only for myself." We don't want our students to know that cold and lonely credo as the only basis for public policy.

When a new baby came to our house, so too came the deluge of advertisements for all the new things to buy for babies. As Nana flipped through the glossy catalogs brimming with three-hundred-dollar strollers and endless paraphernalia, she said sadly, "Think of others." These days Dr. Margaret Morgan Lawrence speaks in shorthand, because she holds the lessons of her life in a form both absolute and distilled. Nights spent in a Harlem ambulance treating emergencies that would not have happened if people had regular health care; days spent helping troubled families to recover their emotional strengths; years spent arguing, cajoling, testifying and running ragged to get local governments to provide mental health services for children and their families; a lifetime of knowing how much people need and how little they get and how it doesn't have to be that way — all this is conveyed in her terse comment over a glossy catalog.

We will repeat to the children her lesson: think of others. You don't need everything your money can buy; you don't have to grab every gift that is laid before you while others go without. If you do, you will lose the most important things you own: your heart, your humanity, your chance at grace.

This is not the altruism of the ascetic. It comes from Nana's Mississippi childhood, from a place where people of limited means piled Sunday tables high for feasting, in abundant celebration of life. This is the altruism of *joy,* one of Nana's favorite words.

We began this book introducing our families and what they taught us. Honor yourself, celebrate life, share the bounty you have, find a place where you will care for others and they will always care for you. We learned this from our parents, and in their spirit, we make the case for affirmative action.

Acknowledgments

On June 16, 1976, a young school child named Hector Peterson was shot dead by the police, the first to die in the student-led SOWETO uprising. It was not until nearly twenty years later that a monument was erected marking the spot where Hector fell. After the historic peaceful revolution in South Africa, a granite marker was erected "In memory of Hector Peterson and all other young heroes and heroines of our struggle who laid down their lives for Freedom, Peace, and Democracy."

Someday those plaques and markers will rise all over America, marking the spots where ordinary people stood their ground for freedom. We acknowledge those historic teachers who engaged in direct struggle for civil rights throughout the history of the United States, and who made our lives as law professors of color possible. We acknowledge Hector Peterson and the international community of human beings who have fought and continue to fight for their own liberation as part of the inexorable, worldwide movement for freedom and dignity that is our inspiration to write.

We acknowledge as well our home teachers: the parents who taught us as soon as we could walk to walk proud of our racial heritage, and to walk with loving appreciation among the many peoples who make up this nation. This book is their work product as much as it is ours.

Many colleagues and friends made this book possible. Those law professors and activists who choose to affiliate with the jurisprudential traditions of critical race theory and feminist theory helped develop many of the ideas we rely on. Specific responses and suggestions received from the following people strengthened this book immeasurably: Pat Cain, Peggy Davis, Dolly Gee, Angela Harris, Marina Hsieh, Kenzo Kawanabe, Kiya Kato, Lisa Lim, Shauna Marshall, Carrie Menkle-Meadow, Doris Ng, Michael Olivas, Glenn Omatsu, Steven Ow Yang, Elizabeth Patterson, Eva Jefferson Patterson, Marita Rivero, J. Clay Smith, Gerald Torres, and Ling Chi Wang. Joel Dreyfuss, co-author with Charles Lawrence of *The Bakke Case: The Politics of Inequality,* made many intellectual contributions to that work which reverberate throughout this book.

We received helpful position papers and research documents from community organizations, including the Asian Law Caucus, Chinese for Affirmative Action, Equal Rights Advocates, Lawyers Committee for Civil Rights Under Law, Leadership Conference on Civil Rights, Mexican American Legal Defense and Educational Fund, NAACP Legal Defense and Educational Fund, National Asian Pacific American Legal Consortium, National Rainbow Coalition, National Urban League, National Women's Law Center, and the Puerto Rican Legal Defense and Education Fund.

Anita Allen, Stephen Arons, David Cole, Irving Hamer, Girardeau Spann, Robin West, and Stephanie Wildman took the time to read early drafts and offered invaluable criticism.

Students in our classes were persistent in offering insights, critiques, challenges, and examples from their own lives. We are grateful to them, and in particular to the research assistants who worked on this book: Gi Hyun An, Kimani Paul-Emile, Susan Epps, Elliot Hines, Boris Gaviria, Gina Kim, Maureen Masters, Hannibal O'Bryan, Chan Park, and Kimberlee Smith.

Dean Judith Areen and the Georgetown University Law Center are consistent supporters of faculty research and writing. Without the support of the law school we could not have finished this book. Dean Larry Foster of the William S. Richardson School of Law graciously allowed us to borrow an office and a computer, and the staff and faculty of that law school created an atmosphere conducive to serious scholarship during our summer sojourns there.

The staff of the Georgetown Law Center provided significant and cheerful support. Ms. Jennifer Fairfax helped prepare the manuscript. Librarians responded to numerous requests for articles and information. It was important to us that in the midst of the stress of preparing the manuscript, all our daily encounters with the people who make the law school work, including technical support staff, secretarial staff, the childcare center, the cafeteria, security, and computer technicians, were rich with care, friendship, humor, and good will.

We encountered gifted professionals in the process of turning our manuscript into a book. Ike Williams was an early supporter who found a notable publisher for us; Wendy Strothman immediately understood our purpose and urged us to write in our own voices. This book is in print because of her generous talents. Wendy Holt provided a detailed, involved, and important substantive critique of the manuscript, along with a large dose of warmth and optimism. Frances Apt was more than a manuscript editor and someone we never want to do a book without.

To our portrait subjects, who bravely and honestly spoke of their own lives, we are particularly indebted. Our sister Sara has said, "For a portraitist to see her subject clearly, she must fall in love." The reader can't help knowing how hard we fell for LaDoris Cordell, Robert Demmons, Bernadette Gross, Diane Ho, Lawrence Levine, and Anthony Romero. We offer humble thanks to our subjects, who were willing to be the human face of affirmative action in this book.

The loving support of our kinship circle — Sara Lawrence, Irving Hamer, Paula and John Wehmiller, Bill Matsuda, Jim Matsuda, Tracy Langhurst, Wes, Abe, Tolani, Martin, Ben, and Lucas — surrounded us and fed us as we worked. Our angels, Maia Thembi, Kimiko Margaret, and Paul Robeson, gave hugs and kisses and constant inspiration. Finally, we thank the friends who fed us, shared childcare, listened to complaints, loved our children, and made our lives sane as we worked. Especially the godparents: Stephen Arons, Shelley Brazier, Tom Williamson, and Carolyn Wong.

Throughout this book we have argued for a community spirit, believing that no individual makes it on her or his own. Certainly our writing is not ours alone, although we take responsibility for its flaws. We had help and care from a large tribe, and in their precious faces we see a better world to come.

Notes

Preface and Introduction

1. Henry Wallace was the Progressive Party candidate for President in 1948.
2. Charles Lawrence's sister has written a biography of their mother, Margaret Morgan Lawrence. See Sara Lawrence-Lightfoot, *Balm in Gilead: The Journey of a Healer* (New York: Addison Wesley, 1988).
3. Examples of supporters of affirmative action using the chemotherapy analogy include: "Seeking Peace at Home," editorial, *Washington Post,* Oct. 31, 1988, p. A10. ("Much of the preferential enterprise that goes by the name of affirmative action, like busing for desegregation, is an extreme remedy, a kind of chemotherapy to be used only with great care for limited purposes and limited periods of time.")

   Stanley Fish, "Reverse Racism or How the Pot Got to Call the Kettle Black," *Atlantic Monthly,* Nov. 1993, p. 128 ("A cancer is an invasion of the body's equilibrium, and so is chemotherapy; but we do not decline to fight the disease because the medicine we employ is also disruptive of normal functioning"); Jack L. Levin, "Affirmative Action Is Still a Necessary Remedy," *Baltimore Sun,* Sept. 11, 1995, p. 9A ("Chemotherapy can destroy . . . but doctors continue to use it to fight cancer. . . . Side effects of affirmative action must be corrected and held to a minimum, but they should not be the excuse for discontinuing the main medication"); Doug Caruso, "OSU Panel Touts Need for Affirmative Action," *Columbus Dispatch,* Jan. 24, 1996, p. 5B (quoting Leroy Pernell, vice provost for minority affairs at the Ohio State University, likening racism to cancer and affirmative action to painful chemotherapy).
4. Congresswoman Susan Molinari's Testimony before House Judiciary Committee, Subcommittee on the Constitution, Dec. 7, 1995, Equal Opportunity Act of 1995, H.R. 2128.
5. Kingsley R. Browne, Wayne State University Law School, Testimony before House Judiciary Committee, Subcommittee on the Constitution, Dec. 7, 1995, Equal Opportunity Act of 1995, H.R. 2128.

6. Testimony of Marcia Greenberger regarding the Equal Opportunity Act of 1995 (H.R. 2128) to House Judiciary Committee, Subcommittee on the Constitution, Dec. 7, 1995 (citing Federal Glass Ceiling Commission, *Good for Business: Making Full Use of the Nation's Human Capital*, iii–iv [1995] and U.S. Bureau of the Census, *Current Population Reports*, "Money Income of Households, Families, and Pensions, in the United States: 1992," Series P-60, No. 184, Table 31).

7. Jonathan D. Galter, "Racial Gap in Pay Gets a Degree Sharper," *Washington Post*, Nov. 2, 1995, p. D13.

8. Tom Dunkel, "Team Effort," *Washington Post* magazine, Dec. 31, 1995, pp. 5, 6.

9. Patty Cantrell, "Blue-Collar Workers: Breaking Through the Brick Ceiling," *Ms.*, Jan.–Feb. 1996, pp. 34–38.

10. Patricia Williams, *The Rooster's Egg* (Cambridge: Harvard University Press, 1995), p. 97.

11. Ibid.

12. Testimony of Carl Cohen, professor of philosophy, University of Michigan, regarding Equal Opportunity Act of 1995 (H.R. 2128) to the House Judiciary Committee, Subcommittee on the Constitution, Dec. 7, 1995.

13. Alice Demba, "Campus Racial Lines May Be Blurring," *Boston Globe*, April 5, 1994, p. 1.

1. Born in Rebellion

1. From "A Testament of Hope," in *A Testament of Hope: The Essential Writings of Martin Luther King, Jr.*, ed. James M. Washington (San Francisco: Harper & Row, 1986), p. 315.

2. For a compelling narrative of the sit-ins, the Freedom Rides, and the history of the Student Nonviolent Coordinating Committee from 1960 to 1964, see Howard Zinn, *SNCC: The New Abolitionists* (Boston: Beacon Press, 1964).

3. U.S. Department of Labor, 9 Employment and Earnings 10 (April 1963), p. 4.

4. Ibid.

5. Julius Lester, *Look Out Whitey! Black Power's Gon' Get Your Mama!* (New York: Grove Press, 1969), p. 98.

6. Ibid.

7. "The New Racism," *Time* magazine, July 1, 1966, p. 11.

8. Lester, *Look Out Whitey!* p. 98.

9. Manning Marable, *Race Reform and Rebellion: The Second Reconstruction in Black America, 1945–1982* (Jackson, MS: University Press of Mississippi, 1984), p. 105.

10. See "Black Power: A Statement by the National Committee of Negro Churchmen," July 31, 1966, in Floyd B. Barbour, ed., *Black Power Revolt* (Boston: Extending Horizons Books, 1968), p. 264.

11. Stokely Carmichael and Charles Hamilton, *Black Power: The Politics of Liberation* (New York: Random House, 1967), p. 46.
12. Malcolm X, "To Mississippi Youth" (Dec. 31, 1964), in *Malcolm X Speaks*, ed. George Breitman (New York: Grove Weidenfield, 1990, 1st Grove Press ed. 1966), p. 145.
13. *Report of the National Advisory Commission on Civil Disorders* (Washington, D.C.: U.S. Government Printing Office, 1968), p. 110.
14. Martin Luther King, Jr., *The Trumpet of Conscience,* quoted in Vincent Harding, *Hope and History: Why We Must Share the Story of the Movement* (Maryknoll, NY: Obis Books, 1991), p. 100.
15. Manning Marable, *Race Reform and Rebellion,* p. 103.
16. Dale Russakoff, "Rutgers Proud of Law School's Set-Asides; Affirmative Action Program Has Been Changing the Face of New Jersey's Bar," *Washington Post,* April 10, 1995, p. A1.
17. Juan Gomez-Quinones, *Mexican Students Por La Raza: The Chicano Student Movement in Southern California, 1967–1977* (Editorial La Causa, 1978), p. 43.
18. Ibid.
19. Ibid.
20. For a discussion of the political insights informing the Japanese American redress and reparations movement, see Eric Yamamoto, "Friend or Foe or Something Else: Social Meanings of Redress and Reparations," 20 *Denver Journal of International Law and Policy* 223 (1992). The history of the Japanese American redress and reparations movement is well documented. See, e.g., William Minoru Hohri, *Repairing America* (Seattle: Washington State University Press, 1988); Peter Irons, *Justice Delayed: The Record of the Japanese-American Internment Cases* (Middletown, CT: Wesleyan University Press, 1989).
21. Mora Dolan, "Boalt's Asian Student Protest," *San Francisco Examiner and Chronicle,* Oct. 26, 1975, reprinted in *Suspended Sentence,* vol. 75, no. 10, p. 1, Oct. 27, 1975.
22. Letter from Asian American Law Students Association at the University of California (no date). See also Asian American Law Students Position Paper on the Asian Admissions Program (1975).
23. For a discussion of the influence of the Black power movement on Hawaiian nationalism in the 1960s and 1970s, see Haunani K. Trask, "Birth of the Modern Hawaiian Movement: Kalama Valley, O'ahu," *Hawaiian Journal of History,* vol. 21, 1987, pp. 126–153, cited in Trask, *From a Native Daughter: Colonialism and Sovereignty in Hawai'i* (Monro, ME: Common Courage Press, 1993.)
24. See "Black Battleground," *Time* magazine, Sept. 5, 1969, p. 78.
25. See "A Rush of Action to Get More Jobs for Negroes," *U.S. News & World Report,* Sept. 15, 1969, p. 67.
26. Ibid.
27. See Marion K. Sanders, "James Haughton Wants 500,000 More Jobs," *New York Times* magazine, Sept. 14, 1969, p. 124.

28. *Report of the National Advisory Commission on Civil Disorders*, p. 110.
29. Executive Order No. 11246 of Sept. 24, 1965, 30 Fed. Reg. 12319, as amended by Exec. Order No. 11375 of Oct. 13, 1967, 32 Fed. Reg. 14303.
30. For an affirmative action program to be "result oriented" originally meant that it had "to increase materially the utilization of minorities and women," 41 C.F.R. Sec. 60–2.10 (1973). Later it was changed to require an employer "to achieve prompt and full utilization of minorities and women," 41 C.F.R. Sec. 60–2.10 (1978).
31. Anita L. Allen, "Affirmative Action," in 1 *Encyclopedia of African-American Culture and History*, ed. Jack Salzman, David Lionel Smith, and Cornel West (New York: Macmillan, 1996), pp. 31–34.
32. "Equality for Women Benefits Industry, Too," *Industrial Week*, Feb. 12, 1973, p. 59, as cited in "Rethinking Weber: The Business Response to Affirmative Action," 102 Harvard Law Review 658, 671 (1989).
33. Anne B. Fisher, "Businessmen Like to Hire by the Numbers," *Fortune*, Sept. 16, 1985, p. 28 [hereinafter "Hire by the Numbers"].
34. "Rethinking Weber," 102 Harvard Law Review 658 (1989), p. 662.
35. See Peter C. Robertson, "Why Bosses Like to Be Told to Hire Minorities," *Washington Post*, Nov. 10, 1985, p. D1, col. 5; Fisher, "Hire by the Numbers," *Fortune*, Sept. 16, 1985, p. 28.
36. President Johnson's Howard address is reprinted in *The Moynihan Report and the Politics of Controversy*, ed. Lee Rainwater and William Yancey (Cambridge: MIT Press, 1967), pp. 125–132.
37. Frederick Douglass, "No Progress Without Struggle," in Floyd B. Barbour (ed.), *The Black Power Revolt* (Boston: Extending Horizons Books, 1968), p. 42.
38. Bill Stall, "After the Riots: The Search for Answers; Campbell Blames 'Evil People' in the Thefts, Fires," *Los Angeles Times*, May 7, 1992, p. A8.
39. Mike Downey, "Mike Downey: Said and Done, But Scott Is Sorry," *Los Angeles Times*, May 14, 1992, p. C1.

Anthony Romero

The portrait of Anthony Romero is based on the authors' interviews.

2. *"We Won't Go Back"*

1. For a detailed account of the litigation of the Bakke case in the California courts and a discussion of the inadequacies of the trial court record see Joel Dreyfuss and Charles Lawrence III, *The Bakke Case: The Politics of Inequality* (New York: Harcourt, Brace, Jovanovich, 1979). See also Charles Lawrence, "When the Defendants Are Foxes Too: The Need for Intervention in Reverse Discrimination Cases," 34 *Guild Practitioner* 1 (1977).

2. *The Regents of the University of California* v. *Allan Bakke,* Law Reprints; U.S. Supreme Court Records and Briefs, No. 76–811.

3. The shift in the attitudes of most white Americans toward race relations, the collapse of the old civil rights coalition, and the evolution of a "New Racism" marked by the rhetoric of victim blaming and reverse discrimination is discussed in Joel Dreyfuss and Charles Lawrence III, *The Bakke Case: The Politics of Inequality,* pp. 141–162.

4. Ibid., p. 143.

5. Ibid., p. 142.

6. Ibid., p. 144.

7. Ibid. See also Robert H. Weibe, "White Attitudes and Black Rights from Brown to Bakke," *Have We Overcome* (Jackson, MS: University Press of Mississippi, 1979).

8. Bernard E. Anderson, et al., *The State of Black America 1978* (New York: National Urban League, Inc., 1978), p. 197.

9. Ibid.

10. Warren Brown, "Urban League Hits Broad Tax Plan; Urban League Opposes Broad Tax Cut," *Washington Post,* Jan. 18, 1978, p. A1.

11. Sociologist Stephen Steinberg traces the beginnings of anti–affirmative action rhetoric as far back as the early 1960s, well before the first affirmative action programs were in place. Stephen Steinberg, *Turning Back: The Retreat from Racial Justice in American Thought and Policy* (Boston: Beacon Press, 1995).

12. Nathan Glazer, "Negroes and Jews: The New Challenge to Pluralism," *Commentary* (Dec. 1964), p. 34.

13. Daniel Patrick Moynihan, "The New Racialism," in Moynihan, *Coping: Essays on the Practice of Government* (New York: Random House, 1973), p. 205.

14. Stephen Steinberg uses the terms "scholarship of confrontation" and "scholarship of backlash" in describing this phenomenon. Steinberg, *Turning Back: The Retreat from Racial Justice in American Thought and Policy* (Boston: Beacon Press, 1995), pp. 97–175.

15. The Moynihan Report and the ensuing controversy it evoked are reproduced in *The Moynihan Report and the Politics of Controversy,* ed. Lee Rainwater and William Yancey (Cambridge: MIT Press, 1967).

16. Nathan Glazer, "Negroes and Jews: The New Challenge to Pluralism," *Commentary* (Dec. 1964), p. 34.

17. Richard J. Herrnstein and Charles Murray, *The Bell Curve* (New York: Free Press, 1994); Dinesh D'Souza, *The End of Racism* (New York: Free Press, 1996).

18. Nathan Glazer, *Affirmative Discrimination: Ethnic Inequality and Public Policy* (New York: Basic Books, 1975), p. 201.

19. Helms's advertisement is quoted in Andrew Hacker, *Two Nations: Black and White, Separate, Hostile, Unequal* (New York: Charles Scribner, 1992), p. 202.

20. For a detailed account and discussion of the U.S. Supreme Court oral argument in the Bakke case, see Joel Dreyfuss and Charles Lawrence III, *The Bakke Case: The Politics of Inequality*, pp. 172–202. See also Peter Irons and Stephanie Guiton, eds., *May It Please the Court* (New York: New Press, 1993), pp. 305–321.
21. Nicholas Lehman, "What Happened to the Case for Affirmative Action?" *New York Times* magazine, June 11, 1995, p. 54.
22. *Hopwood v. State of Texas*, 861 F. Supp 551 (1996).
23. Ibid.
24. *Hopwood v. State of Texas*, from the opinion of the U.S. Court of Appeals for the Fifth Circuit, 78 F.3d 932 (1996), p. 934.
25. Mari Matsuda, et al., *Words That Wound: Critical Race Theory, Assaultive Speech and the First Amendment* (Boulder, CO: Westview Press, 1993), p. 43.
26. *Hopwood v. State of Texas*, 861 F. Supp 551, p. 555.
27. "Court Is Urged to Consider Race in College Admissions," *New York Times*, May 25, 1996, p. 9.
28. In 1992, when Hopwood and her co-plaintiffs were denied admission, the law school was using a two-track admissions system similar to the one that was struck down in *Bakke*. The law school had subsequently changed its admissions procedure, merging the two tracks, so that while race was still used as one factor, white and minority applicants were evaluated in the same pool. The new system was identical with the one endorsed by Justice Powell in *Bakke*. Because the *Hopwood* plaintiffs had been denied admission under the old system, the Fifth Circuit could have ordered their admission based on the unconstitutionality of that program. That part of the Fifth Circuit's opinion which held that the new system was also unconstitutional was unnecessary to the resolution of the case and therefore merely advisory. Calling the issue of whether race or national origin could be used as a factor in admissions "an issue of great national importance," Justice Ginsberg said the Court "must await a final judgement on a program genuinely in controversy" (*Texas v. Hopwood*, 95–1773).
29. Robert Reich, quoted in Susan Cohen, "The American Anxiety Dream," *Washington Post* magazine, Feb. 25, 1996, p. 13.

Robert Demmons

The portrait of Robert Demmons is based on interviews with Chief Demmons, Eva Jefferson Patterson, and Shauna Marshall and the following articles: Shauna Marshall, "Class Actions as Instruments of Change: Reflections on Davis v. City and County of San Francisco," University of San Francisco Law Review, vol. 29 (1995), pp. 911–949; Pamela A. McLean, "Fire Department Racism Prompts Jail Threat," U.P.I., January 14, 1988; Paul Rockwell, "Blacks Challenge the I.A.F.F.: Fighting the Fires of Racism," *The*

Nation, Dec. 11, 1989, vol. 249, no. 20, p. 714; George Cothran, "The Fire Next Time," *San Francisco Weekly,* April 3, 1996.

3. The Big Lie

1. Malcolm Gladwell, "Symbol of Suburban Separatism; Until Teen's Death, Mall Had Refused Bus Stop for Inner-City Shoppers," *Washington Post,* Feb. 5, 1996, p. A1.
2. William J. Wilson, *The Truly Disadvantaged* (Chicago: University of Chicago Press, 1987).
3. Evan McKenzie, *Privatopia: Homeowner Associations and the Rise of Residential Private Government* (New Haven: Yale University Press, 1994).
4. Gladwell, "Symbol of Suburban Separatism," *Washington Post,* Feb. 6, 1996.
5. Lynne Duke, "Whites' Racial Stereotypes Persist, Most Retain Negative Beliefs About Minorities, Survey Finds," *Washington Post,* Dec. 24, 1991, p. A4.
6. Martilla and Kiley, "Anti-Defamation League Survey on Racial Attitudes in America" (1993), p. 20.
7. Lynne Duke, "Racial 'Perception Gap' Emerges as Young Whites Discuss Blacks," *Washington Post,* Dec. 24, 1991, p. A4.
8. Lee Sigellman and Susan Welch, "The Contact Hypothesis Revisited: Black-White Interaction and Positive Racial Attitudes," 71 *Social Forces* 781, 787 (1993).
9. The study prepared for the Office of Policy Development and Research, U.S. Department of Housing and Urban Development found that "[o]verall, black and Hispanic homebuyers as well as black renters experience some form of discrimination more than half the times they visit a rental or sales agent in response to an advertisement in a major metropolitan newspaper, and Hispanic renters experience discrimination almost half the time." Margery Turner, Raymond Struyk, and John Yinger, "Housing Discrimination Study, Synthesis" (The Urban Institute and Syracuse University, 1991), p. 37.
10. Douglass Massey and Nancy Denton, *American Apartheid: Segregation and the Making of the Underclass* (Cambridge: Harvard University Press, 1993).
11. Gary Orfield, "The Growth of Segregation in American Schools; Changing Patterns of Separation and Poverty Since 1968" (National School Boards Association, 1993), p. 9.
12. Claudette E. Bennett, U.S. Department of Commerce, *The Black Population in the United States: March 1994 and 1993* (1994), p. 25.
13. National Center for Health Statistics, "Health, United States 1994" (Hyattsville, MD: Public Health Service, 1995), pp. 97–98. See also Paul Solie, et al., "Black-White Mortality Difference by Family Income," 340 *The Lancet* 346, 347 (1992).

14. U.S. Bureau of the Census, "Income, Poverty, and Valuation of Noncash Benefits: 1993," in P-60 *Current Population Reports* 188, Nov. 1994.

15. National Center for Health Statistics, "Health, United States 1994" (Hyattsville, MD: Public Health Service, 1995), pp. 47–48.

16. *Plessy v. Ferguson*, 163 U.S. 537, at 559 (1896) (Harlan, J. Dissenting).

17. Ibid. at 551.

18. Ibid. at 560.

19. *Adarand Constructors v. Pena*, 115 S.Ct. 2097, p. 2118 (1995) (Scalia, A. Concurring).

20. *Washington v. Davis*, 426 U.S. 229 (1976).

21. *City of Richmond v. J.A. Croson*, 488 U.S. 469 (1989).

22. Ibid. p. 480.

23. Peter Charles Hoffer, "Blind to History: The Use of History in Affirmative Action Suits: Another Look at City of Richmond v. J.A. Croson Co.," 23 Rutgers Law Journal 270 (1992), pp. 289–290.

24. *City of Richmond v. Croson*, 488 U.S. 469 (1989), pp. 499, 502.

25. Dinesh D'Souza, *The End of Racism: Principles for a Multiracial Society* (New York: Free Press, 1995).

26. Albie Sachs, "Towards a Bill of Rights in a Democratic South Africa," 6 *South African Journal of Human Rights* 1 (1990), p. 8.

27. Calvin Butts, "White Racism: Its Origins, Institutions, and the Implications for Professional Practice in Mental Health," 8 *International Journal of Psychiatry* (1969), p. 914.

28. Chester Pierce, "Psychiatric Problems of Black Minority," 2 *American Handbook of Psychiatry* (G. Caplan, 2d ed.), 1974, pp. 512, 513.

29. "Insight," *Los Angeles Times*, Jan. 12, 1995, p. A5.

30. Marc Elrich, "The Stereotype Within," *Washington Post*, Feb. 13, 1994, p. C1.

4. On Meritocracy

1. Mink tells her father's story in *Called from Within: Early Women Lawyers of Hawaii*, Mari Matsuda, ed., (Honolulu: University of Hawaii Press, 1992), p. 253.

2. See Derrick Bell, "Racial Remediation: A Historical Perspective on Current Conditions," 52 Notre Dame Law Review 5, 9–11 (1976) (discussing historical connections between military participation by Blacks and advances in civil rights). See also Mari Matsuda, "Looking to the Bottom, Critical Legal Studies and Reparations," 22 Harvard Civil Rights Civil Liberties Law Review 323 (1987).

3. See Rita Koselka, Fleming Meeks, and Laura Saunders, "Family Affairs," *Forbes*, Dec. 11, 1989, p. 212.

4. U.S. Department of Education, Office of Civil Rights, Compliance Review No. 01–88–6009 (Oct. 4, 1990).

5. Statistics in this paragraph are all from the Glass Ceiling Commission, "Good for Business: Making Full Use of the Nation's Human Capital," (Washington, D.C.: Bureau of National Affairs, 1995).

6. William J. Clinton, "Remarks at the University of Texas at Austin, Oct. 16, 1995" in *Weekly Compilation of Presidential Documents*, vol. 31, no. 42, pp. 1847–1853.

7. See M. Granovetter, "Getting a Job: A Study of Contacts and Careers, 2d ed." (Chicago: University of Chicago Press, 1995). Granovetter's empirical study concludes that "personal contacts are of paramount importance in connecting people with jobs. Better jobs are found this way, and the best ones . . . are most apt to be filled this way" (at p. 22).

8. See Leslie Espinoza, "The LSAT: Narratives and Bias," 1 *American University Journal Gender & Law* 121 (1993). See also Mark Kellman, "Concepts of Discrimination in 'General Ability' Job Testing," 104 Harvard Law Review 1158 (1991).

9. Horace Mann Bond, *The Search for Talent* (Cambridge, MA: Harvard University, Graduate School of Education, 1959), p. 23. See also Jonathan Tilove, "Here's a Tip: Get Yourself Born to the Right Folks, Affirmative Action or Not, Lineage Means Plenty at Nation's Top Schools," *San Francisco Examiner*, April 6, 1995, A16; Elaine Woo, "Belief in Meritocracy and Equal-Opportunity Myth Preferences: It Appeals to the Notion of Fairness, but Distorts Realities of Social Mobility, Historians Say," Series: Affirmative Action: Fairness or Favoritism?, *Los Angeles Times*, April 30, 1995, p. A–1.

10. American Association of University Women, "How Schools Shortchange Girls — The AAUW Report: A Study on Major Findings on Girls and Education" (New York: Marlow & Company, 1992). Katherine Connor and Ellen Vargyas, "The Legal Implications of Gender Bias in Standardized Testing," 7 Berkeley Women's Law Journal 13 (1992). "Do College-Bound Girls Face a Disadvantage When They Sit Down and Take the SAT Test?," 4 *Congressional Quarterly* 488 (1994).

11. Barbara A. Babcock, speech to the Palo Alto Bar Association, Oct. 6, 1995, unpublished.

12. Irving Bernstein, *The Lean Years: A History of the American Worker 1920–1933* (Boston: Houghton Mifflin, 1960), pp. 3–4, 36–37. See also Don D. Lescohier, "Working Conditions," in *History of Labor in the United States, 1896–1932* (New York: Macmillan, 1952).

13. See Richard Kazis and Richard Grossman, *Fear at Work: Job Blackmail, Labor and the Environment* (Philadelphia: New Society Publishers, 1991), pp. 165–175.

14. "President Bush, whose son Neil has dyslexia and son Marvin has had a colostomy, guaranteed the bill's passage. . . . [Ted Kennedy's sister] Rosemary is retarded and his son Teddy, Jr. . . . lost a leg to cancer. Tom Harkin (D-Iowa), chief Senate sponsor, has a deaf brother and a quadriplegic

nephew. . . . Senate Republican Robert Dole . . . cares about disability issues in part because his right arm was rendered useless by war wounds. . . ." Joseph P. Shapiro, "Liberation Day for the Disabled," *U.S. News & World Report*, Sept. 18, 1989, p. 20.

LaDoris Hazzard Cordell

The portrait of LaDoris Hazzard Cordell is based on authors' interviews with Judge Cordell and the following articles: Sharon Noguchi, "Lawyers Mark Firsts in E. Palo Alto," *Palo Alto Times*, Dec. 4, 1976, p. 1; Phyllis Brown, "She Fights for Rights of Blacks," *The Peninsula Times Tribune*, March 13, 1981, p. B9; Rebecca Salner, "Popolizio's Bird Call Backfires in Judge Race," *San Jose Mercury News*, June 9, 1988; LaDoris H. Cordell, "There Must Be Environmental Justice for All," *San Jose Mercury News*, Apr. 7, 1995; LaDoris H. Cordell, "Equal Justice for All Is in Danger," "The Brutal Season," *San Jose Mercury News*, Dec. 30, 1995; Loretta Green, "From Heart to Hand, Drawings Show Judge's Empathy," *San Jose Mercury News*, Jan. 7, 1996, p. B6.

5. Tokens and Traitors

1. Malcolm X, "Message to the Grass Roots," in *Malcolm X Speaks*, George Breitman, ed. (New York: First Grove Weidenfield Evergreen, 1990), p. 10.
2. United States Congress, Senate Committee on the Judiciary, *The Complete Transcripts of the Clarence Thomas — Anita Hill Hearings:* Oct. 11, 12, 13 (1991).
3. Henry J. Reske, "Marshall Retires for Health Reasons: First Black Justice Fought Discrimination as Litigator, Supreme Court Dissenter," 77 *American Bar Association Journal*, p. 14.
4. Associate Justice Clarence Thomas from his separate opinion in *Adarand v. Pena*, 115 S. Ct. 2097 (1995), ". . . remedial racial preferences may reflect a desire to foster equality in society, but there can be no doubt that racial paternalism and its unintended consequences can be as poisonous and pernicious as any other form of discrimination. So-called 'benign' discrimination teaches many that because of chronic and apparently immutable handicaps, minorities cannot compete with them without their patronizing indulgence" (p. 2119).
5. Shelby Steele, "A Negative Vote on Affirmative Action," *New York Times* magazine, May 13, 1990, p. 46; reprinted in Steele, *The Content of Our Character* (New York: St. Martin's Press, 1990), p. 120.
6. *Adarand v. Pena*, 115 S. Ct. 2097 (1995).
7. From the separate opinion of Justice Clarence Thomas, "These programs

stamp minorities with a badge of inferiority and may cause them to develop dependencies or to adopt an attitude that they are 'entitled' to preference" (p. 2119).

8. Charles Krauthammer, "Quota by Threat," *Washington Post,* May 18, 1990, p. A19.

9. Shelby Steele, "A Negative Vote on Affirmative Action," *New York Times Magazine,* May 13, 1990, p. 46.

10. Stephen Carter, *Reflections of an Affirmative Action Baby* (New York: Basic Books, 1991), p. 57.

11. Ibid., p. 54.

12. Ibid., p. 60.

13. Ibid.

14. Ibid., p. 16.

15. Sara Lawrence-Lightfoot, *I've Known Rivers: Lives of Loss and Liberation* (New York: Addison Wesley, 1994), p. 4.

16. Joan Biskupic, "'I Am Not an Uncle Tom,' Thomas Says at Meeting; Justice Speaks to Select Group of Blacks," *Washington Post,* Oct. 28, 1994, p. A1.

17. Ibid.

18. Ibid.

19. Trevor W. Coleman, "Doubting Thomas," *Emerge,* Nov. 1993, p. 39.

20. Ibid., p. 41.

21. Ibid., p. 40.

22. Dele Olojede, "Quandary for Black Leaders," *Newsday,* Aug. 1, 1991, p. 4.

23. Maya Angelou, "I Dare to Hope," *New York Times,* Aug. 25, 1991, Section 4, p. 15, column 2.

24. United States Congress, Senate Committee on the Judiciary, *The Complete Transcripts of the Clarence Thomas — Anita Hill Hearings: October 11, 12, 13* (1991), p. 118.

25. In four different voting rights cases, *Johnson* v. *DeGrandy,* 114 S. Ct. 2647 (1994), *Shaw* v. *Reno,* 509 U.S. 630 (1993), *Miller* v. *Johnson,* 115 S. Ct. 2475 (1995), and *Holder* v. *Hall,* 114 S. Ct. 2581 (1994), Thomas voted to restrict severely the reach of the Voting Rights Act and to subvert its purpose to ensure minorities a real opportunity to elect state and federal office holders. In *Shaw* v. *Reno* and *Miller* v. *Johnson,* the most significant of these because they threatened to preclude significant Black representation in Congress, Thomas joined a conservative majority to cast the deciding vote in 5 to 4 decisions. In three employment discrimination cases, *St. Mary's Honor Center* v. *Hicks,* 509 U.S. 502 (1993), *Rivers* v. *Roadway Express,* 114 S. Ct. 1510 (1994), and *Adarand* v. *Pena,* 115 S. Ct. 2097 (1995), Thomas voted to make it more difficult to prove job bias against white employers, to restrict the application of the 1991 Civil Rights Act, and to cast doubt on the constitutionality of federal set-asides for minority contractors. Here too the conservative wing of the Court needed his vote to advance their anti–civil rights agenda. In an immigration case involving alleged discrimination against

Haitian boat people, *Sale v. Haitian Centers Council Inc.*, 509 U.S. 155, (1993), Thomas voted to uphold the INS policy of picking up Haitian refugees on the high seas and returning them home. In a desegregation case where the trial judge had ordered the state to create a top-flight magnet school in a Black neighborhood in an effort to discourage white flight in a public school system with a long history of discrimination, *Missouri v. Jenkins*, 115 S. Ct. 2038 (1995), Thomas cast the deciding vote to overturn the trial judge's order. In *Hudson v. Mcmillan*, 503 U.S. 1, (1992), a case involving the rights of prisoners, the Court held 7 to 2 that the severe beating of an inmate who was hog-tied on the floor by Louisiana prison guards was a violation of the Eighth Amendment's guarantee against cruel and unusual punishment. Thomas, in his first written dissent, argued that while the injuries inflicted on Hudson might be deplorable they were not remediable under the Eighth Amendment of the Constitution. This from the same man who as a nominee had described how, when he looked from the window of his chambers in the Court of Appeals in Washington, D.C., he could see the busloads of prisoners, mostly Black, brought to court for trials. "Every day," Thomas told the Senate Judiciary Committee, "I looked at the bus and said, 'But for the grace of God, there go I.'" (Reuters, "The Thomas Hearings; Excerpts from Senate's Hearings on the Thomas Nomination," *New York Times*, Sept. 13, 1991, p. A13.)

26. Trevor W. Coleman, "Doubting Thomas," *Emerge*, Nov. 1993, p. 40.

27. Stanley M. Elkins, *Slavery: A Problem in American Institutional and Intellectual Life*, 3rd ed. (Chicago: University of Chicago Press, 1976).

28. John Dollard, *Caste and Class in a Southern Town* (Madison, WI: University of Wisconsin Press, 1937), p. 255.

29. Excerpt from 1980 speech made by Clarence Thomas at a conference of Black conservatives. See Martin Gottlieb, "Jim Crow's Ghost; Savannah and Civil Rights — A Special Report: Ways of Older South Linger in City of Thomas's Boyhood," *New York Times*, Aug. 8, 1991, p. A1.

30. For a discussion of Thomas's scapegoating of his sister, see Nell Irving Painter, "Hill, Thomas, and the Use of Racial Stereotype," *Race-ing Justice, En-Gendering Power: Essays on Anita Hill, Clarence Thomas, and the Construction of Social Reality*, in Toni Morrison, ed. (New York: Pantheon Books, 1992). Painter writes, "His point was to contrast her laziness with his hard work and high achievement to prove, I suppose, that any black American with gumption and a willingness to work could succeed. Thus, a woman whom he had presumably known and loved for a lifetime emerged as a one dimensional welfare cheat, one of the figures whom black women cite as an example of the pernicious power of negative stereotype" (p. 201).

31. Eric Lipton, "400 Activists Protest Outside Justice's Home; Clarence Thomas's Record on Civil Rights Denounced," *Washington Post*, Sept. 13, 1995, p. D3.

32. Jack E. White, "The Pain of Being Black," *Time* magazine, Sept. 16, 1991, p. 24.

Bernadette Gross

The portrait of Bernadette Gross is based on author's interviews.

6. Feminism and Affirmative Action

1. Statistics in this section are from: U.S. Department of Agriculture, *Work Force Data Book 1992–93.* (The percentage of women employees increased from 21.6 percent in 1976 to 29 percent in 1980 and 39.7 percent in 1992. At this rate, the Forest Service estimates that the number of women employees will exceed 44 percent by year 2000.) These figures were confirmed by the author's interview with Dr. Tom Martin, who conducted this study. Asian Americans for Affirmative Action, "Equal Opportunity Fact Sheet," Oct. 14, 1995; National Research Council Office of Scientific and Engineering Personnel, Summary Report 1991: Doctorate Recipients from United States Universities (Washington, D.C.: National Academy Press, 1993), p. 11; The Feminist Majority, Affirmative Action: Expanding Employment Opportunities for Women, Citing Office of Federal Contract Compliance Programs, Employer Information Reports; Federal Glass Ceiling Commission Report, *Good for Business: Making Full Use of the Nation's Human Capital* (1995); San Francisco Fire Department: statistics are from author's interview with Judith Kurtz of Equal Rights Advocates.
2. "Good for Business," p. 14.
3. Ibid., p. 31.
4. Ibid., p. 34.
5. Ibid., p. 148.
6. Ibid., p. 13–14; Bette Woody and Carol Weiss, "Barriers to Workplace Advancement," Report to the Department of Labor Glass Ceiling Commission, Dec. 20, 1993. (Ten years after receiving Stanford MBA's, 16 percent of men were CEO's, as opposed to 2 percent of women; and on average, women made 73.1 percent of the salaries of men.)
7. American Medical Association, "Women in Medicine in America," 1991, p. 27.
8. U.S. Department of Education, National Center for Education Statistics, 1994.
9. See, e.g., Diana Pearce, "The Feminization of Poverty: Women, Work and Welfare," in *Urban and Social Change Review,* Feb. 1978, pp. 28–36.
10. See "Nontraditional Occupations for Women in 1990," U.S. Dept. of Labor, March 1990; Leslie Brody, "Women Exploring the Trades," *The Record,*

Northern New Jersey, June 6, 1994, p. C1. "Often single mothers who earn $200 to $400 a week as nurses' aides, secretaries, or day-care workers barely make enough to pay childcare bills. But with five to twelve months of training as electricians, machine repairers, or plumbers, they can work towards wages topping $500 a week. And federal affirmative action goals for contractors hold out the promise of jobs waiting for them." Ibid.

11. Lauren Sugarman, executive director of Chicago Women in Trades, says, "Affirmative action is our life's blood. We know we wouldn't exist as women in the trades without it." Author's interview, Apr. 9, 1996.

12. Patty Cantrell, "Blue-Collar Workers: Breaking Through the Brick Ceiling," *Ms.*, Jan.–Feb. 1996, pp. 35, 36.

13. Philip S. Foner, Frederick Douglass on Women's Rights (Westport, CT: Greenwood Press, 1976), p. 107.

14. Patty Cantrell, "Blue-Collar Workers: Breaking Through the Brick Ceiling," *Ms.* magazine, Jan.–Feb. 1996, pp. 35, 36.

15. Ibid, p. 36.

16. Chicago Title and Trust Family of Title Insurers Survey, January 1995, p. 6, as cited in *The Feminist Majority, Affirmative Action: Expanding Employment Opportunities for Women.*

17. Suzanne Pharr, *Homophobia, Weapon of Sexism* (Inverness, CA.: Chardon Press, 1988).

18. U.S. Dept. of Commerce, *Statistical Abstract of the United States 1995*, Chart No. 591, "Persons Participating in Selected Means Tested Government Assistance Programs 1987–1991" (19,104 x 1,000 whites versus 10,302 x 1,000 Blacks in major means-tested assistance programs; 10,902 x 1,000 whites versus 7,029 x 1,000 Blacks receiving food stamps); see also Population Reference Bureau, study of 1994 census, reported in *Jet*, Oct. 7, 1996, p. 4.

19. ABA Commission on Women in the Profession, *Basic Facts from Women in the Law: A Look at the Numbers*, American Bar Association (1995).

20. Catharine MacKinnon, *Feminism Unmodified* (Cambridge: Harvard University Press, 1987), p. 37.

21. Statistics cited in this paragraph are from American Bar Association Commission on Women in the Profession, *Basic Facts from Women in the Law: A Look at the Numbers*, Dec. 1995, pp. 2, 3–5 (reporting the number of women attorneys in private practice, women in the judiciary, and women lawyers in education, as of December 1995). Ann J. Gellis, "Great Expectations: Women in the Legal Profession, a Commentary on State Studies," 66 Indiana Law Journal 941, 947–950 (1991) (reporting the findings of the Indiana Bar Report on women in the profession that clearly showed "women lawyers make less than their male counterparts," that "when we compare compensation levels of women and men, controlling for the year of graduation from law school, we find statistically significant differences," and that "even controlling for variables such as experience and type of organization, women earn significantly less than men"). For similar conclusions, see

North Carolina Bar Association, *Final Report of the Commission on the Status of Women in the Legal Profession in North Carolina* (Raleigh, NC: North Carolina Bar Association, 1993), p. 34. New Mexico State Bar, *Final Report of the Task Force on Women and the Legal Profession*, Nov. 1990, pp. 10–12; American Bar Association Commission on Women in the Profession, *Perspectives: A Newsletter for and About Women Lawyers*, vol. 3, no. 1, Fall 1993, p. 3 (reporting a survey of Case Western Reserve University Law School graduates of the class of 1981 that found a wide gap between female and male salaries, and reporting another new salary survey that looked at salaries of University of Michigan Law School alums and found that factoring in a lawyer's law school grades, number of years working full-time, the area of law practiced, and firm size, the results showed that the wage gap between men and women was 15 percent).

22. See, e.g., Washington State Commission on African American Affairs, *Who Is Really Benefiting*, 1995–1996.
23. Jacquelyn Dowd Hall, *Revolt Against Chivalry: Jessie Daniel Ames and the Campaign Against Lynching* (New York: Columbia University Press, 1993).

Barbara Babcock

The portrait of Barbara Babcock is based on authors' interviews with Professor Babcock and the following articles: Babcock, "Defending the Guilty," 32 Cleveland State Law Review 175 (1983–1984); David A. Kaplan, "Almost Nobody Wants to Be Dean," National Law Journal, March 24, 1986, p. 1; Marsha Ginsburg, "Californians on Clinton Attorney General List — Two Women Being Considered Say They Don't Want the Job; Van de Kamp Also May Be in Running," *San Francisco Daily Journal*, Jan. 26, 1993; Barbara Bailey Kelley, "The Road Not Taken: Stanford Law Professor Barbara Babcock Could Have Been a Contender for U.S. Attorney General," *San Jose Mercury News*, Mar. 21, 1993; Jim Muzzanghera, "'Because I've Seen It Work': Ex-Carter Aide Joins the Fight to Defend Affirmative Action," *San Jose Mercury News*, Apr. 19, 1995.

7. Affirmative Action, Class, and Interethnic Conflict

1. Lawrence Fuchs, speaking on "All Things Considered," National Public Radio, March 4, 1995.
2. Facts in this paragraph are from "Making the Cut: Graduate School Demographics, Ph.D. Pipeline: Short Supply of Black Graduates," *Minority Markets Alert*, May 1993; Jeffrey M. Millem and Helen S. Astin, "The Changing Composition of Faculty," *Change*, March 1993.

3. Federal Glass Ceiling Commission, *A Solid Investment: Making Full Use of the Nation's Human Capital* (Washington, D.C.: Bureau of National Affairs, 1995), p. 10.

4. See, e.g., Thomas Sowell, *Compassion versus Guilt, and Other Essays* (New York: Morrow, 1982). See also Thomas Sowell, "Even Some Liberals Are Having Doubts," *Atlanta Journal and Constitution*, Feb. 22, 1995, p. 12.

5. Andrew Hacker, "The Crackdown on African Americans," *The Nation*, July 10, 1995, p. 45.

6. California Senate Office of Research, "The Status of Affirmative Action in California," March 1995, pp. 36, 42, and 45.

7. Edwin M. Lee, "Public Contracting Opportunities for Minority and Women Entrepreneurs," in *Perspectives on Affirmative Action and Its Impact on Asian Americans* (Leadership Education for Asian Pacifics [LEAP], Asian Pacific American Policy Institute, 1995), p. 28.

8. The Supreme Court recognized this in *Metro Broadcasting* v. *FCC*, 497 U.S. 547, 549, 580 (1990), quoting CRS, "Minority Broadcast Station Ownership and Broadcast Programming: Is There a Nexus?" June 29, 1988, J. Jeter, "A Comparative Analysis of the Programming Practices of Black-Owned, Black-Oriented Radio Stations and White-Owned, Black-Oriented Radio Stations," at 130, 139 (1981). Minority-owned broadcasting changes images on television and in news content. See Fife, "The Impact of Minority Ownership on Minority Images in Local TV News," in *Communications: A Key to Economic and Political Change, Selected Proceedings from the 15th Annual Howard University Communications Conference*, 113 (Washington, D.C.: Howard University Press, 1986).

9. Affirmative Action Review Report to President Clinton, July 19, 1995, 1995 Daily Labor Report 139, d30 ("Minority-owned businesses have a tendency to hire more minority employees than other firms," citing T. Bates, "Do Black-Owned Businesses Employ Minority Workers? New Evidence," 16:4 *Review of Black Political Economy* 51 (Spring 1988).

10. Michael Kinsley, "The Spoils of Victimhood," *New Yorker*, March 27, 1995, pp. 62, 69.

11. Thomas Sugrue, "Crabgrass-Roots Politics: Race, Rights, and the Reaction Against Liberalism in the Urban North, 1940–1964," *Journal of American History*, Sept. 1995, p. 570.

12. Little-known historical studies attempt to explain when and how such fragile coalitions have worked. See Alex Lichtenstein, "Racial Conflict and Racial Solidarity in the Alabama Coal Strike of 1894: New Evidence for the Gutman-Hill Debate," *Labor History*, vol. 36, no. 1, Winter 1995; Thomas Almaguer, "Racial Domination and Class Conflict in Capitalist Agriculture: The Oxnard Sugar Beet Workers Strike of 1903," 25 *Labor History* 325–50 (1984).

13. Cable News Network, Feb. 22, 1995, House Speaker's News Conference.

14. Richard A. Posner, "Comment, Duncan Kennedy on Affirmative Action," 1990 Duke Law Journal 1157.

15. Patrick J. Buchanan, Tribune Media Services, Jan. 23, 1995.

16. Laurie Kretchmar, "Up from Inscrutable," *Fortune*, April 6, 1992.

17. "UC Davis Admissions Scrutinized, US Civil Rights Office Probes Medical School's Asian American Policies," *Sacramento Bee*, Oct. 10, 1992.

18. Richard Posner, "Duncan Kennedy on Affirmative Action,"1990 *Duke Law Journal* 1157 (1991), p. 1157.

19. U.S. Bureau of Census, 1990 Census; Asian and Pacific Islander Center for Census Information and Services, *Our Ten Years of Growth: A Demographic Analysis of Asian and Pacific Islander Americans* (San Francisco: ACCIS, 1992).

20. Thomas Sowell, "Weber and Bakke, and the Presuppositions of Affirmative Action," in *Discrimination, Affirmative Action and Equal Opportunity*, Walter Block and Michael A. Walker, eds. (Vancouver, B.C.: Fraser, 1982), p. 37.

21. See, e.g., Richard J. Herrnstein and Charles A. Murray, *The Bell Curve: Intelligence and Class Structure in American Life* (New York: Free Press, 1994).

22. *Good for Business: Making Full Use of the Nation's Human Capital.* Federal Glass Ceiling Commission Report (Washington, D.C.: Bureau of National Affairs, March 1995), p. 107.

23. Cf. Matsuda, "Voices of America," 100 Yale Law Journal 1329 (1991) (discussing the life story of Manuel Fragante, who, despite possessing B.S. and J.D. degrees from universities in the Philippines, had difficulty obtaining a minimum-wage job). One research assistant tells us the story of her father, who despite a B.S. in civil engineering and twenty years of experience working for multinational firms, found that U.S. companies would not accept his degree and experience and refused to hire him for any position other than the entry level.

24. See, e.g., Daniel A. Bell, "The Triumph of Asian-Americans: America's Greatest Success Story," *New Republic*, July 15, 1985, p. 24; Anthony Ramirez, "America's Super Minority," *Fortune*, Nov. 24, 1986, p. 148.

25. In a press conference opposing recent proposals to cut off federal benefits to legal immigrants, for example, twenty-four-year-old Jennifer Kim, fighting back tears, told the story of how her family was forced to use welfare: "I am here today as a taxpaying citizen." But, she admitted, for a time her family relied on public assistance out of necessity. "And I would not be where I am without it." Ms. Kim described her parents' work — her mother was a waitress and her father a pool cleaner — and her father's refusal of charity even when a school nurse warned him that his daughter was undernourished. When her father died of cancer, the family was forced to move out of their home and accept public assistance for a short period. Government loans allowed Kim and her brother to graduate from Ivy League schools. Kim was willing to testify in order to "put a human face" on Asian American welfare recipients. Her story was reported only in the ethnic press. Source: *Rafu Shimpo*, June 8, 1995.

26. *Good for Business*, p. 111.
27. "Asian/Pacific Islanders Trail Whites in Earnings — Comparable Education Fails to Close the Gap," *Washington Post*, Sept. 18, 1992, p. A3, citing U.S. Census data.
28. See, e.g., Robert Reich, *The Work of Nations: Preparing Ourselves for 21st Century Capitalism* (New York: Vintage Books, 1992).
29. For general background on the Lowell High School case, see *Berklemen v. San Francisco Unified School District*, 501 F.2d 1264 (9th Cir. 1974); "A Question of Fairness: A Hard Lesson in Affirmative Action," *San Francisco Chronicle*, June 19, 1995, p. A1; "Caught on the Wrong Side of the Line," *Los Angeles Times*, July 13, 1995, p. A1; Selena Dong, "Too Many Asians: The Challenge of Fighting Discrimination Against Asian Americans," 47 Stanford Law Review 1027 (1995); Dana Y. Takagi, *Retreat from Race: Asian Americans and Racial Politics* (New Brunswick, NJ: Rutgers University Press, 1992).
30. Prof. Michael Olivas shared this insight at a discussion of interethnic conflict at the Association of American Law Schools annual meeting, New Orleans, 1995.
31. "If Lowell were to establish minimum qualifications or a uniform cut-off score for all racial groups and then admit students by lottery within Consent Decree enrollment guidelines, Lowell could maintain its status as a 'merit-based' school and eradicate resentment caused by differential admission scores." Henry Der, "The Asian American Factor: Victim or Short-sighted Beneficiary of Race Conscious Remedies?" in *Perspectives on Affirmative Action and Its Impact on Asian Pacific Americans*, p. 14. See also "New Admissions Policy Offered," *New York Times*, Jan. 11, 1996, p. B10.
32. *Washingtonian* magazine, interview by Ken Adleman, July 1996, p. 21.

Lawrence Levine

The portrait of Lawrence Levine is based on authors' interviews with Professor Levine and the following books: Lawrence W. Levine, *The Unpredictable Past: Explorations in American Cultural History* (New York: Oxford University Press, 1993); Levine, *The Opening of the American Mind: Canons, Culture, and History* (Boston: Beacon Press, 1996).
1. Carl Brindenbaugh, "The Great Mutation," *American Historical Review*, LXVII (Jan. 1963), pp. 322–23.

8. It's All the Same Thing

1. The quotes that appear in this opening are paraphrases of comments that we have heard on countless occasions. The last quote is a paraphrase of Laurence Auster, "Avoiding the Issue," *National Review*, Feb. 21, 1994. Aus-

ter writes: "There is no ignoring the unsettled feeling many people experience upon walking into a New York City subway car or a Los Angeles public school — the feeling of being, as the saying goes, in a third world country . . . Citizens should not be made to feel like strangers in their own land" (p. 48).

2. Hector St. John de Crèvecoeur, "Letter III: What Is an American?" in Crèvecoeur, *Letters from an American Farmer* (1782; New York: Penguin, 1981), pp. 66–70.

3. Arthur Schlesinger, Jr., "Multiculturalism and the Bill of Rights," 46 Maine Law Review, 191 (1994). Schlesinger cautions against the "disuniting of America" and the rise of a "cult of ethnicity." The primary perpetrators of the assault on the fragile fabric of our nationhood are "non-white minorities — all joining to denounce the ideas of assimilation, integration, the melting pot, and to protect, promote and perpetuate separate ethnic and racial communities" (p. 199).

4. W.E.B. Du Bois, *The Souls of Black Folk* (Bantam Classic Edition, New York: Bantam Books, 1989), p. 5.

5. *Knoxville Daily Tribune*, Feb. 2, 1888.

6. Gunnar Myrdal, *An American Dilemma: The Negro Problem and Modern Democracy* (New York: Harper & Row, 1944).

7. Catharine A. MacKinnon, *Toward a Feminist Theory of the State* (Cambridge, MA: Harvard University Press, 1989), p. xv.

8. Allan Bloom, *The Closing of the American Mind: How Higher Education Has Failed Democracy and Impoverished the Souls of Today's Students* (New York: Simon and Schuster, 1987); E. D. Hirsch, *Dictionary of Cultural Literacy: Things Our Children Should Know* (Boston: Houghton Mifflin, 1988); Dinesh D'Souza, *Illiberal Education: The Politics of Race and Sex on Campus* (New York: Free Press, 1991).

For a lucid and compelling criticism of the right-wing assault on multiculturalism and the university see Lawrence Levine, *The Opening of the American Mind: Canons, Culture, and History* (Boston: Beacon Press, 1996). Levine cites no fewer than a dozen books and dozens of articles published during the past decade that were part of "a small growth industry" of writers claiming in a relentlessly apocalyptic tone that "something has turned suddenly sour in the academe, that the Pure Aims and Honest Values and True Worth of the past have been sullied and fouled by politics . . ." (p. 4).

9. Dinesh D'Souza, "Illiberal Education," *Atlantic*, March 1991, p. 51. Reprinted in *Illiberal Education: The Politics of Race and Sex on Campus*.

10. Ibid.

11. William Bennett, "Why the West? Why Western Studies Should Be Required in Universities," *National Review*, May 27, 1988, p. 37.

12. William Chace, "There Was No Battle to Lose at Stanford," *Washington Post*, May 9, 1988, p. A15.

13. Anthony Day, "Stanford Weathers the Storm; Curriculum Revised to Introduce Freshmen to Their Intellectual and Moral Heritage. It Has Brought Both Satisfaction and Continuing Ferment," *Los Angeles Times*, May 3, 1990, p. A1.

14. Renato Rosaldo, quoted in "The Nation: A Campus Forum on Multiculturalism; Opening Academia Without Closing It Down," *New York Times*, Dec. 9, 1990, sec. 4, p. 5.

15. Tom Hundley, "Black Students Take Action," *Chicago Tribune*, April 23, 1989, p. 4.

16. Jon Wiener, "Racial Hatred on Campus," *The Nation*, Feb. 27, 1989, p. 260.

17. Howard Erlich, "Campus Ethnoviolence and Policy Options" (National Institute Against Prejudice and Violence, Institute Report No. 4, March 5, 1990).

18. Federal Bureau of Investigation, U.S. Dept. of Justice, Criminal Justice Information Services, *Hate Crimes — 1993–1994*.

19. Southern Poverty Law Center, *Klanwatch Intelligence Report*, June 1995, p. 1.

20. See, e.g., Nat Hentoff, "The Final Nail in the Coffin of College Speech Codes," *San Diego Union-Tribune*, May 14, 1995, p. G-1; George Will, "On Campuses, Liberals Would Gag Free Speech," *Newsday*, Nov. 6, 1989, Sec. Viewpoints, p. 62.

21. Heather McLeod, "Students Criticize Class as Racially Insensitive," *Harvard Crimson*, Feb. 9, 1988, p. 1; Jon Wiener, "What Happened at Harvard?" *The Nation*, Sept. 30, 1991, p. 384.

22. Abraham H. Miller, "Radicalism in Power: The Kafkaesque World of American Higher Education," *Heritage Foundation Reports*, Heritage Lecture #273, July 1, 1990.

23. Timur Kuran, "Race and Social Mistrust; Seeds of Racial Explosion," *Current*, December, 1993, p. 4.

24. Ibid.

25. Abraham H. Miller, "Radicalism in Power."

26. Alice Dembner, "Campus Racial Lines May Be Blurring: Study Counters Notion That Minorities Segregate Selves," *Boston Globe*, April 5, 1994, p. 1.

27. For a discussion of the liberating consequences of coming out, see Bill Eskridge, "Gay Legal Narratives," 46 Stanford Law Review 607 (1994); Marc Fajer, "Can Two Real Men Eat Quiche Together? Storytelling, Gender Role Stereotypes, and Legal Protection for Lesbians and Gay Men," 46 Univ. of Miami Law Review 551 (1992).

9. The Telltale Heart

1. Notes on the State of Virginia (available on microfiche: *Nineteenth Century Legal Treatises* No. 32487–32490, Woodbridge, CT: Research Publications).

2. Deuteronomy 32:35; Romans 12:19.

3. Klaus-Friedrich Koch, Soraya Altorki, Andrew Arno, and Letitia Hickson, "Ritual Reconciliation and the Obviation of Grievances: A Comparative Study in the Ethnography of Law," 16 *Ethnology: An International Journal of Cultural and Social Anthropology* 269 (1977) pp. 279–283.

4. For further discussion of theory and reparation, see Matsuda, "Looking to the Bottom: Critical Legal Studies and Reparations," 22 Harvard Civil Rights–Civil Liberties Law Review 2 (1987).

5. Edward Countryman, *Americans, A Collision of Histories* (New York: Hill and Wang, 1996), p. 7.

6. Lyric from "The Wagoners Song," a traditional Appalachian ballad.

7. Nathan Glazer, "Race Not Class," *Wall Street Journal*, April 5, 1995, p. A12; Lawrence Fuchs, speaking on "All Things Considered," National Public Radio, Mar. 4, 1995.

8. Stephen Steinberg, *Turning Back: The Retreat from Racial Justice in American Thought and Policy* (Boston: Beacon Press, 1995). Writing of another remembrance, Steinberg writes: "Indeed, the animating force behind the vast Holocaust literature is that remembering is a moral imperative, that it is the only way that we can honor the victims and exact a kind of retribution over history. To forget the victims, to allow the past to recede into oblivion, even in the truncated memories of later generations, is morally repugnant because it abets the obliteration of the obliterated. We become like the Germans who pleaded that they 'did not know'" (p. 162).

Diane Ho

The portrait of Diane Ho is based on authors' interviews.

10. And Also with You

1. Cf. Sally Frank, "The Key to Unlocking the Clubhouse Door: The Application of Antidiscrimination Laws to Quasi-Private Clubs," 2 Michigan Journal of Gender Law 27 (1994).

2. Statistics and facts about women in the workplace referred to in this paragraph are from the Federal Glass Ceiling Commission, *Good for Business: Making Full Use of the Nation's Human Capital* (Washington, D.C.: Bureau of National Affairs, 1995); The American Association of University Women, "The Time for Affirmative Action Has Not Passed," March 15, 1994; Edward Frost and Margaret Cronin Smith, "The Profession after Fifteen Years," National Law Journal, Aug. 9, 1993, p. 1; Mark J. McGarry, "Short Cuts," *Newsday*, June 14, 1994, p. A42; Statistical Abstract of the United States, 1993, Table No. 637, p. 426; Arden Moore, "Women in Educa-

tion Review Gains," *Orlando Sentinel,* March 11, 1994, p. C5; Testimony of
Marcia Greenberger, to House Judiciary Committee on the Constitution,
Dec. 7, 1995; Marion Crain, "Between Feminism and Unionism: Working-
Class Women, Sex Equality and Labor Speech," 82 Georgia Law Journal
1093, 1913–1914 (1994).
3. Ibid.
4. Ibid.
5. Ibid.
6. Prepared testimony of Edward I. Koch, before the Senate Judiciary Committee Subcommittee on Constitution, Federalism, and Property Rights on
Affirmative Action, Oct. 23, 1995.
7. Craig T. Ramey and Sharon Landesman Ramey, *At Risk Does Not Mean
Doomed,* National Health/Education Consortium Occasional Paper #4, Civi-
tan International Research Center, June 1992, p. 5 ("children who received
early education intervention had, on average, IQ scores that were 20 points
higher than those in the control condition"); p. 6 ("the children who received the full day, 5 day a week center-based program, supplemented by
home visits as well, showed much higher intellectual performance than did
the children in the home-based only treatment group or the control group");
Sharon Landesman Ramey and Craig T. Ramey, "Early Educational Intervention with Disadvantaged Children — to What Effect?", *Applied & Preventive Psychology,* 1:131–140 (1992), p. 135 (citing Abecedarian Project's
finding that at age twelve, "children who had received the early educational
intervention continued to show benefits in terms of both academic achievement and IQ scores and a reduction of nearly 50 percent in the rate of
repetition of at least one grade in the elementary school years"). Cf. Frances
A. Campbell and Craig T. Ramey, "Effects of Early Intervention on Intellectual and Academic Achievement: A Follow-up Study of Children from Low-
Income Families," *Child Development,* 65, 684–698 (1994).
8. See, e.g., Lawrence J. Schwineheart, Helen V. Barnes, David P. Weikart,
Significant Benefits: The High/Scope Perry Preschool Study through Age 27 (Ypsi-
lanti, MI: High/Scope Press, 1993), p. 59 ("the program group had a significantly higher regular high school graduation rate than did the no-program group"); p. 83 ("As compared with the no-program group, the
program group averaged a significantly lower number of lifetime [juvenile
and adult] criminal arrests . . . and a significantly lower number of adult
criminal arrests"); p. 60 ("38 percent of the program group and 21 percent of
the no-program group had at some time enrolled in what appeared to be
academic or vocational post-secondary programs"); p. 97 ("The most recent
evidence . . . indicates that, compared with the no-program group, the program group at age 27 . . . had significantly higher monthly earnings . . .
[and] nearly significantly higher annual earnings"); p. 106 ("significantly
fewer members of the program group than of the no-program group had

received social services sometime in the ten years before the age-27 interview and records searches").

9. Children's Defense Fund, *Wasting America's Future: The Children's Defense Fund Report on the Costs of Child Poverty* (Boston: Beacon Press, 1994), p. xxiii.

10. Ibid., pp. 29–38.

11. Joe Donnelly, "A Run at Night Basketball," *Washington Post*, Aug. 18, 1994, p. A1.

12. Children's Defense Fund, *Wasting America's Future*, pp. 105–115.

13. Ibid.

14. Ibid., p. 116.

15. John Dewey, *Democracy and Education: An Introduction to the Philosophy of Education* (New York: Macmillan Co., 1916), p. 101.

16. Alexander Meiklejohn, *Education Between Two Worlds* (New York: Harper Bros., 1942), p. 282.

17. Adrienne Rich, *Blood, Bread, and Poetry* (New York: Norton, 1986).

18. For a longer discussion of accent discrimination, see Mari Matsuda, "Voices of America: Accent, Antidiscrimination Law, and a Jurisprudence for the Last Reconstruction," 100 Yale Law Journal 1329 (1991).

19. Based on the theory that foreigners were more dangerously extreme than native-born Americans, the Alien Act of 1789 gave the President power to deport those foreign agitators he deemed a threat to the welfare and security of the country. What was more, the chief executive could expel an alien "without accusation, without defense, and without counsel." William Preston, Jr., *Aliens and Dissenters: Federal Suppression of Radicals, 1903–1933* (Urbana, IL: University of Illinois Press, 1994), pp. 21–22.

20. The Palmer Raids, sometimes called the "deportations delirium," climaxed during the Red Scare of 1919–1920. During this period of nativism, aliens were equated with subversives and were subject to harsh deportation and exclusion rules. This atmosphere led to the Immigration Act of 1918, which was used for widespread, undemocratic, and extrajudicial treatment of aliens and dissenters. See, generally, William Preston, Jr., *Aliens and Dissenters: Federal Suppression of Radicals, 1903–1933* (Urbana, IL: University of Illinois Press, 1994).

21. The House Un-American Activities Committee (HUAC) held hearings alleging subversion among entertainers, civil rights activists, labor union officials, members of academia, and others. Dissent was repressed through the threat and reality of prison sentences for those deemed to endanger national security because of their political opinions. Dissent was also repressed by the fear of the witch-hunt tactics of HUAC. To be called before HUAC, or to be named in a HUAC hearing, was to be branded a subversive, regardless of the facts. Those who were so branded were blacklisted, lost jobs and friendships, and were disabled from participation in political activism. See, generally, Bud Schultz and Ruth Schultz, *It Did Happen Here,*

Recollections of Political Repression in America (Berkeley: University of California Press, 1989).

22. For a collection of narratives from those who suffered violations of their civil rights and liberties, as well as other losses, under McCarthyism, see Schultz and Schultz, *It Did Happen Here.*

23. For background facts on the internment, see Mari Matsuda, "Looking to the Bottom: Critical Legal Studies and Reparations," 22 Harvard Civil Rights — Civil Liberties Law Review 323 (1987).

24. Also known as "pigpile," "pile-on," or "pile-up," in which several children pounce upon and pile up on a randomly designated target child.

25. See, generally, South African Constitution, Chapter 2 Bill of Rights, especially §§9 (Equality), 10 (Dignity), 26 (Housing), 27 (Health Care, Food, Water and Social Security), 28 (Children), 29 (Education).

11. *A New Heart and a New Spirit*

1. The authors thank David Florenzo for permission to quote from his essay.

Index

Ability grouping, 105

Academic freedom: and *Bakke,* 51–52; and multiculturalism, 213–14

Academic scholarship on race, 47–48

Affirmative action, 1–2, 7–8; Americans with Disabilities Act as, 108; Asian Americans' exclusion from, 21; business set-asides, 186–90, 254; community-control model of, 22–23, 25–26, 101–2, 186, 190, 266; co-optation through, 26; debate over, 1, 2–3, 272–74; deep meaning of, 27–28, 32; disadvantaged vs. privileged as beneficiaries of, 21, 26, 53, 181–92, 252–53; discussion of avoided, 1, 271; as dream of freedom, 259; employers' avoidance of, 148; exercise on, 271–72; federal mandates on, 23; and feminism, 152, 157–67; as healthy balance, 233; and hierarchy, 29, 192, 264 (*see also* Subordination); history behind, 5, 18–26; inadequate progress of, 223–24, 250–51; and institutionalized racism, 28, 76; and interethnic relationships, 180–81, 191–93, 206; and merit(ocracy), 101, 107–8, 109–11, 184–86, 272–73; and Native Hawaiian lawyers, 246, 248; opponents of, 2; as political battle, 57, 58; as redistribution, 76, 82, 83, 272, 273–74; as relative to time and place, xii; and reparation, 233–34, 235, 242–44; segregation from ending of, 5; shallow meaning of, 27, 29, 30; Thernstrom text on, 220; and women, 2, 6, 152, 160–61, 167

Affirmative action, expanded notion of, 159–60, 243, 251–52, 269; and Clinton speech in defense, 268–69; for disabled persons, 261–62, 264; distributional decisions on, 265–67, 268; for economically disadvantaged, 21, 252–57; fear of, 264–65; for gays and lesbians, 251, 258–62, 267; for immigrants or multilinguals, 262–64; as inclusive, 215, 257–58, 278–79; and justice for community, 186; and women, 160, 165–66

Affirmative action, opposition to, 3–4, 5, 6–7, 48–49, 91, 252; in academic scholarship, 47–48; fear of, 69–70, 76–77, 108, 139; *Bakke* decision, 43–53, 289n.28; "bell curve" arguments, 272, 273; and benefits to undeserving, 26, 178, 183–90, 252; and Black Power opponents, 15, 46–47; California Civil Rights Initiative, 57, 58, 84; and "colorblind" principle, 75–76, 84, 158, 167; from minority critics, 125–26; and community-based movements, 46–47; in "culture of poverty" argument, 80; and denial of effects of past, 78–80; and economic/political developments, 47, 57–58; and forgotten identities, 227–28; free-speech champions in, 219; by Gingrich, 69–70, 92, 193; Hopwood case (Bakke II), 53–56, 289n.28; and individual vs. group, 80–81; and intent requirement, 77–78, 79; and interethnic conflict, 48, 178, 191; and meritocracy, 92–93 (*see also* Meritocracy and merit); and other controversies, 209–10; political force of, 249; "redistribution" arguments, 272, 273–74; rhetorical arguments of, 49; "special rights" rhetoric, 252; stigmatization argument, 117, 124–30; in student response, 270; in universities, 212–15; University of California resolution, 41–42, 58; and women, 162, 163–64